Instant JavaScript

Hewlett-Packard Professional Books

Atchison	Object-Oriented Test & Measurement Software Development in C++
Blinn	Portable Shell Programming: An Extensive Collection of Bourne Shell Examples
Blommers	Practical Planning for Network Growth
Caruso	Power Programming in HP OpenView: Developing CMIS Applications
Cook	Building Enterprise Information Architecture
Costa	Planning and Designing High Speed Networks Using 100VG-AnyLAN, Second Edition
Crane	A Simplified Approach to Image Processing: Classical and Modern Techniques
Fernandez	Configuring the Common Desktop Environment
Fristrup	USENET: Netnews for Everyone
Fristrup	The Essential Web Surfer Survival Guide
Grady	Practical Software Metrics for Project Management and Process Improvement
Grosvenor, Ichiro, O'Brien	Mainframe Downsizing to Upsize Your Business: IT-Preneuring
Gunn	A Guide to NetWare® for UNIX®
Helsel	Graphical Programming: A Tutorial for HP VEE
Helsel	Visual Programming with HP-VEE
Holman, Lund	Instant JavaScript
Kane	PA-RISC 2.0 Architecture
Knouse	Practical DCE Programming
Lee	The ISDN Consultant: A Stress-Free Guide to High-Speed Communications
Lewis	The Art & Science of Smalltalk
Lund	Integrating UNIX® and PC Network Operating Systems
Madell	Disk and File Management Tasks on HP-UX
Madell, Parsons, Abegg	Developing and Localizing International Software
Malan, Letsinger, Coleman	Object-Oriented Development at Work: Fusion In the Real World
McFarland	X Windows on the World: Developing Internationalized Software with X, Motif®, and CDE
McMinds/Whitty	Writing Your Own OSF/Motif Widgets
Phaal	LAN Traffic Management
Poniatowski	The HP-UX System Administrator's "How To" Book
Poniatowski	HP-UX 10.x System Administration "How To" Book
Poniatowski	Learning the HP-UX Operating System
Ryan	Distributed Object Technology: Concepts and Applications
Thomas	Cable Television Proof-of-Performance: A Practical Guide to Cable TV Compliance Measurements Using a Spectrum Analyzer.
Weygant	Clusters for High Availability: A Primer of HP-UX Solutions
Witte	Electronic Test Instruments
Yawn, Stachnick, Sellars	The Legacy Continues: Using the HP 3000 with HP-UX and Windows NT

Instant
JavaScript

Brian Holman
Brigham Young University

and

William Lund
Brigham Young University

To join a Prentice Hall PTR internet mailing list,
point to **http://www.prenhall.com/register**

Prentice Hall PTR
Upper Saddle River, New Jersey 07458
http://www.prenhall.com

Library of Congress Cataloging-in-Publication Data
Holman, Brian
    Instant JavaScript / Brian Holman and William Lund
      p. cm.
    Includes index.
    ISBN 0-13-268434-9
    1. JavaScript (Computer program language) I. Lund. William.. II. Title
QA76.73.J39H64   1996
005.2--dc20   96-28762
                                            CIP

Editorial/production supervision: *Joanne Anzalone*
Manufacturing manager: *Alexis R. Heydt*
Acquisitions editor: *Karen Gettman*
Editorial assistant: *Barbara Alfieri*
Cover design: *DeFranco Design Inc.*
Cover design director: *Jerry Votta*
Manager, Hewlett-Packard Press: *Patricia Pekary*

 Published by PTR Prentice Hall
Prentice-Hall, Inc.
A Simon & Schuster Company
Upper Saddle River, New Jersey 07458

The publisher offers discounts on this book when ordered in bulk quantities.

For more information, contact:
Corporate Sales Department
Prentice Hall PTR
1 Lake Street
Upper Saddle River, NJ 07458

Phone: 800-382-3419, Fax: 201-236-7141
E-mail: corpsales@prenhall.com

All product names mentioned herein are the trademarks of their respective owners.

Printed in the United States of America
10 9 8 7 6 5 4 3 2 1

ISBN 0-13-268434-9

Prentice-Hall International (UK) Limited, *London*
Prentice-Hall of Australia Pty. Limited, *Sydney*
Prentice-Hall Canada Inc., *Toronto*
Prentice-Hall Hispanoamericana, S.A., *Mexico*
Prentice-Hall of India Private Limited, *New Delhi*
Prentice-Hall of Japan, Inc., *Tokyo*
Simon & Schuster Asia Pte. Ltd., *Singapore*
Editora Prentice-Hall do Brasil, Ltda., *Rio de Janeiro*

To Julie, Andrew, and Spencer.
— Brian

To Annemarie, Patricia, and Elisabeth.
— Bill

Contents

Preface   **xiii**

What You Will Learn   xiii
Benefits for Internet or Intranet Application Developers.   xiii
Benefits for Webmasters.   xiii
Benefits for Database Administrators and Developers.   xiii

What You Should Know   xiv

Brief History of the Internet and World Wide Web   xiv

The Problem JavaScript Solves   xiv

Brief Introduction to JavaScript   xiv

How JavaScript relates to Java   xv

Chapter Overview   xv

Conventions used in this Book   xvii

The Software Used with this Book   xvii

Installing Netscape Navigator from the CD-ROM   xviii

Using Netscape Navigator to Access the Examples on
    CD-ROM   xix

Acknowledgments   xix

About the Authors   xix

i

CHAPTER 1
Introduction to the JavaScript Architecture   1

What is JavaScript?   1

Noteworthy Attributes of the JavaScript Language   1

Relationship between client-side and server-side JavaScript   4

Using JavaScript to develop Internet applications   4

Independence of client-side and server-side JavaScript   5

CHAPTER 2
Hello World!
Introduction to JavaScript   7

Hello World 1   7
    Components of Hello World I HTML Page   9
    <HTML> Tag of Hello World 1   9
    <!-- --> HTML Comments   10
    <HEAD> Tag   10
    <TITLE> Tag in Hello World 1   12
    <SCRIPT> Tag   13
    The Script Itself   13
    Comparing JavaScript to other Object-Oriented Languages   14
    Object-Oriented Programming   15
    What Is a "document" in JavaScript?   15
    The Rest of the "document" in Hello World 1   16
    Review of HTML   16

Hello World 2   19
    Review The New Components   19
    <SCRIPT> Tag in Hello World 2   23
    Changing the Contents of a Document Once it is Written.   24
    The Contents of the JavaScript in Hello World 2   25
    <FORM> Tag in Hello World 2   26
    Within the <SCRIPT> Tag   27

Hello World 3   29
    <FRAMESET> Tag in Hello World 3   31
    <FRAME> Tag in Hello World 3   40
    Hello World 3 HTML   41

Summary   43

CHAPTER 3
Getting Started with Server-side JavaScript   45

Overview   45

Differences between Client-side and Server-side JavaScript   45

Your First Server-side JavaScript Application—"Hello Net"   46
    Creating the Source Files   46
    Packaging the Application for LiveWire   49
    Installing the Application with the Application Manager   50
    Running the Application   51

"Hello Net" Source Explained   52
    The <SERVER> Tag   52
    Calling External Functions   52
    Dynamic HTML   53
    Server-side Objects   53
    Storage of Server-side Objects.   54
    Variable Initialization.   54

Summary   55

CHAPTER 4
The Browser   and JavaScript   57

The "Window" and the "Document"   57

Documents and Frames   63

Printing   67

Making HTML Interactive   70

CHAPTER 5
The JavaScript Language 71

Similarities to Other Programming Languages 71

Where To Put JavaScript 72
    <SCRIPT> Tag 72

Basic Components of the Language 75
    Defining Variables 75
    Math Data Type 76
    Boolean Data Type 77
    String Data Type 77
    Strong vs. Weak Data-typing 78
    Special Data Values, Null and <Undefined> 81
    Defining Arrays 81
    Populating an Array When Created 83
    How Do I Add Elements To An Array Once It Is Defined? 83

Expressions 84
    Assignment Operator 84
    Binary Operators 84
    Unary Operators 85
    Bitwise Operators 86
    Representing Numbers As 32-Bit Quantities For Bitwise
      Operations 87
    Defining Bitwise Operations 90
    Comparison Operators 91
    Logical Operators 94
    String Operators 95
    Operator Precedence 100
    Conditionals 102
    GOTO Missing in Action 102
    Partial Evaluation 102
    JavaScript Conditional Expressions 110
    while 111
    for 112
    for (...;...;...) {} 112
    for (var in obj) {} 113
    continue 116

break	117
if … then … else	118
function Statement	118
return Statement	121
Scope of Variables, Defining Global and Local Variables	122
Passing Parameters	123
HTML and JavaScript Comments	126
Definition of HTML and JavaScript Comments	127
HTML Comments	127
JavaScript Comments	128
Comments To Hide Javascript From Non-Javascript Capable Browsers	128
Using Server-side JavaScript to Redirect non-JavaScript-Capable Browsers	131

CHAPTER 6
Objects, Methods, and Properties 133

JavaScript Compared	133
Objects and Methods and Props, Oh My!	133
Objects and Properties	134
Methods	138
Events	139
Javascript Objects With Their Associated Properties, Methods, and Events	140
navigator Object	141
Example	143
window Object	144
window Synonyms	148
window	149
self	149
top	149
windowReference	149
window Properties	150
defaultStatus	150

status	151
window Methods	151
alert	152
confirm	152
prompt	153
open	154
Examples	155
close	156
setTimeout	156
clearTimeout	157
window Events	157
onLoad	158
onUnload	158
Frames Are Windows Within Windows	**159**
frame Object	**161**
frames Array	168
parent Synonym	168
document Object	**169**
document Properties	175
alinkColor	175
bgColor	176
cookie	176
fgColor	177
lastModified	177
linkColor	177
referrer	177
title	178
vlinkColor	179
document Methods	179
clear	180
close	180
open	180
write	181
writeln	181
document Objects	181
anchors Array Object	182
forms Array and Object	184

history Object 186
history.back() Method 186
history.forward() Method 187
history.go() Method 187
links array Object 187
onClick Event 190
MouseOver Event 190
location Object of the document Object 190
Examples 192

form Object 192
elements Array 196
form Objects 197
button Object 198
Example of onClick 200
checkbox Object 200
hidden Object 204
password Object 206
radio Object 208
reset Object 212
select Object (Options Array) 214
submit Object 221
text Object 224
textarea Object 227

focus, select, and blur Methods and Events 231

Built-in Objects 232

Math Object 233

string Object 244

Date Object 250
Date 250
getYear 256

Built-in Methods 256
escape() and unescape() 258
eval() 258
parsefloat() and parseint() 260
isNaN() 261

Scope of Statements   268
   with   268
   this   269

CHAPTER 7
Developing Applications with LiveWire   271

Overview   271

Creating the Source Files   272
   Creating HTML Files   272
   The <SERVER> Tag   272
   The Backquote (`) Character   273
   Creating JavaScript Function Files   273

Compiling the Source Files   274
   The LiveWire Command-line Compiler   275

Using the LiveWire Application Manager to Install and
   Debug your Applications   277
   Adding and Modifying an Application   277
   Deleting an Existing Application   278
   Starting, Stopping, or Restarting an Application   278
   Running or Debugging an Application   280
   Controlling Access to your LiveWire Applications   283
   Creating a LiveWire Application for your Web Server's Root   283
   Changing Application Manager Settings   284

Summary   284

CHAPTER 8
Server-side JavaScript Language   285

Overview   285

Objects and Functions Shared with client-side JavaScript   286

Top-level Functions   286
   Generating Output   287

Redirecting a page to a new URL   288
Maintaining the Client Object   289
Adding Values to URL Query Strings   289
Calling External Libraries   290
Re-mapping Top-level Functions   290

Pre-defined Objects, their Properties, and Methods   290

The `request` Object   292
Using the `request.agent` Property to Verify a Browser   292
Automatically Setting Properties of the `request` Object   293
Submitting a Form   293
Adding a Query Component to a URL   295
The `client` Object   296
Maintenance Techniques for the `client` Object   297
Using `client-cookie` to Maintain the client object   298
Using the `client-cookie` Technique to Communicate between
   Client-side and Server-side JavaScript   298
Using `client-url` to Maintain the `client` Object   303
Using `server-ip` to Maintain the `client` Object   304
Using `server-cookie` to Maintain the `client` Object   305
Using `server-url` to Maintain the `client` Object   305
The `project` Object   306
Locking the `project` Object   307
The `server` Object   307
The `database` Object   308
Establishing Database Connections   309
Non-locking Database Connection   309
Locking Database Connection   311
Sending SQL Statements to the Database   312
Creating Database Transactions   314
Detecting Database Error Conditions   315

Object-Types, their Properties, and Methods   317

The `database.cursor` Object-type   317
Opening and Closing a Cursor   318
Retrieving the Results of the Query Associated with a Cursor   319
Linking to and Displaying Database BLOB Fields   321
Updating, Deleting, and Inserting Rows in a Cursor   325
Data-type Conversion between the DBMS and JavaScript   327
The `File` Object-type   329

Ensuring File Integrity   330
Opening and Closing a File   330
Getting and Changing the Current Position in a File   331
Getting Information about a File   331
Reading from a File   333
Writing to a File   333
Byte/String Data Conversion   338
Detecting Errors   339

Summary   339

CHAPTER 9
Pulling It All Together   **343**

Overview   343

Message Board Application Requirements   343

Message Board Design Constraints   344

Message Board Design   345
Program Logic   345
User Interface   346
Functional Organization of Message Board Application   347
Partitioning the Application between the Client and the Server   348

Implementing the Message Board Application   349
Creating the Main Application Page   349
Implementing Message Storage Using a Server-side File   356
Implementing Message Storage Using an SQL Database   359

Compiling and Installing the Message Board Application   361

Testing and Verifying the Message Board Application   363

Summary   365

CHAPTER 10
Active Pages with JavaScript   367

Introduction   367

Java/JavaScript Communications   368
    Creating Applets that are JavaScript Friendly   369
    Accessing a Java Applet from JavaScript   369
    Accessing JavaScript from a Java Applet   370
    An Example of Java/JavaScript Communication   374
    Accessing the Standard Java Packages from JavaScript 380

Updateable Images   381

Updateable Form Select Options   382

Summary   384

Index   389

Preface

What You Will Learn

In this book you will learn by example how to create interactive Internet applications on the World Wide Web using JavaScript. You will learn how to program in JavaScript on both the Web browser and Web server. You'll be able to start creating your first interactive Web pages immediately as the examples build on each other.

Benefits for Internet or Intranet Application Developers.

This book will be extremely valuable for Internet application developers considering the use of JavaScript over other Internet development options such as Microsoft's Active X. You will be able to leverage your existing knowledge of the Web and programming languages to get up to speed on JavaScript very quickly. At the conclusion of the book, you will have created a non-trivial JavaScript application that demonstrates many of the language's most valuable features. You will be able to use these components in your own applications.

Benefits for Webmasters.

Webmasters will find this book useful in giving them a clear vision of the kinds of things that are possible with JavaScript and how best to use JavaScript on their sites.

Benefits for Database Administrators and Developers.

Database administrators and developers will be able to quickly understand how JavaScript can interface with their existing database environment. They will also learn about JavaScript's methods for data access and manipulation and gain a clear understanding of how to migrate existing database applications to the Web.

What You Should Know

You should have a general understanding of the Internet and World Wide Web. You should also have some experience with HTML (Hyper-Text Mark-up Language) and be able to recognize its tags. Some programming experience and a knowledge of HTML forms will be useful. For the server-side database features, a knowledge of SQL (Structured Query Language) is important.

Brief History of the Internet and World Wide Web

Over the last few years the Internet has gone from an obscure academic research network to the primary means of disseminating electronic information for the planet. This change was brought about largely by the creation of the World Wide Web. The World Wide Web built upon the existing protocols of the Internet and added protocols and languages that would support hyper-text and multimedia. The cryptic character-cell applications of the Internet gave way to a graphical multimedia interface—the World Wide Web client (sometimes referred to as a browser).

Universities, corporations, and government agencies began creating electronic documents to be served on the World Wide Web on every subject from admissions to product lines to the 1040EZ. This new interface appealed to a much larger audience and users are now flocking to the World Wide Web in droves.

The Problem JavaScript Solves

Most of the World Wide Web to this point is a collection of static documents with very little interactive content. For example, today you may connect to your bank's World Wide Web page and it gives you static information about taking out a loan and the current interest rates available. What you'd really find useful, however, is to fill out a loan application, calculate your monthly payment, view your amortization schedule, and see if the bank will pre-approve the loan based on your current credit rating and income-to-debt ratio. This kind of interactive content is made possible with JavaScript!

Brief Introduction to JavaScript

The JavaScript language was developed by Netscape Communications Corporation as an extension to the Hyper-Text Mark-up Language (HTML) to facilitate the development of interactive, full-featured applications on the World Wide Web. JavaScript statements are embedded in an HTML page and run directly as interpreted commands within the Web client or on the Web server. You can write JavaScript just like HTML code using a simple text editor.

JavaScript has a specific group of objects that it can take advantage of depending on where it is running. On the client, JavaScript can validate form input, pop up confirmation messages, make calculations, and so forth. On the server, JavaScript can create and access server files, perform database operations, and share data among clients. You will be taught the fundamentals of JavaScript so that you can begin to write JavaScript code immediately!

How JavaScript relates to Java

JavaScript is NOT the same as Java. Java was developed at Sun Microsystems and, as stated above, JavaScript was developed at Netscape. The two languages are related, but yet are very different and have different purposes. Java is a full-featured object-oriented programming language that creates separate applets (mini-applications) that don't interrelate with HTML like JavaScript does. Most of these applets just display in a box in the Web client similar to the way an embedded image does. JavaScript is much simpler to program than Java. JavaScript was designed for a more specific purpose—exposing useful properties of the Web client and server to a script programmer.

Chapter Overview

Chapter 1. In this chapter, you will be given an introduction to the JavaScript architecture. Specifically, you will learn about what JavaScript has in common with some of today's most popular languages. In addition, you will learn about some of JavaScript's features that differentiate it from other languages. You will also be taught how JavaScript on the browser and JavaScript on the Web server relate to each other.

Chapter 2. The structure of client-side JavaScript and its usage and placement within an HTML document is introduced using the traditional "Hello World" application in three examples. The first shows the simplest usage of JavaScript to create document text. The second introduces JavaScript as called by HTML forms. And the last example demonstrates using JavaScript in a multi-frame environment crossing frames to display "Hello World" in the language of the user's choice.

Chapter 3. In this chapter, you will be exposed to JavaScript running on the Web server. You will create your first server-side JavaScript application. As part of creating this application, you will learn about server-side Java-Script's powerful shared data structures. You will also be taught how to install JavaScript applications on the Web server using the LiveWire Application Manager.

Chapter 4. Understanding the structure of a browser, including windows, documents, and frames, and how they relate to each other is important before beginning JavaScript programming.

Chapter 5. The JavaScript language has some similarities with C++ and some important differences. The structure of the language includes common elements such as "if" statements, "while" and "for" loops, and other control structures. Variables are declared either locally within a function or globally to be accessed by JavaScript from any context.

Chapter 6. The core of JavaScript are the objects, methods, and properties of the language. Each HTML object and tag is associated with a JavaScript object. The language also has built-in objects and methods to handle dates, strings, and math operations.

Chapter 7. This chapter goes into detail about the server-side JavaScript development environment. Specifically, you will learn more about the LiveWire Compiler and LiveWire Application Manager that you used in Chapter 3. You will also learn how to debug server-side JavaScript applications.

Chapter 8. This chapter will focus on the server-side JavaScript Language Components. You will learn about the top-level functions, pre-defined objects, and object-types unique to server-side JavaScript. There will be formal specifications of these components as well as clarifying examples to solidify the concepts. You will also learn about the objects and functions shared with client-side JavaScript.

Chapter 9. The real strength of JavaScript is in using client-side and server-side JavaScript together to develop full-featured Web applications. The best way to show how they work together is to create a non-trivial application that incorporates them both. In Chapter 9, you will create a message board application. This application will include some of the most useful features of client-side and server-side JavaScript. After completing this program and the other examples in the book, you should feel confidant in using JavaScript to develop real-world Web applications.

Chapter 10. This Chapter covers some of the new features of JavaScript as introduced in Netscape Navigator 3.0. It includes information on how to communicate with Java applets and the Java API in JavaScript. It also demonstrates how to update images and select options text in an HTML page.

Conventions used in this Book

The following fonts will used in the text:

- Code - Used to display JavaScript source code.
- **Keyword** - Used to represent JavaScript keywords or built-in objects and methods in the source code.
- *ObjectInstances* - A place holder for an instance of an object. Use the actual instance name defined in your code, instead of the place holder name.
- Result - The result of the execution of some JavaScript code.

The Software Used with this Book

All of the examples from the book are contained on the included CD-ROM. Refer to the READ_ME.TXT file in the root directory of the CD-ROM for more information on its contents.

The following Netscape software products are required to run the examples in the book:

- For client-side JavaScript, you should install <u>Netscape Navigator</u> 2.x or higher. For your convenience, Netscape Navigator 2.02 is included on the CD-ROM. However, you may choose to obtain the latest release from the Netscape site (Netscape Navigator 3.x or higher is required for the examples in Chapter 10).
- For server-side JavaScript, you should obtain and install the latest release of the <u>Netscape FastTrack</u> or <u>Enterprise</u> Web Server. Included with either of these servers is the runtime environment that supports server-side JavaScript. In order to develop your own applications that incorporate server-side JavaScript, you will also need to obtain and install the <u>Netscape LiveWire</u> product.

You may obtain these products from the Netscape site at the URL:

```
http://home.netscape.com/comprod/mirror/index.html
```

For Java/JavaScript communication as covered in Chapter 10, you should obtain and install the latest release of the Java Developer's Kit (JDK) from JavaSoft, a Sun Microsystems Business, at the URL:

```
http://www.javasoft.com/
```

Installing Netscape Navigator from the CD-ROM

As mentioned previously, Netscape Navigator 2.02 is included on the CD-ROM for the MacOS, Windows 3.1, Windows 95/NT, and HP-UX under the NETSCAPE directory. There is a platform-specific sub-directory under the NETSCAPE directory that contains the supported version of Navigator for that platform. See Table P-1 for more information.

TABLE P-1. Installing Netscape Navigator from the CD-ROM.

Platform	CD-ROM File	Installation Instructions
MacOS	MAC\NETSCAPE.202	Execute this program to install the Netscape Navigator on your Macintosh.
Win 3.1	WIN31\SETUP.EXE	Execute this file from the File\Run menu of the Program Manager to start the installation. After installation is complete, there should be a Netscape folder in the Program Manager.
Win 95/NT	WIN95_NT\SETUP.EXE	Execute this file from the Start\Run option of the Taskbar to begin the installation. After installation is complete, there should be a Netscape Navigator folder under the Programs area of the Start Taskbar.
HP-UX	HPUX\NSNAV202.TAR	Extract this .tar file by executing cat /cdrom_path/nsnav202.tar | tar xfv - from a writeable location. This extracts the netscape executable file.

When Netscape Navigator is executed for the first time you are asked to review Netscape's license agreement and either accept or reject it. The inclusion of Netscape Navigator on this CD-ROM gives you no special privileges or licenses to the Navigator software above and beyond those granted by Netscape Communications Corporation. Please be sure to abide by their licensing agreement.

Using Netscape Navigator to Access the Examples on CD-ROM

In addition to being able to view files across the Internet, Navigator can be used to view HTML files on your personal computer. This is done by selecting the `"Open File..."` option from the Navigator `"File"` pull-down menu. From there you are presented with the standard "opening a file" dialog box for your graphical environment. You can view the examples from the CD-ROM by selecting the CD drive and choosing the desired HTML file to load.

Acknowledgments

We gratefully acknowledge the contributions of HP Press and Pat Pekary. Their support and encouragement of this work contributed measurably. We also acknowledge the assistance of Karen Gettman and Joanne Anzalone. We thank Netscape Communications for permission to include their Navigator product on the CD-ROM. Brigham Young University's Lee Library contributed support and encouragement. We also want to thank our wives and children for allowing us the time to complete the project.

About the Authors

Brian Holman is a systems programmer for the Lee Library at Brigham Young University. Brian created his first World Wide Web site in January 1994 as the beginning of an Electronic Libraries Project. Further work on this project led Brian to create an interface to simplify the programming of CGI-based World Wide Web applications. He has also developed gateways between the World Wide Web and database protocols such as SQL and Z39.50. He is now actively working to exploit the strengths of Java and JavaScript in creating more robust and user-friendly Web applications. Brian holds a B.S. in Computer Science from BYU. His email address is brian_holman@byu.edu

Bill Lund is the information systems manager for the Lee Library at Brigham Young University. His background includes a tenure at Hewlett-Packard as a manager in the research and development labs of the Information Networks Division. He is the author of the book *Integrating UNIX and PC Network Operating Systems* published recently by HP Press. Bill holds a B.S. in Mathematics from BYU and a Masters in Operations Research from Stanford University. His email address is bill_lund@byu.edu.

Introduction to the JavaScript Architecture

What is JavaScript?

JavaScript is an object-based scripting language that has expression syntax and flow control similar to C, C++, and Java. However, JavaScript is not compiled to some low-level machine code as is the case with the aforementioned languages. It is a runtime-interpreted language with an architecture similar to HyperTalk and Perl.

In addition to the language, the JavaScript environment includes several built-in objects that could be considered the "standard libraries" of JavaScript. These objects are JavaScript's interface to the key components of the Web browser and Web server environments. For example, on the client, the `document.title` property refers to the title of the current HTML document and the `history.back()` method loads the previous URL in the history list.

Noteworthy Attributes of the JavaScript Language

Familiar. JavaScript has much in common with some of today's most popular languages. Those familiar with C, C++, or Java will not have to relearn the syntax for loops, conditionals, expressions, or operators since they are much the same in JavaScript. However, in some cases, the semantics are different than in C, C++, or Java. In those cases, we will attempt to highlight the differences. The following example illustrates some of JavaScript's similarities to C, C++, and Java with regard to loops, assignments, conditionals, and expressions:

1

```
for (i=0; i < 10; i++) document.write(i + " ");

while (i >= 5)
{
        i--;
}
document.write(i);

if (i == 4)
        i+=3;
else
        i=2;
document.write(i == 7 ? " seven" : " NOT seven");
```

```
0 1 2 3 4 5 6 7 8 9 4 seven
```

Embedded in HTML. In addition to JavaScript's similarities to other languages, the language also has elements that make it unique. JavaScript statements are embedded in HTML pages. HTML generated from JavaScript appears in the order in which it was placed in the HTML source file. Java-Script is generally executed only once per document load and cannot be changed once it is displayed. However, JavaScript functions assigned as event handlers may be executed more than once. You'll learn more about this in Chapter 6. This is an example of how JavaScript is embedded in HTML:

```
<HTML>
....
<SCRIPT>
client-side JavaScript code
</SCRIPT>
....
<SERVER>
server-side JavaScript code
</SERVER>
....
</HTML>
```

Object-based, but not object-oriented. Like object-oriented languages such as C++ and Java, JavaScript allows you to have objects and those objects can have associated properties and methods (functions associated with a specific object). However, the concept of inheritance where one object definition builds on another does not exist. The concept of data hiding is also nonexistent—every property and method is accessible from the global scope.

Listing 1-1 demonstrates defining an `Employee` object with its properties (`name, title, salary`) and associating the function `Raise()` as the method `raise()` for that object type. It also shows how to create and manipulate a new object of that type.

```javascript
// Define Raise() method for Employee() object
function Raise()
{
    this.salary = this.salary + (0.10 * this.salary);
}

// Define the Employee object definition
function Employee(name, title, salary)
{
    this.name = name;
    this.title = title;
    this.salary = salary;
    this.raise = Raise;
}

// Create a new Employee() object
emp1 = new Employee("John Doe", "Programmer", 40000.00);

// Call the raise() method and output the result
emp1.raise();
document.write(emp1.name);
document.write("'s new salary after a raise is ");
document.write(emp1.salary);
```

LISTING 1-1   DEMONSTRATES JAVASCRIPT'S OBJECT-BASED FEATURES.

```
John Doe's new salary after a raise is 44000
```

Loose Data-typing. With JavaScript, it is not necessary to declare the type of a variable. JavaScript offers a great deal of flexibility on what the type of a variable is and this can change during the variable's lifetime. This example illustrates the loose data-typing in JavaScript:

```
var money = "Famous Painter";
document.writeln(money);
money = 25 + 7;
document.writeln(money);
```

```
Famous Painter
32
```

Relationship between client-side and server-side JavaScript

JavaScript can be used to develop client/server Internet applications using the same consistent language on both the client and server. As of this writing, client-side JavaScript is supported in Netscape Navigator 2.x or higher. It is also expected that Microsoft Internet Explorer will support client-side JavaScript in version 3.0. Server-side JavaScript is supported on any of the Netscape Web servers with LiveWire or LiveWire Pro installed.

Client-side JavaScript gives a developer access to the key features of the browser, including such things as frames, form elements with their events and content, and document location. These JavaScript statements are embedded in an HTML page and interpreted by the browser.

Server-side JavaScript is executed on the Web server and its source is *not* viewable by the client browser. Instead, the results are sent to the client along with the standard HTML in the page and any client-side JavaScript code.

Server-side JavaScript has facilities for state management and database access. State management is important because connections between the browser and Web server are not maintained, but are issued independently on an as-needed basis. And of course, keeping state is important to many data-oriented applications, i.e., knowing what the user last entered as input, knowing what the previous result was, and so forth.

In addition, having a facility for database access is critical to developing any serious enterprise application. Server-side JavaScript contains support for the most popular commercial databases including Oracle, Informix, Illustra, and Sybase. Additional databases are supported through ODBC.

Using JavaScript to develop Internet applications

Let's say you want to check for available flights via the Web. You want to be able to select the origin and destination airports from an HTML form and enter the desired date and maximum ticket price you are willing to pay. Once you enter this information, you would like to see a display of a table of flights that match your query. Finally, you would like to be able to select the flight you are interested in and make a reservation. Table 1-1 demonstrates the way this application would most likely be partitioned between the client and server.

TABLE 1-1. Application partitioning example with JavaScript.

Client-side JavaScript	Server-side JavaScript
Verify that the user entered a valid date and alert the user if it is invalid. Verify that the user entered a valid dollar amount for the maximum ticket price (can't be less than zero and must be a valid number) and alert the user if it is invalid.	Query the database for possible airports and generate an HTML form for airport selection. Query the database for flights that meet the user's requirements and display them in a HTML table.

In any client/server development project, design decisions must be made as to which components of the application should reside on the client and which should reside on the server—this is known as application partitioning. The general idea is to have the server do what is absolutely necessary for it to do and to have the client do the rest. However, "which component resides where" is application- and environment-specific. For example, you may want to use client-side JavaScript for form validation and use server-side JavaScript for database access. During the design phase, you discover that 50% of your users are not using a JavaScript-compatible browser, so you move form validation to the server. You make this trade-off of requiring the server to do more work for the client so that you can provide access to a larger group of users. As a result, the client is not much more than a screen painter, whereas the server may pose a potential bottle-neck for transaction processing.

Independence of client-side and server-side JavaScript

Client-side and server-side JavaScript can be used independent of each other. For example, you could use client-side JavaScript to validate a form and submit it via CGI to a Perl script running on an NCSA Web server.

Using the same language on the client and server has significant advantages. Application development is much less complicated and partitioning code between the client and server is much more straightforward. Any serious application developer should consider this elegant approach to developing full-featured Web applications.

Hello World!
Introduction to
JavaScript

- **Three Hello World Scripts Using JavaScript**
- **Hello World 1 Using Inline JavaScript**
- **Hello World 2 Using Forms**
- **Hello World 3 Using Frames**
- **JavaScript Functions**
- **HTML and JavaScript Comments**
- **Frames And How To Define Them**

In this chapter we're going to write our first HTML pages that use client-side JavaScript in three simple "Hello World" pages. These examles will demonstrate the basic structures and components of the language. The chapters which follow will go through the particulars of the language, including the syntax, built-in objects that can be controlled by JavaScript, and some examples of interesting JavaScript applications.

For you to follow along with this book, you will need to have access to the NetScape 2.0 browser for your client platform. If you have a version greater than 2.0, that will work too. As of this writing, JavaScript was still being developed by Netscape Communications so some of the scripts you find here may need to be changed to work on your client if the language has been modified. Netscape Communications maintains current JavaScript documentation on their home page at <URL: http://www.netscape.com>.

Hello World 1

Figure 2-1 and Listing 2-1 show our first, very simple implementation of an HTML page which uses JavaScript.

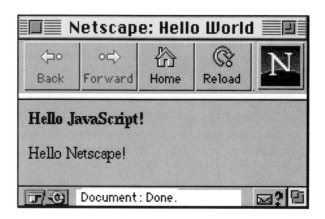

FIGURE 2-1   Hello World 1 as seen on a Netscape browser.

```
<HTML>
<!-- File: LIST2_01.HTM
     Usage: A simple HTML page with embedded
            JavaScript which is displayed when the
            page is loaded.
  -->
<HEAD>
<TITLE>Hello World</TITLE>
<SCRIPT LANGUAGE="JavaScript">
document.write("<B>Hello JavaScript!</B>")
</SCRIPT>
</HEAD>

<BODY>
<P>Hello Netscape!
</BODY>

</HTML>
```

LISTING 2-1   THE HELLO WORLD 1 HTML SCRIPT WHICH GENERATED THE BROWSER WINDOW IN FIGURE 2-1

Components of Hello World I HTML Page

Our first foray into JavaScript is admittedly a very simple one showing only one new HTML tag that isn't common to HTML version 3. These are the `<SCRIPT>` ... `</SCRIPT>` tags which contain the JavaScript itself. All of the other tags in this example are standard to HTML. JavaScript extends the HTML language with other components, such as event handlers for forms. so that when the content of a form changes, specific JavaScript functions or code will be executed. But, more on those later...

Let's review all of the components of this script. Although we've assumed that you are already familiar with enough HTML that a detailed discussion of HTML components isn't really necessary, we'll mention a few items of particular interest to JavaScript programming.

`<HTML>` Tag of Hello World 1

```
<HTML>  ...  </HTML>
```

info	Although the official documentation indicates that the <HTML> tag should enclose the entire document, most browsers allow you to get away without including it.

The `<HTML>` tag tells the browser that you're going to be using HTML scripting language. Depending on the browser, this is often not required if the end of the document name is ".HTML" or ".HTM". For consistency's sake, it is good to use the `<HTML>` tag. Another good reason is that some browsers will not expect a document to contain HTML unless the file name has the ".HTML" extension, or unless the first line contains the `<HTML>` tag. It won't hurt to include the tag and may save some confusion.

As we would expect the `</HTML>` tag terminates the `<HTML>` tag. All HTML tags and text should appear between the `<HTML>` and `</HTML>` tags, although experience shows that most browsers don't really care where the tags and text are and will continue to interpret HTML tags and text even after the closing `</HTML>` tag. As we'll see in a later chapter which discusses ways to hide JavaScript code from browsers that don't interpret the `<SCRIPT>` tag, browsers aren't consistent in their interpretation of SGML or HTML specifications.

<!-- --> HTML Comments

Formally, HTML itself does not have any way to embed comments in the text; however "meta-commands" provide a way to do this. A "meta-command" is used to give commands to the browser itself, in practice, however this part of the SGML and HTML specifications is rarely used by HTML writers. The meta-command begins with "<!" and ends with ">". The double dashes "--" are comments within the meta-command. Frequently, you'll see the "<!-- ... -->" characters used as a comment field within HTML, however you could just as easily separate the "<!" and ">" from the double dashes as demonstrated in Listing 2-2. This may seem like a small point, but you'll see

```
<!-- This is a comment within HTML
     which stretches across two lines -->

<!
  -- This is also a comment          --
  -- which uses the double dashes     --
  -- to embed each line in a separate --
  -- comment field.  The meta-command --
  -- will end on its own without a    --
  -- double dash.                     --
>
```

LISTING 2-2   EXAMPLE OF HTML COMMENTS

later in this chapter what happens when you try to hide JavaScript from a browser which doesn't understand JavaScript by enclosing it within the meta-command comment structure.

<HEAD> Tag

<HEAD> ... </HEAD>

Implemented in HTML version 2.0.

Tags which appear under the <HEAD> tag:

- <BASE> - defines the base URL for the document from which all relative references are defined.
- <ISINDEX> - defines a searchable index for the document.

- `<TITLE>` - defines a title for the document to be displayed on the title bar of the page.

The `<HEAD>` tag is for components of the page which apply to the entire document. Typically, information that would appear here would describe aspects of the entire document, such as the title of the page which appears at the top of the window displaying the page's contents. Often, this tag can be left out since the other tags which appear under this section are unique to the `<HEAD>` section and the browser just processes them as they occur. The most commonly used tag here is the `<TITLE>` tag, which gives the document a title for the title bar on the window.

Although a strict interpretation of what you would expect from the `<HEAD>` tag and its sub-tags might lead you to believe that untagged text within the `<HEAD>` … `</HEAD>` pair would not appear on the page, this isn't the case on most browsers. In particular, the Netscape browser will display any untagged text inside the `<HEAD>` section as if it were inside the `<BODY>` section. Figure 2-2 and Listing 2-3 show what happens to text that is scattered

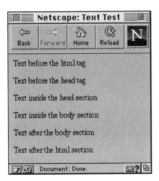

Many browsers do not care where text appears in the document; if it isn't directly attached to another tag, it will be displayed. This can lead to some messy practices for the HTML page writer, and as we'll see, it also causes some confusion to browsers that don't understand the <SCRIPT> tag.

FIGURE 2-2   Text locations within an HTML document.

in all areas of the document, outside of the `<HTML>` tags, within the `<HEAD>` tags, and elsewhere. As Figure 2-2 shows, the Netscape 2.0 browser splashes all of it on the page.

This is an important issue because when a browser that does not interpret the `<SCRIPT>` tag gets your JavaScript code, even though the text is within the `<HEAD>` tags, buried somewhere else in the document or even enclosed within HTML comments, it will most likely display on the page and produce a page that looks messy and unprofessional. Chapter 8 will discuss some ways around this problem

```
<!-- File: LIST2_03.HTM
     Usage: Demonstrate what happens to text outside of
            the BODY tag
  -->

<P>Text before the HTML tag

<HTML>
<P>Text before the head tag

<HEAD>
<P>Text inside the head section
<TITLE>Text Test</TITLE>
</HEAD>

<BODY>
<P> Text inside the body section
</BODY>

<P>Text after the body section
</HTML>

<P>Text after the HTML section
```

LISTING 2-3   THE HTML THAT GENERATED THE BROWSER WINDOW SHOWN IN FIGURE 2-2 USING THE
NETSCAPE BROWSER.

<TITLE> Tag in Hello World 1

```
<TITLE> ... </TITLE>
```

Implemented in HTML version 2.0.

The <TITLE> tag should only appear within the <HEAD> tag. If the title is not provided, the name of the document file is used instead.

Returning to our example in Figure 2-1 and Listing 2-1, let's review each line of code to see what it is doing.

```
<TITLE>Hello World</TITLE>
```

The first tag we see in the heading is the <TITLE> tag. This is probably familiar to most people who have used HTML before. It simply puts a text string into the browser window for this document. It is a nice touch that gives the user a feeling for what kind of information is being provided in the document.

<SCRIPT> Tag

```
<SCRIPT> ... </SCRIPT>
```

<SCRIPT> contains the JavaScript of the document. It may appear in the <HEAD> or <BODY> sections of the document.

LANGUAGE=" *text* " attribute defines the scripting language being used.

```
<SCRIPT LANGUAGE="JavaScript">
```

The next tag after <TITLE> is new and is the first encounter we've had with JavaScript. This particular script executes immediately when it is encountered by the browser as the document is loaded and, as we've seen in Figure 2-1, displays the text message "Hello JavaScript". Before we move on, let's look at the sub-tags.

LANGUAGE Sub-tag. The authors of JavaScript are being very forward-looking and flexible. At this writing only one value is legal for the "LANGUAGE" sub-tag and that is "JavaScript"; however, if someone else were to develop another scripting language, the <SCRIPT> tag is extensible to allow for this.

At this writing the only officially released browser which supports JavaScript is the Netscape Navigator. Microsoft has announced support for JavaScript in their Internet Explorer product.

The Script Itself

```
document.write("<B>Hello JavaScript!</B>")
```

With `document.write()` we've run into the first component of the JavaScript language. "document" is the name of an object which can receive messages in the context of an object-oriented language. The "`write(...)`" message sent to the document object tells the browser to display some text defined in the `write()` message as a document. We'll see a little later that you need to be careful when you're sending text to the document because you can overwrite what is already there. (See Figure 2-3.)

Comparing JavaScript to other Object-Oriented Languages

For those familiar with other object-oriented languages, JavaScript has defined objects that can send and receive messages as shown in Figure 2-3. In

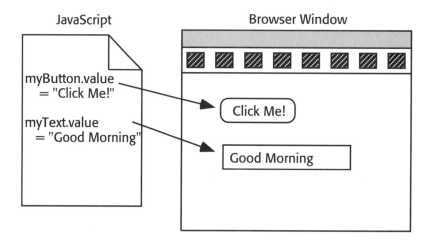

FIGURE 2-3   JavaScript sending "messages" to "objects", which changes the content of the document.

this respect, JavaScript is an object-oriented language, like C++, Java, Small-Talk, HyperTalk, and others. Each language differs in the degree to which the principles of object-oriented programming are implemented, but in general all share similar concepts. For instance, JavaScript defines objects to which messages are sent. If you aren't familiar with the model of object-oriented programming, it looks like you are making procedure function calls. Those who are familiar already with C++ and Java will recognize the syntax we just saw in our very short example, `document.write(...)`. "document" is the name of the object and `write()` is a method, message, or function (depending on your background, you might use any one of those terms). By putting them together as we have done, `document.write(...)` says that we're calling a procedure, in this case, `write()`, and we want to apply it to an object, in this case, "document". The result is that the text within the `write()` method is sent to the document and will be displayed with the data stream when the document is closed, usually at the end of the document load or when the JavaScript is finished executing, whichever occurs last.

Object-Oriented Programming

If you're not familiar with object-oriented languages, let's discuss the syntax we've just seen. In a procedural language like Pascal, a function or procedure call is made just using the name of the function. In our example for Hello World 1, the procedure call is actually the "`write(...)`" statement. In Pascal, `write()` would have been defined so that it already knew who it was writing to, or perhaps it would have been called "`document_write()`" so that the programmer could see the difference between writing to a document and writing to a text field which might have been called "`txt_fld_write()`".

We don't have room here for a complete discussion of object-oriented programming (OOP), but one of the virtues of OOP is that the same function call, in this case, `write()`, can be used for different types of structures. So, `document.write()` and `formname.textarea.write()` both use the specifications for `write()`, but the JavaScript interpreter works out the differences between writing to a document and writing to a text field. Perhaps an easy way to think about this is to consider `write()` as if it had been defined to have a parameter which determined the type of write to call. So, `document.write()` could be thought of as `write( document, "text")` and `formname.textarea.write()` could be thought of as `write( formname, textarea, "text")`, where a very clever programmer had set up the first parameters to capture the type of data structure on which `write()` was operating.

What Is a "document" in JavaScript?

So what is a "document"? As you might expect, a `document`, in this case, refers to the entire HTML code which the browser is currently displaying in the top-most page of the top-most window. Because we're calling it directly in the `<HEAD>` section, it writes the contents of `write(...)` to the screen at the point where it is writing the header.

Could you just call `write()` without referring it to an object? Not really. Within JavaScript, `write()` and the other functions, or methods, as they are more properly called, apply to specific objects, and JavaScript does not allow for overloading, or redefining an existing method to do something other than what the language allows. Therefore objects will have a `write()` method and others will not, depending on what type of object we're talking about and what makes sense.

Within the `document.write(...)` call, you see a string which is enclosed within "...". Whenever you see quotation marks, the text within the marks is considered a string. In this case we've put an HTML tag to make the following string bold `<B>`, then the text, and the tag to end the bold text `</B>`. In fact, any HTML code could have been found in here. We've put something very simple, but it could have been any HTML you wanted to write.

As a follow-on to the question we posed in Figure 2-2 concerning what happens if text appears around or in the `<SCRIPT>`? Just like in Figure 2-2, any text which isn't directly associated with a tag is interpreted by many browsers as text to be displayed on the screen and will appear as such.

The Rest of the "`document`" in Hello World 1

The rest of the HTML is very pedestrian and doesn't deserve much explanation. We just begin the formal body of the document, remembering that the Netscape browser doesn't really care where unattached text appears, it is willing to display it anywhere. We say hello to the browser itself and end the document.

Review of HTML

Now that we've seen our first JavaScript example, albeit a very small one, let's review some HTML concepts so that we don't get confused later. First, the browser doesn't really care about the formatting you've done in the original file which contains the HTML. Although our example Hello World 1 in Listing 2-1 is nicely laid out with separate lines for the tags and text appearing on each line, the browser could have done just as well with the text in Listing 2-4. Even though all of the tags and text are continuous, the browser interprets this just like Figure 2-1. The formatting is really for the human reader, to make it clear what is happening in the script. With that in mind, it is a very good idea to use this flexibility to make your scripts as readable as possible. Good programmers, who have experience in complex systems, know the value of writing readable code. Six months after you create even a moderately complex piece of code, you won't have a clue about what it is trying to do without good structured techniques and comments.

```
<HTML><HEAD><SCRIPT LANGUAGE="JavaScript">
document.write("<B>Hello JavaScript!</B>")</SCRIPT>
<TITLE>Hello World</TITLE></HEAD><BODY><P>Hello
Netscape!</BODY></HTML>
```

LISTING 2-4   HELLO WORLD 1 WITHOUT PRETTY FORMATTING. THE BROWSER DOESN'T CARE ABOUT
SPACING AND LINE FEEDS WHEN OUTSIDE OF THE TEXT AREA. COMPARE WITH LISTING 2-1

The only exception to the "non-formatting" of HTML is the <PRE> tag,
which says to the browser, I've already formatted this text, display it just like
I have written it here. The danger in using the <PRE> tag too much is that the
browser makes the text independent of any particular visual display system.
Therefore using the <PRE> tag, you are defeating the independence of the
browser. It is a better idea to use HTML formatting tags to create the text the
way you want it to appear. Figure 2-4 and Listing 2-5 show what happens

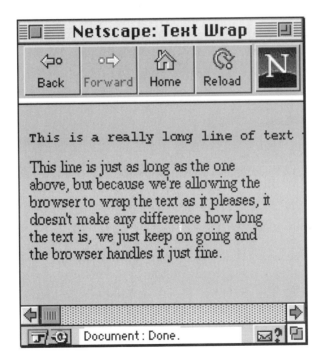

FIGURE 2-4   The first line of text scrolls off the screen because the document uses
the <PRE> tag to prevent formatting. See Listing 2.5 for the HTML.

```
<HTML>
<!-- File: LIST2_05.HTM
     Usage: Demonstrate the line formatting of HTML
  -->

<HEAD>
<TITLE>Text Wrap</TITLE>
</HEAD>

<BODY>
<PRE>
This is a really long line of text that most browsers would
eventually get really upset about and it would  go off the
end of the page and you'd have to scroll over to read all
of it.
</PRE>

<P>
This line is just as long as the one above, but because we're
allowing the browser to wrap the text as it pleases, it
doesn't make any difference how long the text is, we just
keep on going and the browser handles it just fine.

</BODY>

</HTML>
```

LISTING 2-5   THE POINT OF USING A BROWSER WITH FORMATTING TAGS IS TO LET THE BROWSER WORRY ABOUT HOW TO ACTUALLY DISPLAY THE INFORMATION YOU ARE PRESENTING. USE OF THE <PRE> TAG PREVENTS THIS.

when the <PRE> tag is used to force formatting rather than letting the browser do it for you. People frequently want to use the <PRE> tag when trying to format a document. Make the effort to use HTML tables and frames to display the information instead.

Having said all of that, you must keep in mind that the browser will not glue pieces of a word together. Be sure that no word has a break, either a space or carriage return, in the middle. This convention seems reasonable, but after making a big deal out of how HTML is really non-formatted text, we thought we'd better include this comment.

Hello World 2

It's always good to start out with something simple and then get more complex. We've seen a very simple document which was for all intents nothing more than what you could have done without JavaScript. Now let's move on to something a little more interesting and interactive. Figure 2-5 and Listing 2-6 show JavaScript changing the content of a document on the fly based on user input.

FIGURE 2.5A   An example of using JavaScript to interact with the user. The form allows the user to select the language in which "Hello World" will be displayed. Hello World 2 as it appears when first loaded.

Review The New Components

Since we're not going to go over all the basics of writing HTML, and our first example covered everything that was used, we'll go straight to the new components after looking at the execution of the script.

FIGURE 2.5B   Hello World 2 after the user has clicked on the menu item.

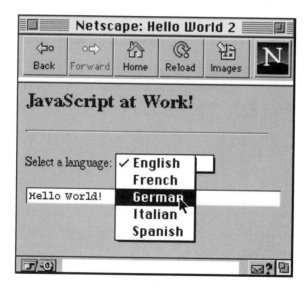

FIGURE 2.5C   The user scrolls down to the item "German" and selects it.

FIGURE 2.5D   Hello World 2 after the user has selected a language.

```
<HTML>
<!-- Hello World 2
     File: LIST2_06.HTM
     Usage: Demonstrate the use of forms to communicate
     between the user and the JavaScript code.
  -->

<HEAD>
<TITLE>
   Hello World 2
</TITLE>
<!-- Put scripts under the HEAD tag so that they are
     available to the rest of the document.
  -->
<SCRIPT LANGUAGE="JavaScript">
```

LISTING 2-6   THE HTML CODE USED TO GENERATE HELLO WORLD 2 SHOWN IN FIGURE 2-5.

```
// This function will receive the name of
// a form and based on the selected index from
// the form itself will great you in that language.

function sayHi(my_form)
{
    // Retrieve the value of the index selected
    // in the form
    var idx = my_form.seLang.selectedIndex

    // Based on the index of the select field,
    // put a greeting in the text field of the form.
    if ( idx == 0 )
        my_form.inHello.value = "Hello World!"
    if ( idx == 1)
        my_form.inHello.value = "Bonjour tous le monde!"
    if ( idx == 2)
        my_form.inHello.value = "Guten Tag Welt!"
    if ( idx == 3 )
        my_form.inHello.value = "Buon giorno tutto il" +
                                " mondo!"
    if ( idx == 4 )
        // You can't use the i acute by typing it in.
        // you must call it out of the ISO Latin
        // character set.
        my_form.inHello.value = "Buenas d" +
            unescape( "%92" ) + "as el mundo!"

return
}

</SCRIPT>
</HEAD>

 <BODY>

<H2>JavaScript at Work!</H2>

<HR>

<FORM NAME="foLang">
    Select a language:
```

LISTING 2-6   (CONTINUED) THE HTML CODE USED TO GENERATE HELLO WORLD 2 SHOWN IN FIGURE
2-5.

```
<SELECT NAME="seLang" ONCHANGE="sayHi(this.form)">
    <OPTION SELECTED>English
    <OPTION>French
    <OPTION>German
      <OPTION>Italian
    <OPTION>Spanish
</SELECT>
<BR><BR>
<INPUT TYPE="TEXT" NAME="inHello"
        VALUE="Hello World!" SIZE=40>
</FORM>

</BODY>
</HTML>
```

LISTING 2-6   (CONTINUED) THE HTML CODE USED TO GENERATE HELLO WORLD 2 SHOWN IN FIGURE 2-5.

<SCRIPT> Tag in Hello World 2

Like last time, we're defining the script inside the <HEAD> section. One of the reasons for doing this is to make sure that the function is available when the document needs it. For instance, if a function in the <SCRIPT> section were needed while the page was loading, perhaps to change the date on the document, the function which made that change would have to have been previously defined before it was needed. You can define a <SCRIPT> in many places in a document, but it must be defined before it is used..

 warning   document.write() will overwrite any document which already exists in your browser window. This includes an and all JavaScript functions and objects.

Unlike the last example, this script won't be executed as the document is being loaded because we defined a function which must be called to execute the script

Why didn't we just use document.write() as in the first example to display our "Hello World!" in each language? This is due to the way that the Netscape browser handles a document. From the perspective of the browser, a document is a static thing which never changes until it is replaced or overlaid with another document. Table 2-1 shows the procedure the Netscape browser uses to deliver a document to a window.

TABLE 2-1. Updating a document.

1. Open a document for display.

2. Download the text and tags for the document.

3. Close the document so that there is no updating of the content. Note that the browser considers the form's structure to be separate from its contents. You can update the contents of a form, but not the structure.

Once a document has been displayed, you can not go back and modify it. Your only option is to replace it or open a new document in the same window. For example, if we had used `document.write()` to display the "Hello World" message, the script would have overwritten the existing window and our user input form would have been lost. You'd get one chance to select from the form and then you'd have to reload the form to select something else.

In some instances, this may be adequate. For example, it could be useful when a user is expected to make a selection and move on from there, never returning to the page. In this case, however, we wanted the user to be able to make multiple choices.

Changing the Contents of a Document Once it is Written.

So why do you get to change the contents of the form?We previously said that once a document was written, it could not be changed? But this form consists of input fields which can be modified. Our page and JavaScript specifically allow us to modify the contents of the form. This is one way in which JavaScript can make an HTML page interactive, by allowing output based on the user's input.

Three components of HTML and JavaScript make an HTML page interactive: hypertext links, forms, and frames.

Hypertext Links. The first component of HTML and JavaScript which provide interactive capability to an HTML document is the original concept of hypertext links. This is the familiar point-and-click link to other documents. The user can select the order in which the documents are displayed, but cannot change the content of a document interactively. This also does not allow the current page to change content.

Forms Within an HTML Document. Forms, which were added to the original HTML specifications, allowed a user to input information into a document. This made HTML a two-way vehicle for exchanging information between the user and HTTD server which provided the HTML document.

To use the information a user provided in a form, a program had to be written on the HTTD server using the Common Gateway Interface (CGI). The program on the server used the information provided through the CGI interface and displayed an appropriate response. This required that the document author write in some language such as Perl on the server.

With JavaScript, the contents of the form are available to the document writer through JavaScript objects. You can use the form to gather input from the user and use JavaScript to act on the input. Still, if you want to retrieve and save the information, you need the server to do something with it. That's where server-side JavaScript comes in. Without the server-side of JavaScript, you'd still have to program using the CGI interface. With server-side JavaScript, you are given the power to save and manipulate the data with minimal programming.

Frames Within an HTML Document. Frames are a fairly new concept in HTML and were originally proposed by Netscape Communications. Frames allow the HTML writer to divide up the browser window into multiple independent documents.

Although frames themselves don't allow for user input (you still use forms for that) they do allow you to get around a problem which is present in using forms for all user input. As you might have thought, if you're limited to only putting information into a form, how do you format the information and how do you use some of the advanced features of HTML such as displaying images and hypertext links?

Frames allow you to have multiple documents displayed in the same browser window, where one window can control the content of another window. Hello World 3 will demonstrate this.

The Contents of the JavaScript in Hello World 2

This example of JavaScript differs from our first example in that it does not execute while the document is being loaded. The document displays a form and waits for the user to do something before executing any JavaScript code. Notice that we've put the JavaScript in the <HEAD> section. This insures that the script will be available to execute when needed by any components in the <BODY> section. Since the script uses the objects and attributes of a <FORM> tag, we're going to postpone discussing the remainder of the script until after we've taken a look at the form itself.

<FORM> Tag in Hello World 2

```
<FORM> ... </FORM>
```

Implemented in HTML version 3.0.

Attributes of the <FORM> tag:

- NAME = name of the form. Used by JavaScript to refer to the form and its properties, methods, and objects.

Tags which appear within the <FORM> tag:

- INPUT - single-line text field which the user can type into or JavaScript can write to.
- TEXTAREA - multiple-line text field which can be scrolled if necessary.
- SELECT - multiple-line menu for selecting an item.

<FORM> is an element of HTML that is defined to allow the structured input and output of information between the user and the document in the browser. Even if you are familiar with writing HTML, unless you have been using CGI to incorporate interactive components in your document, you may not have used the <FORM> tag.

```
<FORM NAME="foLang">
```

One of the properties of the <FORM> tag is the NAME="text" attribute, which allows the form to have a name. Assigning a name to the form simplifies accessing it, as well as its properties, methods, and objects. Using our naming standard, the form name begins with "fo" to indicate that this is a form object, and then the name "Lang" follows. A naming standard is not required and is not part of the JavaScript language. It is only intended to help us identify the type of object we're dealing with in the code.

Following the <FORM> tag is the text we want to display within the form. This appears in the document as text.

```
Select a language:
<SELECT NAME="seLang" ONCHANGE="sayHi(this.form)">
    <OPTION SELECTED>English
    <OPTION>French
    <OPTION>German
    <OPTION>Italian
    <OPTION>Spanish
</SELECT>
```

<SELECT> defines a po- up menu from which the user can select an item. The individual items are listed beside their <OPTION> tags. Note that one of them is defined as the default selection using the <OPTION SELECTED> tag.

<SELECT> also has a name associated with it, again with the indicator that it is a <SELECT> item.

<SELECT ONCHANGE="sayHi(this.form)"> tells the browser what to do when the user makes a change in the selected item of the menu. ONCHANGE contains any JavaScript code which is executed when a change in the selected item occurs. In this case, the JavaScript we are calling is the function defined in the <SCRIPT> section within the <HEAD> section.

If sayHi() were not defined in the <HEAD> section, and we were dealing with a very long document with embedded images, it would be possible for the user to see the form before the sayHi() function had been loaded. In this case, the user would be able to trigger the ONCHANGE script before sayHi() was loaded and the JavaScript would fail. For this reason, it is a good idea to put all scripts which are needed elsewhere in the document in the <HEAD> section.

The sayHi() function passes in a single parameter, "this.form". As in C++ "this" refers to the current object and "this.form" refers to the form from which the script is executing. If more than one form in the document had the same structure as this form, passing "this.form" would be sure to differentiate between them.

```
<INPUT TYPE="TEXT" NAME="inHello" VALUE="Hello
    World!" SIZE=40>
```

The last component of the form is an <INPUT> field. The TYPE="TEXT" property designates this as a single-line text field that both the user and JavaScript can write to. Its name is "inHello", using a standard designator for an input field. The initial value is "Hello World!", which matches the initial option selected in the <SELECT> field above. The length of the field is 40 characters.

This completes the <BODY> section of the document. Now that we've seen the <FORM> object and its names, we'll return to look at the script.

Within the <SCRIPT> Tag

```
function sayHi(form) {...}
```

The first line of JavaScript is the function declaration for a function called "sayHi()". This function takes as an input a form which will be passed to it by the <FORM> tag. "function" is a keyword in JavaScript. This function will be able to act on all of the objects within the form that is passed to it. Rather than give details about all of the objects and their properties right now, let's just keep moving through the code. Most of it is self-explanatory.

```
var idx = my_form.seLang.selectedIndex
```

This defines a variable called "idx" and assigns to it the index value of the item which was selected by the user. If the first item of the list is chosen, the value of "selectedIndex" for that item will be 0, the second will be 1, and so forth. "selectedIndex" is a property of the <SELECT> object with the <FORM>.

```
// Based on the index of the select field,
// put a greeting in the text field of the form.
if ( idx == 0 )
   my_form.inHello.value = "Hello World!"
if ( idx == 1)
   my_form.inHello.value = "Bonjour tous le monde!"
if ( idx == 2)
   my_form.inHello.value = "Guten Tag Welt!"
if ( idx == 3 )
   my_form.inHello.value = "Buon giorno tutto il mondo!"
if ( idx == 4 )
      // You can't use the i acute by typing it in.  You
      // must call it out of the ISO Latin character set.
   my_form.inHello.value = "Buenas d" +
         unescape( "%92" ) + "as el mundo!"
return
```

At this writing, JavaScript does not have a "switch" or "case" statement, so you must write individual "if" statements for each possible case. Looking at the first case, if the "selectedIndex" value were 0, the text field "inHello" would get the value "Hello World!". For each language, we assign the appropriate value to the text field.

You can't type international characters in from your workstation. I wrote the Hello World 2 HTML on a Macintosh which easily supports the i acute character, "í". However, when you type this into the HTML file and load the file, you end up with a different character. HTML attempts to be the lowest common denominator between display systems and does not directly support anything outside of the 7-bit ASCII character set. However, you can get the browser to display international characters by using the ISO Latin character set and JavaScript `unescape()` function. Some browsers also support ISO Latin 1 characters. For example, Í also defines the "í" character.

The last line of the function is the `return` statement. This statement can appear anywhere in the function and will terminate the execution of the function and return control to the calling procedure or script. Optionally, you can define a value to return to the calling statement.

Hello World 3

So far, we've seen how to execute a JavaScript when a document is being loaded by including the JavaScript directly in the document between the `<SCRIPT>` … `</SCRIPT>` tags. We've also seen that once a document is loaded, it can't be changed.

The second example of "Hello World" showed a script which did not execute when loaded, but waited for a user event to change the contents of a form. However, the form is limited in what it can display. There's no way to format text within a form's input fields and it cannot display an image.

Hello World 3 will show how to use frames and forms to gain complete control over the display and to provide the full support of HTML including the dynamic loading of documents under control of JavaScript. See Table 2-2 Figures. 2-6 and 2-7 show what Hello World 3 looks like. The documents is created by the HTML in Listings 2-7 through 2-10.

TABLE 2-2. Points where JavaScript can execute

1. Execute at load. JavaScript calls and statements within `<SCRIPT>` tags. Note that a JavaScript function will not execute on load unless called directly by a JavaScript statement outside of a function. See Hello World 1.
2. Execute at an event. JavaScript executes as a result of a user action, such as clicking on a button or selecting a menu item. See Hello World 2.
3. Execute at an event to cause a load. JavaScript can cause a load to occur, which itself can cause JavaScript statements to execute.. See Hello World 3.

TABLE 2-3. Advantages to using Frames for Interactive Web Pages

1. More than one document can be viewed at a time.
2. With JavaScript, one frame can control the contents of another frame in which the full scope of HTML formatting and scripting are available.

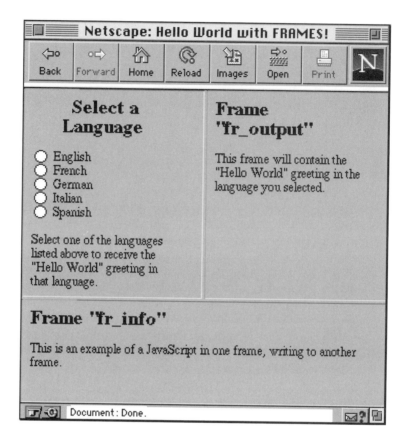

FIGURE 2-6   Hello World 3 shows the use of frames which allow user input, while at the same time display content that is under control of the script. See Listings 2-7 through 2-10 for the HTML and JavaScript which generates this page.

The big difference between Hello World 2 and Hello World 3 is in the use of frames to display information rather than forms. Frames allow more than one document to be displayed at one time in the same window. In addition, one frame can control the content of another frame, including full use of HTML scripting and formatting. See Table 2-3.

The use of frames makes for a more complex example than what we saw in the last example. Whereas all of the objects were in the same window or frame in Hello World 2, we now must reference objects by the name of their frame to make sure that we're putting information where it belongs. Let's start by looking at Listing 2-7 where the frames were defined.

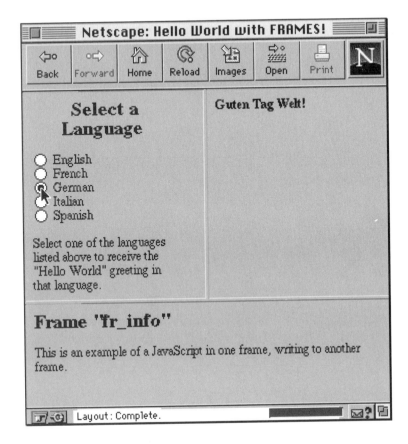

Netscape: Hello World with FRAMES!

FIGURE 2-7   The content of one of the frames has changed based on user input. See Listings 2-7 through 2-10 for the HTML and JavaScript which generated this page.

<FRAMESET> Tag in Hello World 3

```
<FRAMESET>  ...  </FRAMESET>
```

Implemented in the Netscape Navigator version 2.0. Proposed for adoption in future HTML versions.

Attributes:

- COLS - a definition of how the window space is divided into columns.
- ROWS - a definition of how the window space is divided into rows.

```
<HTML>

<!-- Hello World using frames and JavaScript between frames

    File: LIST2_07.HTM
    Usage: demonstrate forms, frames, and JavaScript
    Calls: LIST2_08.HTM, LIST2_09.HTM, LIST2_10.HTM
-->

<HEAD>
<TITLE>Hello World with FRAMES!</TITLE>
</HEAD>

<!-- Notes:
• FRAMESET should NOT appear within the BODY tag.  When you
  do that, FRAMESET stops working.  Some versions of the
  documentation are incorrect in saying that FRAMESET should
  or can appear within BODY.
-->

<!-- Define two FRAMESETs, one within the other. -->
<FRAMESET ROWS="67%,33%" COLS="100%">
    <!-- The first FRAMESET defines two frames in rows
         where the first one takes up 67% of the available
         space and the second row takes up 33% of the space
      -->
    <FRAMESET COLS="50%,50%">
        <!-- The second FRAMESET defines two frames within
             the first frame of the first frame set (the
             frame taking up 67% of the window).  Each of
             the frames takes up 50% of the space within the
             first frame.
          -->
        <FRAME SRC=LIST2_08.HTM NAME="fr_control"
         SCROLLING="auto">
        <FRAME SRC=LIST2_09.HTM NAME="fr_output"
         SCROLLING="auto">
    </FRAMESET>
    <FRAME SRC=LIST2_10.HTM NAME="fr_info"
     SCROLLING="AUTO">
</FRAMESET>
</HTML>
```

LISTING 2-7   THE INITIAL HTML WHICH DEFINES THE FRAMES ON THE SCREEN AND POINTS TO THE DOCUMENTS WHICH WILL BE LOADED INTO EACH FRAME.

```
<HTML>

<!-- File: LIST2_08.HTM
     Usage: fill the frame named "fr_control"
     Called by: LIST2_07.HTM
  -->

<HEAD>

<SCRIPT LANG="JavaScript">

function processAction( btn_value )
{
parent.fr_output.document.open( "text/HTML" );

if (btn_value == "en")
   parent.fr_output.document.write("<B>Hello World!")
if (btn_value == "fr")
   parent.fr_output.document.write("<B>Bonjour tous le" +
      " monde!")
if (btn_value == "ge")
   parent.fr_output.document.write("<B>Guten Tag Welt!")
if (btn_value == "it")
  parent.fr_output.document.write("<B>Buon giorno tutto" +
      " il mondo!")
if (btn_value == "sp")
   parent.fr_output.document.write("<B>Buenas d" +
      "&iacute" + "as el mundo!")

parent.fr_output.document.close();
return;
}

</SCRIPT>

</HEAD>

<BODY>

<H2 ALIGN=CENTER>
   Select a Language
</H2>
```

LISTING 2-8   THE HTML WHICH IS LOADED INTO THE FIRST FRAME CALLED "FR_CONTROL".

```
<FORM NAME="selectLang">
   <INPUT TYPE=RADIO NAME="btn_"
    onClick="processAction( selectLang.btn_.value='en')" >
   English<BR>
   <INPUT TYPE=RADIO NAME="btn_"
    onClick="processAction( selectLang.btn_.value='fr')" >
   French<BR>
   <INPUT TYPE=RADIO NAME="btn_"
    onClick="processAction( selectLang.btn_.value='ge')" >
   German<BR>
   <INPUT TYPE=RADIO NAME="btn_"
    onClick="processAction( selectLang.btn_.value='it')" >
   Italian<BR>
   <INPUT TYPE=RADIO NAME="btn_"
    onClick="processAction( selectLang.btn_.value='sp')" >
   Spanish
</FORM>

<!-- By naming all of the buttons the same thing, they will
     automatically turn each other off as you go from one
     to the other.
  -->

<P>Select one of the languages listed above to receive the
"Hello World" greeting in that language.

</BODY>

</HTML>
```

LISTING 2-8   (CONTINUED) THE HTML WHICH IS LOADED INTO THE FIRST FRAME CALLED "FR_CONTROL".

Tags used with <FRAMESET>:

- <FRAME> - defines the contents and properties of a frame within a <FRAMESET>.

<FRAMESET> defines how frames are to appear on a document. Each <FRAMESET> entry defines rows and columns which are filled by individual <FRAME> definitions. A single <FRAMESET> divides up the window it is in. Up to six frames can be specified.

Placing a <FRAMESET> statement within another <FRAMESET> statement allows non-tiled windows. Figure 2-8 shows examples of how the <FRAMESET> statement divides the space in a window

```
<HTML>

<!-- File: LIST2_09.HTM
     Usage: Initial load into frame "fr_output"
            This document is overwritten by the script
            in the frame "fr_control".
     Called by: LIST2_07.HTM
  -->

<BODY>
<H2>Frame "fr_output"</H2>
<P>
This frame will contain the "Hello World" greeting in the
language you selected.
</BODY>

</HTML>
```

LISTING 2-9   THE HTML WHICH IS INITIALLY LOADED INTO THE SECOND FRAME CALLED "FR_OUTPUT".
THIS DOCUMENT WILL BE OVERWRITTEN BY THE SCRIPT IN THE FRAME "FR_CONTROL".

```
<HTML>

<!-- File: LIST2_10.HTM
     Usage: This is the content of the frame: fr_info
            which is not changed by the script in
            fr_control.
     Called by: LIST2_07.HTM
  -->

<BODY>
<H2>Frame "fr_info"</H2>
<P>This is an example of a JavaScript in one frame, writing
to another frame.
</BODY>
</HTML>
```

LISTING 2-10   THE HTML LOADED INTO THE FRAME "FR_INFO". THIS FRAME IS NOT CHANGED BY THE
SCRIPT IN "FR_CONTROL".

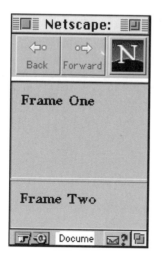

```
<FRAMESET ROWS="67%,33%">
    <FRAME SRC=frameOne.HTML>
    <FRAME SRC=frameTwo.HTML>
</FRAMESET>
```

This `<FRAMESET>` example defines two rows with the first taking 2/3 of the available window space.

FIGURE 2.8A   Defining Frames with rows only within a browser window.

```
<FRAMESET
  COLS="67%,33%">
  <FRAME SRC=
    frameOne.HTML>
  <FRAME SRC=
    frameTwo.HTML>
</FRAMESET>
```

A `<FRAMESET>` creating two columns.

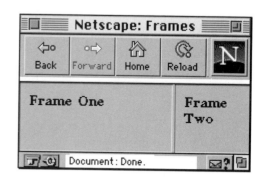

FIGURE 2.8B   Defining Frames with columns only.

```
<FRAMESET
 ROWS="67%,33%"
 COLS="67%,33%">
 <FRAME SRC=
    frameOne.HTML>
 <FRAME SRC=
    frameTwo.HTML>
 <FRAME SRC=
    frameThree.HTML>
 <FRAME SRC=
    frameFour.HTML>
</FRAMESET>
```

Whenever both ROWS and COLS attributes are specified, a grid or tile of frames is created. Regardless of which attribute is specified first, the frames will load in row order, filling the first row first from left to right.

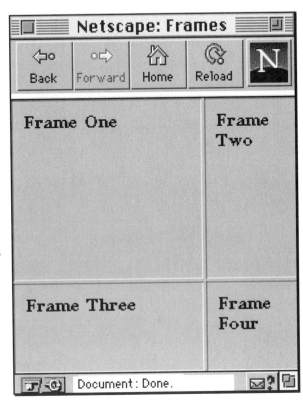

FIGURE 2.8C   Defining a grid of Frames

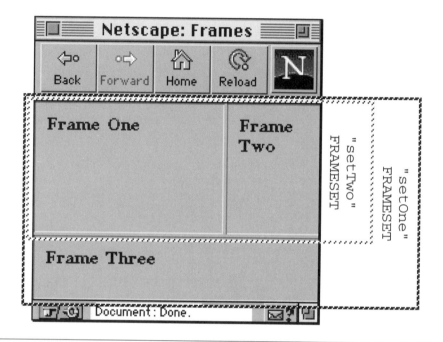

```
<FRAMESET NAME=setOne ROWS="67%,33%">
   <FRAMESET NAME=setTwo COLS="67%,33%">
      <FRAME SRC=frameOne.HTML>
      <FRAME SRC=frameTwo.HTML>
   </FRAMESET>
   <FRAME SRC=frameThree.HTML>
</FRAMESET>
```

To define non-titled frames, define a <FRAMESET> within a <FRAMESET>. This example defines two rows, and within the first row, defines two columns.

FIGURE 2.8D   Defining Non-Tiled Frames.

Let's look at the HTML which defines the <FRAMESET>s for Hello World 3. The following code fragment comes from Listing 2-7.

```
<!-- Define two FRAMESETs, one within the other. -->
<FRAMESET ROWS="67%,33%" COLS="100%">
    <!-- The first FRAMESET defines two frames in rows
        where the first one takes up 67% of the available
        space and the second row takes up 33% of the space
    -->
    <FRAMESET COLS="50%,50%">
        <!-- The second FRAMESET defines two frames within
            the first frame of the first frame set (the
            frame taking up 67% of the window).  Each of
            the frames takes up 50% of the space within the
            first frame.
        -->
```

This HTML divides up the window twice. The first <FRAMESET> divides the entire window into two rows, one taking up 67% of the available space and the other taking up 33%. No columns are defined at this point. This is illustrated in Figure 2-9.

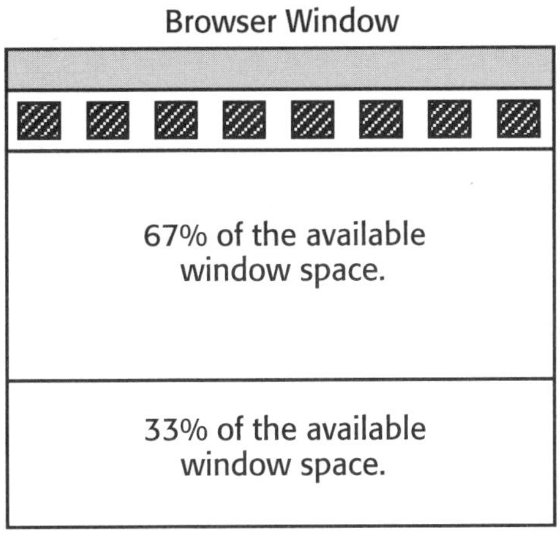

FIGURE 2-9   The first <FRAMESET> division of the window.

The second <FRAMESET> tag is found inside the first command before any <FRAME> tags. This means that it will occupy the space of the first <FRAME>, or the column which has taken up 67% of the window. This <FRAMESET> then divides the frame it is in into two parts, each taking 50% of the frame they are in. Figure 2-10 illustrates this.

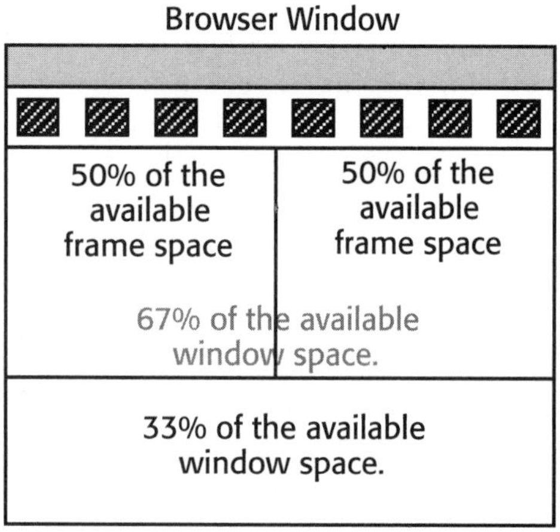

Browser Window

FIGURE 2-10   The second <FRAMESET> division of the window. This creates the two frames within the first row.

<FRAME> Tag in Hello World 3

```
<FRAME>
```

```
Attributes:
```
- NAME - the reference nameof this frame.
- SCROLLING - whether the frame will support scrolling to see contents which cannot fit within the visible part of the frame. The values "yes", "no", and "auto" are legal. "auto" allows the browser to determine if scrolling is needed to see all of the document.
- SRC - a URL indicating where the contents of this frame should be found.

Returning to the HTML of Listing 2-7, the frames are defined, named, and the source for each is defined. Once the frames are defined, each frame is loaded in turn.

```
<FRAME SRC=helloFrame1.HTML name="fr_control"
```

```
     scrolling="auto">
    <FRAME SRC=helloFrame2.HTML name="fr_output"
     scrolling="auto">
   </FRAMESET>
   <FRAME SRC=helloFrame3.HTML name="fr_info"
    SCROLLING="AUTO">
 </FRAMESET>
```

This completes the loading of LIST2_07.HTM in our Hello World 3 example. You'll notice that there wasn't any JavaScript and the forms and content we saw in Figure 2-7 and Listing 2-7 aren't defined. That's because the rest of the content is defined in the documents pointed to by the <FRAME SRC=...> statements.

Hello World 3 HTML

The interesting parts of Hello World 3 are found in Listing 2-8. As with our last Hello World example, let's start with the <FORM> object which is the interface between the user and scripts.

```
<form name="selectLang"> … </form>
```

As in Hello World 2, we've named our form so that referring to it will be easier.

```
<input type=radio name="btn_"
  onClick="processAction( selectLang.btn_.value='en')" >
English<br>
<input type=radio name="btn_"
  onClick="processAction( selectLang.btn_.value='fr')" >
French<br>
<input type=radio name="btn_"
  onClick="processAction( selectLang.btn_.value='ge')" >
German<br>
<input type=radio name="btn_"
  onClick="processAction( selectLang.btn_.value='it')" >
Italian<br>
<input type=radio name="btn_"
  onClick="processAction( selectLang.btn_.value='sp')" >
Spanish
```

Within the <FORM> section we've defined a way for the user to tell us what he or she wants the document to do. This time we're using a radio button for input. The <INPUT TYPE=radio> specifies the radio button for each item. Notice that all of the buttons have the same name, "btn_". The browser will only allow one of the buttons to be highlighted at a time. If the buttons had different names, each set of names would have only a single button highlighted.

We also see a new event handler, the onClick="..." handler, which like the onClick handler we saw in Hello World 2, causes JavaScript code to be executed when the button is clicked. In this case, the JavaScript function processAction() is called and the value of the button is changed to identify the language that was selected. Note that the processAction() call contains a JavaScript statement. This is a legal JavaScript construct. Also, within the onClick="text", any number of JavaScript statements could have been included.

After each <INPUT> definition, the label text which will appear after the button is included. This is standard HTML text and any legal HTML text formatting tags could have been included.

Let's return now to the JavaScript for processAction() to see what happens when the user clicks on one of the radio buttons defined in the form. (See Figure 2-7 to see what the form looks like.)

processAction() Function. Similar to sayHi() in Hello World 2, processAction() receives a value, in this case the value of the button which was pressed. Note that the value of the button is an arbitrary value and is not the same thing as the name of the button.

```
parent.fr_output.document.open( "text/HTML" );
```

The first statement of the script is different than what we saw in Hello World 2. In that example, we were writing side of the current document and only defined the form and input fields we were using. This time we use the construct "parent....". "parent" defines the first document which was loaded in this set and usually includes the HTML which defined the forms themselves. In this case, parent would be the document found in Listing 2-7. This was where the frames were defined and named. "parent.fr_output..." says go to the parent of this document, and then go to the frame named "fr_output".

Because the frame "fr_output" already has content, we have to re-open that frame for output which is what ...document.open() does for us. We tell the browser that the information we will be passing to it is text in HTML format.

```
if (btn_value == "en")
   parent.fr_output.document.write("<B>Hello World!")
if (btn_value == "fr")
   parent.fr_output.document.write("<B>Bonjour tous
                                   le monde!")
if (btn_value == "ge")
   parent.fr_output.document.write("<B>Guten Tag
                                   Welt!")
if (btn_value == "it")
   parent.fr_output.document.write("<B>Buon giorno
                                   tutto il mondo!")
if (btn_value == "sp")

   parent.fr_output.document.write("<B>Buenas d" +
                            "&iacute" + "as el mundo!")
```

From here, the code looks a lot like what we saw in Hello World 2. Without a "case" or "switch" statement we have a series of "if" statements. The only difference is that now, instead of placing a string in the text field of a form, we're writing HTML into a document frame. Because we are writing from the frame named "fr_control" to the frame named "fr_output", we have to specify the whole chain which gets us there, going up to the parent, then down into the frame we want. "…document.write()" sends the HTML into that frame, just like we did in Hello World 1.

```
parent.fr_output.document.close();
```

The last statement of the function closes the output stream to the frame and forces it to be displayed.

Summary

This completes our introduction to client-side JavaScript. We've seen how JavaScript can execute while a document loads. In later chapters we'll have more information about how to use information available to JavaScript to change how a document appears.

We've also seen how to use forms and frames to individualize a document so that a user can specify what he or she wants to have displayed on the screen, and how to receive input so that JavaScript can interact with the user.

From here on, we'll discuss server-side JavaScript and in more detail the object, properties, methods, and language functions available to you as a JavaScript programmer. We'll also discuss some of the pitfalls you might fall into with JavaScript in its current form, including what happens if you try to access a document with JavaScript from a browser which does not understand JavaScript.

Getting Started with Server-side JavaScript

- Create your first server-side JavaScript application.
- Learn about server-side JavaScript's powerful shared data structures.

Overview

Whereas client-side JavaScript is supported through the Navigator client, server-side JavaScript is supported through the LiveWire compiler and server extensions. The LiveWire compiler packages HTML files with embedded Java-Script into a single entity referred to simply as a Web file. A single Web file comprises a distinct JavaScript application. Many JavaScript applications can exist on the same server.

The LiveWire server extensions allow a standard Netscape Web server to understand JavaScript and provide a facility to manage JavaScript applications.

Differences between Client-side and Server-side JavaScript

The language itself is the same on both the client and server, but the built-in objects are different. Server-side Java-Script does not have access to any of the client-specific objects such as `window` and `document`. It does, however, have access to some common objects such as `Date`. It also has some of its own server-side objects such as `request`, `database`, and `File`.

Your First Server-side JavaScript Application—"Hello Net"

To begin, we will create a "Hello Net" application that demonstrates the use of some of the properties of server-side objects. It will also demonstrate how to generate dynamic HTML based on the current state of an application.

Figure 3-1 illustrates the steps we will follow to develop the "Hello Net" application.

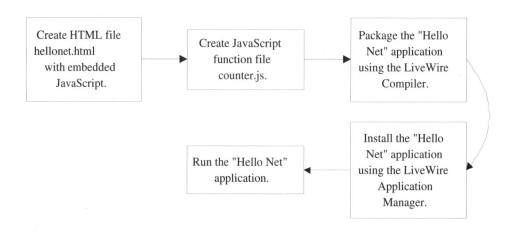

FIGURE 3-1   The steps to creating the "Hello Net" application.

Creating the Source Files

It is probably a good idea to create a `develop` sub-directory under the Web server directory in which to store our examples. For this example, let's create a `hellonet` sub-directory under `develop`. We will create and store two files in the `hellonet` sub-directory:

- `hellonet.htm` - This file will contain standard HTML, as well as embedded server-side JavaScript. It will not contain any client-side JavaScript, but it could if necessary.
- `counter.js` - This file will contain a server-side JavaScript user function named `counter()` that will illustrate the manipulation of server-side object properties. Files with a `.js` extension will be used to store JavaScript functions so they can be called by multiple HTML files. Since this example has only one HTML file, we could have put the `counter()` function in `hellonet.htm` and eliminated the `counter.js` file.

The source for `hellonet.htm` and `counter.js` is found in Listing 3-1 and Listing 3-2 respectively.

```
<HTML>

<HEAD>
<SERVER>counter();</SERVER>
<TITLE>Hello Net!</TITLE>
</HEAD>

<BODY>
<H1>Hello Net!</H1>
<P>I know the following things about you:</P>
<UL>
<LI>Your IP address is <B><SERVER>write(request.ip);</SERV-
ER></B>.
<LI>Your Browser is <B><SERVER>write(re-
quest.agent);</SERVER></B>.
<LI>Using the <B><SERVER>write(request.protocol);</SERV-
ER></B> protocol, you used the <B><SERVER>write(re-
quest.method)</SERVER></B> method to retrieve this
document.
<LI>You have previously accessed this application <B><SERV-
ER>write(client.counter);</SERVER></B> times.

<SERVER>
// Only report name if value posted from form
if (request.method == "POST")
{
     write("<LI>You reported your name to be <B>"
           +request.yourname+"</B>.")
}
</SERVER>
</UL>

<P>Let me tell you a little about myself:</P>
<UL>
<LI>My hostname is <B><SERVER>write(server.host-
name);</SERVER></B>.
<LI>This application has been accessed <B> <SERV-
ER>write(project.counter);</SERVER></B> times.
<LI>This server has been accessed <B>
<SERVER>write(server.counter);</SERVER></B> times.
</UL>
```

LISTING 3-1   THE SOURCE FOR THE "HELLO NET" SERVER-SIDE JAVASCRIPT PROGRAM.

```
<SERVER>
if (request.method == "GET")
{
    write("<P>Tell me more about yourself:</P>")
   write("<FORM METHOD=\"POST\" ACTION=\"hellonet.htm\">")
    write("<UL>")
    write("<LI>Enter your name: ")
    write("<INPUT TYPE=\"TEXT\" NAME=\"yourname\"
size=20>")
    write("</UL>")
    write("<INPUT TYPE=\"SUBMIT\" VALUE=\"Submit\">")
    write("<INPUT TYPE=\"RESET\" VALUE=\"Reset\">")
    write("</FORM>")
}
</SERVER>
</BODY>

</HTML>
```

LISTING 3-1   (CONTINUED) THE SOURCE FOR THE "HELLO NET" SERVER-SIDE JAVASCRIPT PROGRAM.

```
function counter()
{
    // # of times this client has accessed this application
    // during the current session
    if (client.counter == null)
       client.counter = 0;
    else
       client.counter = parseInt(client.counter,10) + 1;

    // # of times any client has accessed this application
    project.lock();
    if (project.counter == null)
       project.counter = 0;
    else
       project.counter = 1 + parseInt(project.counter,10);
    project.unlock();

    // # of times any client in any application accessed the
server
    server.lock();
    if (server.counter == null)
       server.counter = 0;
    else
```

LISTING 3-2   THE SOURCE FOR THE JAVASCRIPT FUNCTION FILE THAT MAINTAINS THE NUMBER OF
TIMES "HELLO NET" HAS BEEN ACCESSED.

```
server.counter = 1 + parseInt(server.counter,10);
server.unlock();
}
```

LISTING 3-2 (CONTINUED) THE SOURCE FOR THE JAVASCRIPT FUNCTION FILE THAT MAINTAINS THE NUMBER OF TIMES "HELLO NET" HAS BEEN ACCESSED.

Packaging the Application for LiveWire

Now that the HTML and JavaScript function files have been created, they must be packaged together into a single entity for the LiveWire server extensions to be able to process them. This is done by using the LiveWire compiler. The term "compiler" is misleading here because it doesn't actually translate the files into low-level machine code. What the LiveWire compiler actually does is check for syntax errors in the JavaScript code and then package all of the files into a single .web file. The following example illustrates how we packaged our application using the command-line LiveWire compiler:

```
lwcomp -v -o hellonet.web hellonet.htm counter.js
```

```
Livewire Compiler Version xx
Copyright (C) Netscape Communications Corporation xxxx
All rights reserved
Reading file hellonet.htm
Compiling file hellonet.htm
Reading file counter.js
Compiling file counter.js
Writing .web file
```

A file called hellonet.web should now be found in the hellonet subdirectory, in addition to the other two source files.

Installing the Application with the Application Manager

Now that the application has been successfully packaged into a `.web` file, the next step is to install the application on the server using the LiveWire Application Manager. Use the URL "`http://hostname/appmgr/`" to access the Application Manager where `hostname` is the name of your Netscape Web server with LiveWire installed and enabled. Once in the Application Manager, select the Add option to add a new LiveWire application. Table 3-1 shows the information that must be supplied to install the application.

 You must manually enable LiveWire on your Web server before you can access the Application Manager.

TABLE 3-1. *The information supplied to the Application Manager to install "Hello Net".*

Name	hellonet
Object File Path	C:/.../develop/hellonet/hellonet.web
Default URL	hellonet.htm
Initial URL	hellonet.htm
External Libraries	
Client Mode	client-cookie

Please note that the object file path is the full operating system path to the `hellonet.web` file created in the previous section. The example object file path given in the table is for Windows NT with LiveWire being installed in the default location. You will need to alter this path if you are on UNIX or if you installed LiveWire in another location on NT.

Once you have entered the correct information in the Add Application form, submit it to the Application Manager. It should report that the LiveWire configuration has been modified and the application has been started. You have now successfully installed your first LiveWire application!

Running the Application

After the application has been installed, we are ready to run it for the first time. If the name of your Web server with LiveWire extensions installed is www.foo.bar, the URL for the "Hello Net" application would be:

```
http://www.foo.bar/hellonet/hellonet.htm
```

When the above URL is opened in your Web client for the first time, something similar to Figure 3-2 should appear.

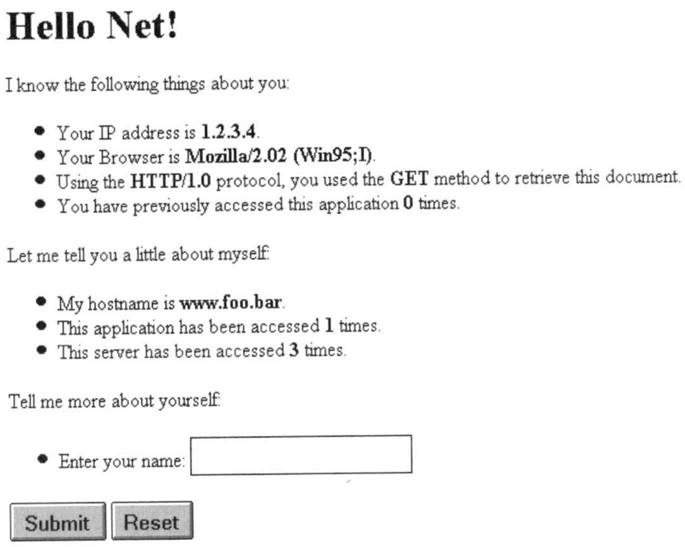

Hello Net!

I know the following things about you:

- Your IP address is **1.2.3.4**.
- Your Browser is **Mozilla/2.02 (Win95;I)**.
- Using the **HTTP/1.0** protocol, you used the **GET** method to retrieve this document.
- You have previously accessed this application **0** times.

Let me tell you a little about myself:

- My hostname is **www.foo.bar**.
- This application has been accessed **1** times.
- This server has been accessed **3** times.

Tell me more about yourself:

- Enter your name: [   ]

[Submit] [Reset]

FIGURE 3-2   Loading hellonet.htm on the browser.

If you view the source in your browser, you will notice that none of the server-side code is sent to the client; only the actual resulting text is sent. Compare what you see in your browser's View Source window to what you entered for hellonet.htm to verify this. A side benefit of only the result being sent is security—you can be sure that passwords or other sensitive data stored in server-side JavaScript will *never* be viewable by the client.

Now, enter your name in the form and click the Submit button. The same page, hellonet.htm, will be displayed by your browser but the content will be changed as shown in Figure 3-3.

Hello Net!

I know the following things about you:

- Your IP address is **1.2.3.4**.
- Your Browser is **Mozilla/2.02 (Win95;I)**.
- Using the **HTTP/1.0** protocol, you used the **GET** method to retrieve this document.
- You have previously accessed this application **1** times.
- You reported your name to be **Brian**.

Let me tell you a little about myself:

- My hostname is **www.foo.bar**.
- This application has been accessed **2** times.
- This server has been accessed **4** times.

FIGURE 3-3   The result of posting your name to "Hello Net".

As shown in Figure 3-3, this page generates dynamic content based on user input. Unlike previous methods involving the Common Gateway Interface (CGI), the same page can both accept and process user input. It is no longer necessary to create a separate CGI script for the posting of form data.

"Hello Net" Source Explained

Now let's dissect the source of the "Hello Net" application and learn more about how server-side JavaScript works.

The <SERVER> Tag

The <SERVER> tag is used to begin any number of server-side Java-Script statements in an HTML page. It requires a closing </SERVER> tag to end the code section. An unlimited number of server-side code sections can be contained in a page and they may appear in either the <HEAD> or <BODY> of the HTML file. However, as with client-side JavaScript, you would not want to generate any HTML in the <HEAD> as it would not be displayed.

Calling External Functions

The counter() function increments the number of times the client (the current browser session), the application, and the server have been accessed. Any functions included in an HTML page can only be called from that page. We do not want to include the counter() function in hellonet.htm because we may want to use the counter() function in other pages in the application or for other applications on the same server. So, we created the counter.js file and stored the counter() function there. A .js file can contain any number of JavaScript functions. In these files, JavaScript statements not contained in functions are ignored.

Dynamic HTML

Server-side JavaScript outputs text using the write() function. This function is very similar to the document.write() function in client-side JavaScript. To generate dynamic HTML, the tags must be included within the write() function. In the following example, the HTML list item will only be displayed if the "POST" method was used to access the page rather than the "GET" method. What this means is that yourname can't be displayed until the user has entered a value for it and the form has been submitted.

```
if (request.method == "POST")
{
    write("<LI>You reported your name to be <B>"
        +request.yourname+"</B>.")
}
```

Later on in hellonet.htm, a similar piece of code will only display the HTML form to input yourname if the "GET" method is used. This way, the same page can both accept and process user input.

Server-side Objects

Up to this point we haven't given any detailed explanation of the objects used in the example. Much of the details concerning these objects and their built-in properties will be saved for Chapter 8. However, we will give a brief explanation of the server-side objects here in the context of this example:

- request - This object contains data from the current transaction. The request object contains properties for each HTML form element submitted. So, in the example, the request.yourname property contains the value from the yourname text box in the form. It also contains some pre-defined properties such as method and agent. As illustrated previously, the method property can be used to ensure that an appropriate response is given to a request.
- client - The client object stores data for an individual Web browser. This is the object used to keep state between each client and the server so the server knows what the client has done previously. In our example, the client.counter property keeps track of the number of times the

current browser has accessed the "Hello Net" application. The `client` object is stored in a number of different ways. We chose `client-cookie` for our example. We will explain the other types in Chapter 8 and in what situations it would be most appropriate to use them.

- `project` - The `project` object contains data common to the entire application. This object can be used to share data between multiple clients using the same application. In our example, the `project.counter` property keeps track of the number of times any client has accessed the "Hello Net" application. Since multiple clients could write to the same property at the same time, a locking mechanism ensures that only one client at a time writes to the object.

```
project.lock();
```
(Changes to properties of the `project` object.)
```
project.unlock();
```

- `server` - The `server` object contains data common to all applications on the server. This is an ideal way for multiple applications to collaborate. In our example, the `server.counter` property stores the number of times any client has accessed any application on the server. For this count to be accurate for the server, we assume that every application page on the server calls the `counter()` function explicitly. As with the `project` object, the `server` object supports a locking mechanism.

Storage of Server-side Objects.

The properties of server-side objects are always stored as strings even if they are numeric values. It is for this reason that the `parseInt()` built-in function is used on the previous counter values in `counter()` before an addition is made to them. The `parseInt()` function converts a string to an integer.

```
server.counter = 1 + parseInt(server.counter,10);
```

Variable Initialization.

These server-side objects have two types of object properties: pre-defined properties such as `request.ip` and `server.hostname`, and user-defined properties such as `client.counter` and `project.counter` created specifically for "Hello Net". The values for pre-defined properties are set without programmer intervention. However, with user-defined properties, we often need to determine if they have been initialized before we use them—it doesn't make any sense to increment an unknown value.

In the `counter()` function contained in the `counter.js` file, we check to see if the counters have been initialized, and if they have not, we set them to zero. If a value has not yet been initialized, it has a value of `null`. This is because JavaScript doesn't need to declare a variable before it uses it and there must be some way to check if a variable has been assigned a value.

```
if (client.counter == null)
```

Summary

As illustrated by the "Hello Net" application, server-side JavaScript is an ideal way to create Web pages that don't merely present static content but also have the ability to *process* information and present dynamic content for each individual client. All of this is done without the need for the less-than-elegant CGI approach. In addition, JavaScript's server-side objects provide techniques to share information between multiple clients in one application and multiple applications on a server. These objects will assist the developer in making Web collaboration a reality.

For a more in-depth presentation of server-side JavaScript concepts, see Chapters 7 and 8.

The Browser and JavaScript

- The Differences Between A Window And A Document.
- Documents and Frames
- Printing JavaScript Has Vanishing Returns
- Making HTML Interactive

The "Window" and the "Document"

In the simplest sense, a document and a window are frequently the same thing; however, in Chapter 6 we will be going over the HTML and browser objects which the JavaScript language defines. A good understanding of the relationships between frames, windows, and documents will be helpful.

When you start a browser, the first thing you see is a window within the desktop environment you are running. If you are on a Macintosh, you see the application menu bar at the top of the screen with the browser window underneath. In UNIX and Windows, the application menu bar is attached to the window itself (see Figure 4-1.).

The document which you identified as the home document, or the first document that the browser will access, is loaded into this window. This is an important point to remember: the window and the document which is loaded into the window are two different things (see Figure 4-2).

A window exists to contain a document, and in fact, a window can contain more than one document at a time. A browser window is like having a stack of papers that you are moving through. As you access links in one document, additional documents are added to the stack. In Figure 4-3, a doc-

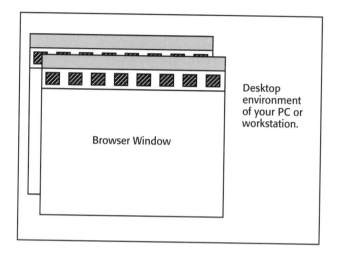

FIGURE 4-1   A Browser opens a window.

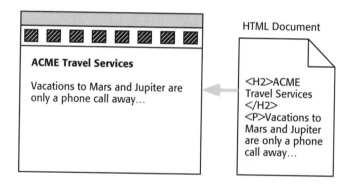

FIGURE 4-2   A document is loaded into an available window.

ument called "Acme Travel Services" has been loaded into the browser's only open window. This document has links to documents called "Mars" and "Jupiter". Until the user clicks on that link, there is still only a single document loaded in the window.

In Figure 4-4, the user has clicked on the hot link to document "Mars" and the visible contents of the window have changed. Now we see the document "Mars" and its links to "The Grand Canal" and "The Polar Icecaps".

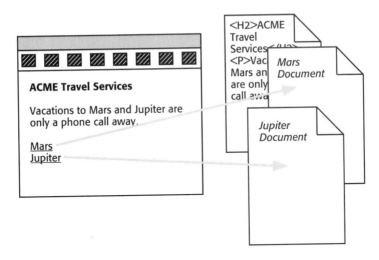

FIGURE 4-3   The document for ACME Travel Services has been loaded into the browser window.

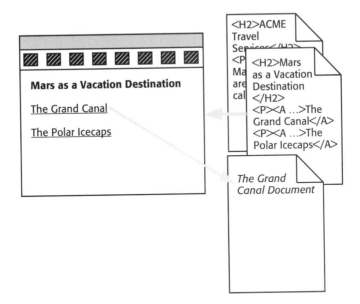

FIGURE 4-4   The user clicked on the hot link "Mars" and a new page has loaded replacing the previous page.

Although we see "Mars" in the window, document "Acme Travel Services" is still there, contained within the window structure, but not displayed (see Figure 4-5). The important thing to remember is that both "Acme Travel Services" and "Mars" are still present in the window, and from the perspective of JavaScript, both are accessible, including accessing any JavaScript functions and data.

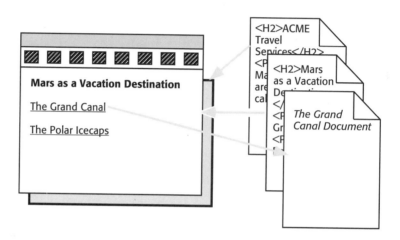

FIGURE 4-5   Although the "Mars" page is visible, the first page "ACME Travel Services" is still in the browser, but "behind" the visible page.

Clicking on the link to "The Grand Canal" will place that document in the browser on top of the stack (see Figure 4-6). Now we have a stack of three documents, "Acme Travel Services" on the bottom, "Mars" in the middle, and "The Grand Canal" on top and visible. Note that we still only have a single window open, containing all three documents, one on top of the other, with only the top one showing.

The "Back" and "Forward" buttons of the browser allow you to navigate through the stack of documents, changing which one is visible at any one time. From the position shown in Figure 4-7, pressing the "Back" button on the browser will result in document "Mars" becoming visible, although all three documents are still present in the window. Pressing "Back" and "Forward" moves you through the stack, changing which of the documents in the window is visible.

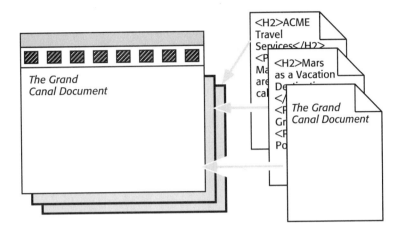

FIGURE 4-6   Three documents: "The Grand Canal", "Mars", and "ACME Travel" are loaded into a single browser window. Only the top document, "The Grand Canal" is visible.

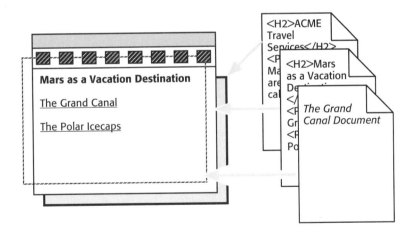

FIGURE 4-7   Pressing "Back" in the browser window changes which document is visible. In this case, the "Mars" document becomes visible, but all three documents are still present in the browser.

We've seen what happens to the stack when you are on top and load a new document, the stack gets larger by adding the new document to the top of the stack. What happens if we are in the middle of the stack and click on a link or access a new document? Let's take a look at our current set-up. Let's assume our window had "Acme Travel Services", "Mars", and "The Grand Canal" loaded, and the document at the bottom of the stack, document "Acme Travel Services", was visible (see Figure 4-8).

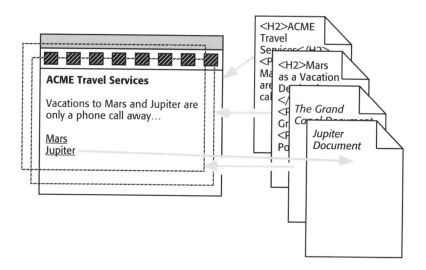

FIGURE 4-8   Pressing "Back" again, makes the bottom document , "ACME Travel" visible. All three documents are still present in the browser.

Now the user clicks on the link to "Jupiter". Documents "Mars" and "The Grand Canal" are discarded from the stack and the document "Jupiter" is loaded on top and made visible (see Figure 4-9). The important point here, particularly for JavaScript writers, is that the functions, and perhaps most importantly, the data contained in JavaScript variables and HTML forms are gone. Not only are they inaccessible, they have been deleted.

The complete list of documents is accessible to JavaScript in the history object.

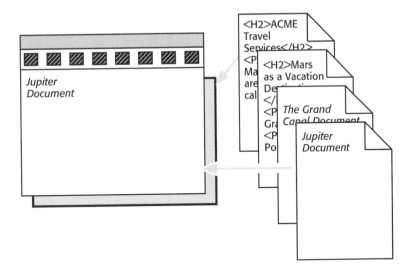

FIGURE 4-9 The user clicked on the "Jupiter Document" while viewing the bottom document "ACME Travel". Because "ACME" was on the bottom, loading the "Jupiter" document replaced the two documents on top, "Mars" and "The Grand Canal".

The examples we've looked at so far have contained only a single window. The browser is capable of creating multiple windows, each with its own stack of documents. Likewise, JavaScript is capable of creating and accessing multiple windows; however, for security reasons, JavaScript can only access those windows which it created. Any windows created by the user, independent of the document which is running a JavaScript application, are not accessible to JavaScript (see Figure 4-10).

So far we've seen one way in which a window contains more than one document. The next section covers how frames provide the second way.

Documents and Frames

Netscape Communications pioneered the concept of frames within a window. Simply put, a frame is a way to divide up one physical window into multiple "virtual" windows, each having its own document (see Figure 4-11).

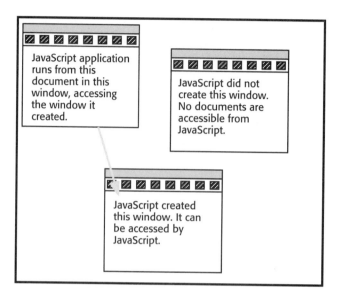

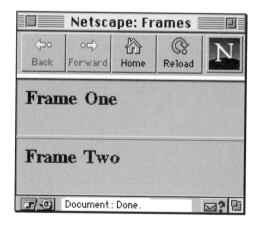

FIGURE 4-10   JavaScript can only access windows which were created by JavaScript itself. Windows not created by JavaScript are not accessible.

FIGURE 4-11   Two frames in a single Netscape Navigator window.

As we'll cover in Chapter 6, JavaScript sees frames as "window-like" objects having many of the attributes of windows, but being contained within a single window. The advantage to using frames is that you can make each frame independent of the others, containing its own history of documents, its own JavaScript data and functions, and its own forms and HTML.

Frames follow many of the same rules as windows. Each frame has its own history of documents, but these are not typically accessible via the "Go" menu on the browser, which refers to the documents of a window and not a frame. However, JavaScript does have access to the history of documents in a frame. Likewise, the upper documents in a frame's stack will be deleted when a new document is introduced in the middle of the stack.

Briefly, the document which creates the frames has no textual content except for the <TITLE> tag and the frame definitions. Listings 4-1 through 4-3 show the HTML which created the simple frame in Figure 4-11. Although this book is not intended as a tutorial on HTML, Chapter 6 contains some information on frames and their attributes as they apply to JavaScript.

```
<HTML>
<!-- File: LIST4_01.HTM
     Usage: Demonstrate creating frames.
     Calls: LIST4_02.HTM, LIST4_03.HTM
  -->

<HEAD>
<TITLE>Frames</TITLE>

<FRAMESET ROWS="50%,50%">
   <FRAME SRC=LIST4_02.HTM>
   <FRAME SRC=LIST4_03.HTM>
</FRAMESET>

</HEAD>
</HTML>
```

LISTING 4-1   HTML DOCUMENT TO CREATE TWO FRAMES AND LOAD THEM WITH HTML DOCUMENTS.

```
<HTML>
<!-- File: LIST4_02.HTM
     Usage: Loaded by LIST4_01.HTM into
            a frame.
  -->

<BODY>
<H2>Frame One</H2>
</BODY>
</HTML>
```

LISTING 4-2   HTML DOCUMENT LOADED INTO THE FIRST FRAME.

```
<HTML>
<!-- File: LIST4_03.HTM
     Usage: Loaded by LIST4_01.HTM into a frame.
  -->

<BODY>
<H2>Frame Two</H2>
</BODY>

</HTML>
```

LISTING 4-3   HTML DOCUMENT LOADED INTO THE SECOND FRAME.

It is important to keep separate the concepts of the window, which ultimately displays everything to the user, the document, which creates the frames and has a special relationship of "parent" to the frames which it defines, the frames, which are contained within a window, and the documents, which inhabit the frames. Let's consider the example in Listings 4-1 through 4-3 and Figure 4-11 (see Figure 4-12).

The window contains the document LIST1.HTM. All this document can do is define the frames and load the title of the window. We'll cover more on this later, but this document is called the "parent" of the frames and is used to access JavaScript and HTML structures from one frame to the next. Without the parent document, the frames would have no way of communicating with each other.

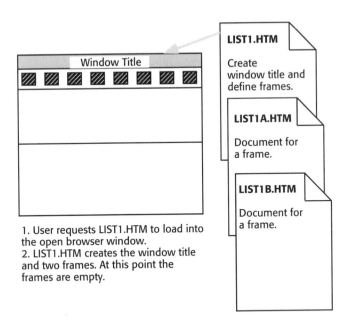

FIGURE 4-12 Loading the parent HTML document into a window to define frames, window title, and frame contents. Except for the window title, the parent document displays nothing in the window itself..

The parent document of the frames should not have a <BODY> tag. If a <BODY> tag is included, it will be ignored. Some documentation on frames indicates that the <FRAMESET> tag should or could appear in the <BODY> section. This is not true. If the <FRAMESET> tag appears in the <BODY> section, it will be ignored.

Having created the frames, the next step is to load them with the documents which have been defined (see Figure 4-13).

Keeping the hierarchy of frames, documents, and windows in mind will help when writing JavaScript code.

Printing

One of the weakness of the Netscape browser at this writing is JavaScript and printing. Any text generated by JavaScript within a document will not be printed out, even though it is displayed in the window. For example, the code in Listing 4-4 would generate the document shown in Figure 4-14.

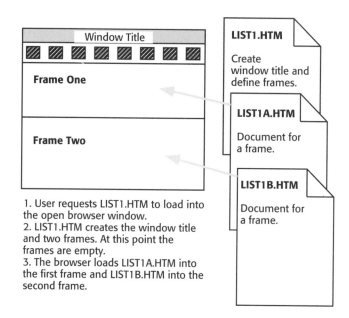

1. User requests LIST1.HTM to load into
the open browser window.
2. LIST1.HTM creates the window title
and two frames. At this point the
frames are empty.
3. The browser loads LIST1A.HTM into
the first frame and LIST1B.HTM into the
second frame.

FIGURE 4-13   Once the parent document is loaded, the frames are loaded as
defined by the <FRAME SRC=...> tags.

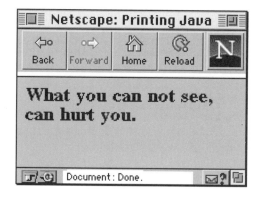

FIGURE 4-14   Document created using Listing 4-14. Note that the word "not" is generated by JavaScript, not HTML text.

```
<HTML>
<!-- File: LIST4_04.HTM
      Usage: Demonstrate JavaScript not
             printing.
  -->

<HEAD>
<TITLE>Printing JavaScript</TITLE>
</HEAD>

<BODY>
<H2>What you can
<SCRIPT LANG="JavaScript">
document.write( "not" )
</SCRIPT>
see, can hurt you.</H2>
</BODY>
</HTML>
```

LISTING 4-4   THE HTML USED TO GENERATE FIGURE 4-14. NOTE THAT THE WORD "NOT" IS GENERATED BY JAVASCRIPT RATHER THAN HTML TEXT.

The document contains the word "not" which was generated by a JavaScript statement instead of by HTML text. Figure 4-15 shows what is printed out.

FIGURE 4-15   A screen capture of the printed document. Note that the word "not" has disappeared without trace. Anything created by JavaScript does not print out, including the contents of forms.

Clearly, the word "not" is missing. This trivial example demonstrates, however, that your users can be inconvenienced by the lack of printing. This problem extends even to forms which have their content provided by Java-Script. The form text fields will print, but not the content which is provided by JavaScript.

It may be useful to monitor Netscape's progress in improving their browser and JavaScript to determine when printing is supported. JavaScript could also be used to determine the browser version and warn the user that printing of JavaScript-generated text may not be possible.

Making HTML Interactive

The point of JavaScript and this book is to demonstrate how to increase the interactive content of HTML documents. There are three ways of doing this, two of which existed prior to the introduction of JavaScript:

- Using links to allow the user to browse what she or he wants,
- Using forms and CGI,
- Using forms, frames, and JavaScript.

Hot links within a document were the first way that documents were made interactive, by allowing the user to chose his or her path through a collection of documents. However, the documents themselves were non-interactive in that once they were displayed, the content could not be changed based on user input.

The introduction of forms by Netscape, along with the Application Program Interface (API) on the server to process the content of forms, allowed the document designer to create a new level of interactive content. The document and its form could pass to the Common Gateway Interface (CGI) application information which would be used to either change form information of the current document or determine which new document would be loaded.

Although this was a step toward more integrated interactive content on the Web, this required the document designer to write in two dissimilar environments, the HTML document and the server application environment, which often required using Perl.

JavaScript introduces the first capability to download in a single document intelligence to provide interactive content right on the user's Web browser. Chapters 5 and 6 will discuss the full JavaScript client-side language so you can begin programming in JavaScript immediately. All you need is Netscape's browser version 2.0 or later and a word processor!

The JavaScript Language

- Similarities Between JavaScript And Other Recent Programming Languages
- Where To Put JavaScript In Your Documents
- Data Types
- Expressions
- Conditionals
- Operators
- Control Statements
- Function Statements And Parameters
- Comments In Javascript And HTML

Similarities to Other Programming Languages

JavaScript on both the client and server owes a lot to languages, such as C and C++ for many of its concepts and syntax. For a C or C++ programmer, this is both an advantage and a disadvantage. On the negative side, many of the components of those languages were not included in JavaScript. On the positive side, the following statements in JavaScript will look very familiar to a C programmer:

```
if ( i == 0 ) { ... }

for ( i = 0 ; i < 100 ; i++ ) { ... }
```

The first is a conditional statement evaluating whether the variable "i" equals zero, and the second is a "for" loop incrementing the variable "i" from 0 to 99 in steps of 1. Both are identical in C.

And, the following method call will look like what you'd expect to find in a C++ program:

```
parent.frame[0].document.write(
    "Hi There!" )
```

The method `write()` is called for a document in the first frame of the parent document to where the JavaScript is executing.

However, JavaScript implements conditional evaluation short circuiting or partial evaluation. What this means (and we'll discuss this more later in the chapter) is that as soon as a conditional statement can be determined to be true or false, evaluation of the statement stops and execution continues based on that value. For example, consider the following code fragment:

```
var i = 0;       // create a variable "i" and assign 0
if ( ( i == 0 ) || my_func() == 3 )
{
    // execute if true
}
```

The question for the reader is, does the function `my_func()` ever get called? In C and C++, you'd expect `my_func()` to be called and do whatever it is supposed to do, which may be to modify other data structures or objects. However, in JavaScript with its short circuited evaluation, `my_func()` is never called because the first part of the conditional statement `i==0` evaluates true and the "or" operator "||" never calls `my_func()` because the outcome of that operation won't change the value of the conditional statement. We can just see some poor programmer tearing his or her hair out trying to figure out why `my_func()` isn't doing what it is supposed to be doing.

In some respects, we believe it would have been better to be completely different, than just a little bit different.

This chapter and the next will go over all of the language statements, structures, objects, and methods of JavaScript, with special attention to the objects of the language.

Where To Put JavaScript

<SCRIPT> Tag

```
<SCRIPT LANGUAGE="JavaScript"> ... </SCRIPT>
```

Implemented in the Netscape Browser version 2.0 and later. <SCRIPT> contains the JavaScript of the document. It may appear in the <HEAD> or <BODY> sections of the document.

Attributes of the <SCRIPT> tag:

LANGUAGE = "text" attribute defines the scripting language being used.

The first issue when writing JavaScript is, where do I put it? As we discussed in Chapter 2, JavaScript must appear between the <SCRIPT> ... </SCRIPT> tags somewhere within your HTML document. At this writing, it appears that the scripts can appear just about anywhere in the document, and you can have multiple <SCRIPT> tags in different parts of the document. In addition to appearing between <SCRIPT> tags, JavaScript can appear in the event handlers defined for certain HTML objects. For example, the radio button within an HTML form, has an event called "onClick" which invokes JavaScript statements when the user clicks on that button. The syntax for that form is: <INPUT TYPE="radio" onClick="//JavaScript">. Listing 5-1 illustrates all of the places within an HTML document that JavaScript can appear. Table 5-1 lists the situations in which JavaScript executes.

```
<HTML>
<HEAD>
<TITLE>This is my title!</TITLE>
<SCRIPT>

// Putting JavaScript function declarations
// in the HEAD section insures that they are
// available when needed by objects in the
// document.

function my_func( my_var)
{

// Place JavaScript of my_func() here.
// Executed only when my_func() is called.

} // end of my_func()

// JavaScript outside of a function is
// executed when script is loaded.

</SCRIPT>
</HEAD>
<BODY>
```

LISTING 5-1   ILLUSTRATE ALL OF THE PLACES THAT JAVASCRIPT CAN APPEAR IN AN HTML DOCUMENT.

```
<H1>My Heading!</H1>

<SCRIPT>

// You could put function declarations here,
// but you run the risk that in a slow load
// or a long load that the functions will not
// have been loaded when they are invoked by
// a document object.

function my_func2()
{

// JavaScript of my_func2() here
// Executed only when my_func2() is called

} // end of my_func2()

// JavaScript outside of a function is
// executed when the script is loaded

</SCRIPT>

<FORM>
    <INPUT TYPE="text" onChange="my_func()">
    <INPUT TYPE="radio" onClick=" // JavaScript">
</FORM>

// JavaScript event handlers can contain any
// JavaScript statements.

</BODY>

</HTML>
```

LISTING 5-1 (CONTINUED) ILLUSTRATE ALL OF THE PLACES THAT JAVASCRIPT CAN APPEAR IN AN HTML DOCUMENT.

TABLE 5-1. Conditions under which JavaScript executes.

• JavaScript functions are executed only when called.
• JavaScript within an event handler is executed only when the event occurs (such as a mouse click on a radio button).
• In line JavaScript executes when loaded.

Basic Components of the Language

The basic components of the JavaScript language include defining variables, JavaScript expressions, operators, conditional expressions, the function statement, and comments.

Defining Variables

```
var varname [= value] [..., varname [= value] ]
```

Client side: YES   Server side: YES

Variable names are defined using both lower-case "a" through "z", upper-case "A" through "Z", the numbers "0" through "9", and the underscore character "_". Variable numbers must begin with an upper- or lower-case alphabetic character or the underscore character. The length of a variable name can be up to 231 characters, however, this is subject to change as the Netscape browser advances.

Examples of legal variable names are: "abc", "_my_var", and "x123". Examples of illegal variable names are "1aaa" and "333".

The var statement explicitly defines a variable which can be initialized to a given value. The variable name can be any legal identifier, however, the programmer should take care to avoid the reserved words of the language. At this writing, the Netscape browser will not give you an error if you define a variable which uses an already existing object, property, or method name.

The scope of the variable name depends on where it is declared. Variables declared within a function are only visible within that function. Variables declared in inline code, outside of a function, are visible to the current application.

The VAR statement is not required to define a variable however, simply assigning a value to a variable name will define that variable. The danger in this is typographical. The following code fragment illustrates this:

```
VAR idx = 4;
VAR i = 3;

ixd = i*2;                    // programmer error in typing!

document.write( idx );
```

Because of the programmer's fumble fingers, the value of `idx` which is printed is not what was expected. Instead of printing "6" the value "4" is printed. When JavaScript encounters "`ixd`" it defines the variable and assigns it the value `i*2`. Again, this is a trap that programmers can fall into. The language is trying to be agreeable, but there are ways to shoot yourself in the foot.

One instance where using an explicit `VAR` declaration is required is if you want to define a local variable within a function which has the same name as a global variable defined outside the function. In this case, declaring the variable is required.

Data Types

JavaScript supports three data types:

- Math data types
- String data types
- Boolean data types

Within the string data type, specially formatted strings can be operated on as Date structures. More on that when we cover the Date object.

Math Data Type

The Math data type is as you would expect numeric data which can be either integer or floating point. Unlike languages which relate strongly to the underlying hardware architecture such as C and C++, JavaScript does not make a big distinction between the two. You can express integer Math literals in one of three forms: decimal (base 10), octal (base 8), and hexadecimal (base 16). As in C and C++, they are represented as follows:

- Decimal numbers begin with any digit other than 0 (zero) and contain the digits from 0 to 9. Example: 39
- Octal numbers begin with the digit 0 (zero) and contain the digits from 0 to 7. Example: 047
- Hexadecimal numbers begin with 0x (zero "x") and contain the digits from 0 to 9 and the letters "a" through "f". The letters may be either upper- or lower-case. Example: 0x27

Floating point Math literals are represented either with a decimal point, or with a number with a decimal point followed by the letter "E", followed by another positive or negative decimal number. The letter "E" may be upper- or lower-case. For example:

- 3.1415 is a floating point number without an exponent.
- 31415E-4 is a floating point number with an exponent.
- 3.1415e0 is a floating point number with an exponent.

Boolean Data Type

The Boolean data type has only two values, `true` and `false`. The result of a boolean operation such as the `&&` (logical "AND") function results in a boolean data type. For example, the following code fragment assigns the result of a boolean operation to a variable:

```
var my_var;          // Define a JavaScript variable.
var i = 3;           // Define "i" and assign the value 3.
my_var = i && 3;     // Boolean "AND" results in my_var
                     //  containing the value "true".
```

String Data Type

The String data type is an arbitrary sequence of characters beginning and ending with either "double" or 'single' quotation marks. You must begin and end a string with the same kind of quote marks, either single or double. A string can also have no characters and be of zero length.

```
"My First String!"        // A valid string
'My Second String!'       // A valid string
"Not a valid string!'     // Different quotation marks
                          //  at the beginning and end
""                        // A string with zero length!
```

Unlike C/C++, a string in JavaScript does not terminate with a null byte.

The number of string characters stored in a variable appears, at this point, to be limitless, however, any individual string literal is limited to 244 characters.

```
var my_var = "xxx…xxx";        // A single string literal
                               // is limited to 244
                               // characters.
my_var = "xxx…xxx" +           // A variable can contain
         "yyy…yyy" +           // multiple 244-character
         "zzz…zzz";            // literals.
```

You can also include non-printing characters in your string. Following is a list of special two-character codes which, when used in a string, will result in a single character as shown.

- `\b` equals a backspace.
- `\f` equals a form feed.
- `\n` equals a new line character.

- \r equals a carriage return.
- \t equals a tab character.
- \" equals a double quote character.

With the exception of the double quote escape character, the values of these characters are marginal. The only time that the non-printing characters are used is when you have turned off browser formatting using the <PRE> tag. As discussed earlier in Chapter 2, this defeats one of the purposes of a common browser, which is to format the incoming data in the best manner for the platform it is being displayed on. By using the <PRE> tag, you take away the browser's ability to do its job. Figure 5-1 and Listing 5-2 show what happens when you use the escape characters in both formatted and unformatted text.

Strong vs. Weak Data-typing

JavaScript is a weakly typed language, which means that variables can contain any legal data type, and can change data types during execution. The following code fragment in JavaScript demonstrates this:

```
VAR i;            // Declare a variable.
i = "My String";// A legal assignment of a string to i
i = 3;            // A legal assignment of an integer to i
i = 3.1415;       // A legal assignment of a floating point
                  //  number to i
```

Some programming languages like Pascal require strong data-typing, which means that if you declare a variable to be of type "integer", you can't put a floating point number in that variable. For example, the following code fragment in Pascal would cause a compiler error:

```
INT i;         { declare an integer variable }
i := 3.1415;   { this statement would generate a compiler
               error. }
```

On the other end of the scale, a language like Apple Computer's Hyper-Talk, which is used to program their HyperCard application, is not typed at all. At one point, you could put an integer into a variable, then a floating point number, and then a string, and HyperTalk wouldn't care. It's up to the programmer to make sure that you don't try to do an inappropriate operation on a data type, such as multiply the string "xyz" times 2. That obviously won't work. The following code fragment in HyperTalk demonstrates weak variable.

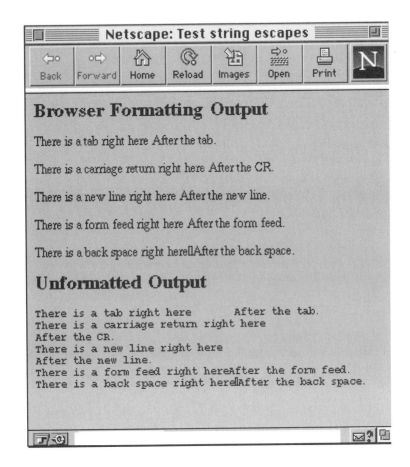

FIGURE 5-1   How the Netscape Navigator interprets the special escape characters embedded in a string. See Listing 5-2 for the HTML and JavaScript which generated this page.

```
<HTML>

<!-- File: LIST5_02.HTM
     Usage: Test how the string escapes are handled
  -->

<HEAD>
<TITLE>Test string escapes</TITLE>
</HEAD>

<BODY>
<SCRIPT LANG="JavaScript">

document.write( "<H2>Browser Formatting Output</H2>" );
document.write( "<P>There is a tab right here\tAfter the " +
                "tab.");
document.write( "<P>There is a carriage return right " +
                "here\rAfter the CR.");
document.write( "<P>There is a new line right " +
                "here\nAfter the new line.");
document.write( "<P>There is a form feed right " +
                "here\fAfter the form feed.");
document.write( "<P>There is a back space right " +
                "here\bAfter the back space.");

document.write( "<H2>Unformatted Output</H2>" );
document.write( "<PRE>" );
document.write( "There is a tab right here\tAfter the " +
                "tab.<BR>")
document.write( "There is a carriage return right " +
                "here\rAfter the CR.<BR>")
document.write( "There is a new line right here\nAfter " +
                "the new line.<BR>")
document.write( "There is a form feed right here\fAfter " +
                "the form feed.<BR>")
document.write( "There is a back space right here\bAfter " +
                "the back space.");

</SCRIPT>
</BODY>
</HTML>
```

LISTING 5-2   HTML FOR FIGURE 5-1 SHOWING THE USE OF STRING ESCAPE CHARACTERS.

```
global myVar              -- Declare a variable in HyperTalk.
myVar = 3.1415            -- A legal assignment of a floating
                          --  point number to myVar
myVar = 3                 -- A legal assignment of an integer
                          --  value to myVar
myVar = "My String"       -- A legal assignment of a string
                          --  to myVar
myVar = myVar * 2         -- This would generate a run-time
                          --  error in HyperTalk because of
                          --  the type of data found in myVar
                          --  at this point.
```

JavaScript is much closer to HyperTalk's concept of data types than to Pascal or C/C++. This means that you, the programmer, need to make sure that you know what type of data is found in a variable before you use it. Otherwise, the person browsing your document will be treated to an error message and your script will crash.

Special Data Values, Null and <Undefined>

JavaScript uses two special values to define variable states. The value null indicates a variable which does not have a value. Any operation or expression with a variable containing the null value will result in null. The <undefined> value is assigned by JavaScript to any variable (or array element, as we'll discuss next) which has not been initialized. The <undefined> value is actually a string which can be manipulated as a string literal.

```
var my_var;              // Create my_var.  JavaScript assigns
                         // the value "<undefined>".
my_var = null;           // Indicate that my_var has no value.
my_var = 2;              // my_var is assigned the value 2.
```

Defining Arrays

Up to this point, we've dealt with simple data types which contained a single value or item. Most languages include some way to collect items into an array so that they can be referred to sequentially. This is an area in which JavaScript is changing. Under Netscape Navigator version 2.0 ,creating an array was not an intuitive process. New to version 3.0 is the array object type.

Recalling that JavaScript does not declare a variable's type when created, the Array operator is very simple to use. Simply declare the variable and use the Array() operator to indicate that the variable should be an array.

```
var my_array = new Array()
```

Besides the `Array()` operator, we have another operator, the "new" operator. We won't go into detail now about "new". Suffice it to say here that "new `Array()`" is how we define a variable as an array.

Now that my_array has been declared, we can begin assigning values to it. We use the same notation as in C/C++ to address the individual elements of the array. Specify the name of the array, followed by a left bracket, then the element number, and a right bracket. The elements begin with number 0 (zero).

```
my_array[0] = 3.1415
my_array[1] = 'foo'
my_array[59] = true
```

Notice that in our array definition, we didn't tell the script the size of the array. In the code above, we assigned values to elements 0, 1, and 59. As an element is assigned, the browser creates enough elements to cover the assignment. In this case 60, elements were created when we were done.

```
my_array[0] = 3.1415    // create element 0
my_array[1] = 'foo'     // create element 1
my_array[59] = true     // create elements 2 through 59
```

As in other variables, elements of an array can contain any legal JavaScript literal, and the same array can contain more than one type simultaneously, although each element contains only a single type and value.

In our example here, after element 59 was created, what did elements 2 through 58 contain that hadn't been defined? They contain the string value "<undefined>" until they were given a value by the script.

```
my_array[2] == "<undefined>"
```

An array can be defined another way, which is to explicitly give it a size when you create it.

```
var my_array2 = new Array(60)
```

After this declaration, my_array2 contains 60 elements, numbered 0 through 59, which are initialized to the string value <undefined>.

Populating an Array When Created

You can also define the values of an array when you create it. The following code fragment would create an array of three elements and initialize them to the values shown.

```
var my_array3 = new Array( 3.1415, 2.34, 56.3 );
```

How Do I Add Elements To An Array Once It Is Defined?

C and C++ programmers are used to being able to dynamically allocate memory as needed. JavaScript doesn't have pointers or the usual `malloc()` or C++ `new()` calls (or at least new works differently in JavaScript than in C++), so how does a programmer allocate memory when more is needed during execution.

We've actually already seen this in `my_array`. Once an array is defined, accessing an array element which isn't already defined causes JavaScript to extend the array up to that element.

```
var my_array4 = new Array(60); // Define an array of 60
                               // elements.
...
my_array4[99] = 6;          // At some point, more is
                            // needed. Just accessing
                            // element 99 causes elements
                            // 61 through 99 to be
                            // created and the value 6
                            // is assigned to element 99.
```

To help determine an array's size during execution, arrays have a property called "`length`" which contains the current length of the array. Note that the last element of an array is its `length-1`. The syntax of this is the name of the array, followed by a period, and then the word "`length`". We're jumping the gun a little here since Chapter 6 covers objects; however, this example is simple. The following code fragment prints out the lengths of all the arrays we've discussed thus far:

```
document.write( "<P>my_array length = " +
                my_array.length );
document.write( "<P>my_array2 length = " +
                my_array2.length );
document.write( "<P>my_array3 length = " +
                my_array3.length );
document.write( "<P>my_array4 length = " +
                my_array4.length );
```

Following is what would appear on the document window showing the lengths:

```
my_array length = 60
my_array2 length = 60
my_array3 length = 3
my_array4 length = 100
```

Expressions

Assignment Operator

As in C/C++ the assignment operator is =. The expression on the right side of the = is assigned to the variable on the left side. Optionally, the assignment operator can be used with the VAR statement to create and initialize a variable at the same time.

```
var my_var1;
my_var1 = 2 + 3;
my_var1 = "My String!";

var my_var2 = 2 * 3;
var my_str  = "My String!";
```

Binary Operators

Arithmetic binary operators are those which require two values. The usual four arithmetic operators are supported as expected.

```
Addition: +
Subtraction: -
Division: /
Multiplication: *

var my_var, i = 2, j = 3;
my_var = i + j;
my_var = i - j;
my_var = i / j;
my_var = i * j;
```

Another binary operator is the modulus operator "%", or the remainder operation. The form of the operator is `X % Y`, where `Y` is divided into `X` and the result of the operation is the remainder. For example, `7 % 3` is 1 since 3 divided into 7 results in 2 with a remainder of 1. 1 is the result of the modulus operation.

```
Modulus: %

7 % 3 == 1
```

Unary Operators

Unary operators are those which require only a single value. C/C++ programmers will recognize the increment and decrement operators. The increment and decrements operators, `++` and `--`, have two forms, a pre-fix form and a post-fix form. The difference is that in the pre-fix notation, `++my_var`, the value of `my_var` is incremented (1 is added to the value) before the value of the variable is used. In the post-fix notation, `my_var++`, the value of the variable is used in the expression and then it is incremented.

```
Increment: ++
Decrement: --
Negation: -

var my_var = 3, your_var; // Create my_var and assign
                          // the value 3.

your_var = my_var++; // your_var is assigned the value
                     // 3 from my_var and then my_var
                     // is incremented to 4.
my_var = 3;
your_var = ++my_var; // my_var is incremented to 4 and
                     // then 4 is assigned to your_var.
my_var = 3;
your_var = my_var--; // your_var is assigned the value
                     // 3 from my_var, and then my_var
                     // is decremented to 2.
my_var = 3;
your_var = --my_var; // my_var is decremented to 2 and
                     // then 2 is assigned to your_var.
```

The negation operation "-" takes the negative of the expression.

```
Negation: -
```

```
var my_var = 3, your_var;
your_var = -my_var;      // your_var is assigned the value
                         // -3
my_var = -5;
your_var = -my_var;      // your_var is assigned the value
                         // 5
```

Bitwise Operators

Bitwise operators operate on integers only. Because JavaScript does not explicitly define integer values as separate and different from floating point values, any numeric expression, whether an integer, floating point, or even a string which can be interpreted as a number, is converted to an integer before being operated on. Floating point numbers have their fractional part truncated, not rounded, so the value 135.999 would end up as the value 135.

Strings which begin with a valid numeric value are converted to that value up to the point that the conversion would fail. For example, the string "123xxx222" would be converted to the number 123, stopping at the point were the conversion stops being a numeric quantity. The string "xxx" would result in an error.

The boolean values true and false are represented as 1 and 0, respectively. Mixing data types in a bitwise operation is fine, as long as all of the operands can be evaluated to numeric quantites. Table 5-2 illustrates these conversions.

TABLE 5-2. Conversion of numbers and strings for bitwise operators.

A number without a fractional part is converted to an integer. 135 converted to 135
A number with a fractional part is truncated and converted 135.999 converted to 135 234.33E1 converted to 2343 234.33E-1 converted to 23
A String is converted to a number, then it is converted as indicated above: "135" converted to 135 "135.999" converted to 135 "135yyy" converted to 135 "xyz" results in an error
The boolean values are converted as follows: true is converted to 1. false is converted to 0.

Representing Numbers As 32-Bit Quantities For Bitwise Operations

When we have a numeric quantity, it is represented as a 32-bit integer for the bitwise operations themselves. Where the quantity cannot be represented as a 32-bit integer, which is the range -2,147,483,648 to 2,147,483,647 (or $-(2**31)$ to $(2**31)-1$), the bit pattern represented by the first 32 bits of the number is used. For example,

```
(2**33)-1 = 11111111111111111111111111111111 (binary)
(2**32)   = 100000000000000000000000000000000
```

AND of these quantities should result in $2**32$ as a result. You end up with: $-(2**31)$ instead. (See Figure 5-2.) What's happening? The first quantity, $(2**33)-1$, is represented as a 32-bit value which drops the high order bit.

```
(2**33)-1 => 11111111111111111111111111111111 (binary)
```

The second value is also represented as a 32-bit value, but this time without dropping any of the bits.

```
(2**32)   => 100000000000000000000000000000000
```

The AND of these two quantities results in $2**32$; but we've got a problem. The high order bit of a 32-bit number is used to indicate a sign using the 2's complement method. Without going into a lot of detail, a 32-bit integer representation of a number follows the pattern illustrated below:

```
0          => 00000000000000000000000000000000
1          => 00000000000000000000000000000001
2          => 00000000000000000000000000000010
...
(2**31)-1 => 01111111111111111111111111111111

-1         => 11111111111111111111111111111111
-2         => 11111111111111111111111111111110
...
-(2**31)   => 10000000000000000000000000000000
```

As you can see, the last pattern matches the result of our bitwise operation $(2**33)-1$ & $(2**32)$ and so the result returned from the operation is the value -2,147,483,648, which is $-(2**31)$.

In summary, numbers outside of the range -2,147,483,648 to 2,147,483,647 or `-(2**31)` to `(2**31)-1`, will be truncated and the results will not be what you would otherwise expect if JavaScript were using more than 32-bit integers.

Figures 5-2 and Listing 5-3 illustrate the results of the AND (`&`) bitwise operation on a number of different data types.

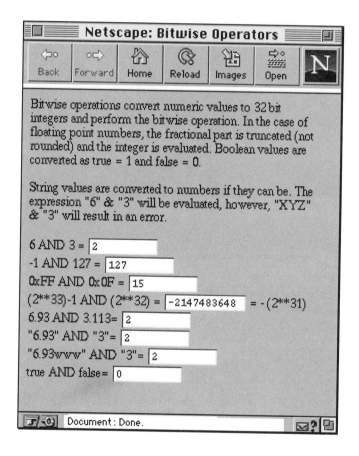

FIGURE 5-2   Results of bitwise AND (&) operations. See Listing 5-3 for the HTML and JavaScript which generated this page.

```
<HTML>

<!-- File: LIST5_03.HTM
     Usage: Demonstrate data type conversions for bitwise
            operations.
  -->

<HEAD>
<TITLE>Bitwise Operators</TITLE>
</HEAD>

<BODY>
<P>Bitwise operations convert numeric values to 32 bit
integers and perform the bitwise operation.  In the case of
floating point numbers, the fractional part is truncated
(not rounded) and the integer is evaluated.  Boolean values
are converted as true = 1 and false = 0.

<P>String values are converted to numbers if they can be.
The expression "6" & "3" will be evaluated; however, "XYZ"
& "3" will result in an error.
<BR>

<FORM NAME=fo_form>
   6 AND 3 =
   <INPUT NAME="in_int1" SIZE=10>
   <BR>
   -1 AND 127 =
   <INPUT NAME="in_int2" SIZE=10>
   <BR>
   0xFF AND 0x0F =
   <INPUT NAME="in_int3" SIZE=10>
   <BR>
   (2**33)-1 AND (2**32) =
   <INPUT NAME="in_int4" SIZE=12>
   = - (2**31)
   <BR>
   6.93 AND 3.113=
   <INPUT NAME="in_float" SIZE=10>
   <BR>
   &quot;6.93&quot; AND &quot;3&quot;=
   <INPUT NAME="in_str1" SIZE=10>
   <BR>
```

LISTING 5-3   THE HTML FOR FIGURE 5-2 DEMONSTRATING BITWISE OPERATIONS.

```
    &quot;6.93www&quot; AND &quot;3&quot;=
    <INPUT NAME="in_str2" SIZE=10>
    <BR>
    true AND false=
    <INPUT NAME="in_bool" SIZE=10>
</FORM>

<SCRIPT LANG="JavaScript">

// The following JavaScript is evaluated as the document is
// loaded.  The form definition must come before the
// JavaScript so that the form objects have been defined
// as the JavaScript executes.

document.fo_form.in_int1.value = 6 & 3;
document.fo_form.in_int2.value = -1 & 127;
document.fo_form.in_int3.value = 0xFF & 0x0F;
document.fo_form.in_int4.value = 8589934591 & 4294967296;
document.fo_form.in_float.value = 6.93  & 3.113;
document.fo_form.in_str1.value = "6.93" & "3";
document.fo_form.in_str2.value = "6.93www" & 3;
document.fo_form.in_bool.value = true & false;

</SCRIPT>

</BODY>

</HTML>
```

LISTING 5-3   (CONTINUED) THE HTML FOR FIGURE 5-2 DEMONSTRATING BITWISE OPERATIONS.

Defining Bitwise Operations

Operands for the bitwise operation are X and Y. N represents a number for shifting bits.

Client Side: YES   Server Side: YES

```
AND: X & Y
110 & 011 => 010

OR: X | Y
110 | 011 => 111
```

```
XOR (exclusive OR): X ^ Y
110 ^ 011 => 101

Left Shift: X << N
Left Shift moves the bits to the left N places, filling
in zeros on the right. Bits which roll off the left are
discarded.
000111 << 2 => 011100
100011 << 2 => 001100

Sign-propagating Right Shift: X >> N
Sign-propagating Right Shift moves the bits to the right
N places. The sign bit is propagated with the shift. Bits
which roll off the right are discarded.
10000000000000000000000111000001 >> 2
    => 11100000000000000000000001110000
00000000000000000000000111000001 >> 2
    => 00000000000000000000000001110000

Zero-fill Right Shift: X >>> N
Zero-fill Right Shift moves the bits to the right N
places. The sign bit remains in place and zeros fill in.
Bits which roll off the right are discarded.
10000000000000000000000111000001 >> 2
    => 10000000000000000000000001110000
00000000000000000000000111000001 >> 2
    => 00000000000000000000000001110000
```

Comparison Operators

Comparison operators compare two quantities and return a boolean value (`true` or `false`) based on the result of the comparison. Note that these comparison operators also work for strings where the comparison is made based on the sorting order of the string itself.

Client Side: YES   Server Side: YES

```
Equal: ==
2 == 3 returns false
2 == 2 returns true

Not Equal: !=
2 != 3 returns true
2 != 2 returns false

Greater Than: >
```

```
2 > 3 returns false
2 > 2 returns false
3 > 2 returns true

Greater Than or Equal To: >=
2 >= 3 returns false
2 >= 2 returns true
3 >= 2 returns true

Less Than: <
2 < 3 returns true
2 < 2 returns false
3 < 2 returns false

Less Than or Equal To: <=
2 <= 3 returns true
2 <= 2 returns true
3 <= 2 returns false
```

Most programming languages use these very same operators for comparisons. They can be part of an assignment,

```
var my_var;              // create my_var, i and j
var i = 2;
var j = 3;
my_var = i < j;          // "true" assigned to my_var
```

or a part of a conditional expression,

```
var i = 2;               // create i, j and k
var j = 3;
var k;
if ( i <= j )            // evaluates to true
{
   k = j - i;            // k assigned the value 1
}
```

For those not familiar with C/C++ the equals operator "==" is a source of endless trouble in programming. Many beginning programmers will confuse the assignment operator "=" with the equals to logical operator "==" in conditional statements. If you do this in JavaScript you'll get an error message indicating that it will use the equals comparison operator rather than the assignment operator. This is another example of where JavaScript differs from C/C++. Let's look at the code in Listing 5-4.

```
<HTML>
<!-- File: LIST5_04.HTM
     Usage: Demonstrate what happens if you use
            assignment (=) instead of equality
            comparison (==) inside an if
            statement.
     NOTE!  This script will generate an error
            on your browser.
  -->
<HEAD>
<TITLE>Test assignment in IF</TITLE>
</HEAD>

<BODY>
<SCRIPT LANG="JavaScript">

window.alert( "This script will generate an error!" );

VAR i,j;
i = 2;
j = 3;

document.write( "<P>i = " + i + " j = " + j );

// The following conditional will generate an
// an error.  The browser will notify the user
// that an assignment is being attempted, but
// the browser will assume that an equality
// comparison was intended.  The browser then
// executes a comparison instead of the assignment.

if ( i = j )
{
   document.write( "<P>Evaluated as true" );
}
else
{
   document.write( "<P>Evaluated as false" );
}
document.write( "<P>i = " + i + " j = " + j );
</SCRIPT>
</BODY>
</HTML>
```

LISTING 5-4   A SCRIPT USING THE ASSIGNMENT OPERATOR (=) INSTEAD OF THE EQUALITIES TEST (==)

The statement

```
if (i = j)
```

will generate an error in JavaScript. Although the browser will replace the statement with

```
if ( i == j)
```

which is a legal comparison statement, this is very sloppy. Any time the user is faced with an error condition, the quality of the script is in question. For C/C++ programmers the first statement is legal and could be a source of confusion. C/C++ would assign the value of j to i and if it were non-zero would evaluate the expression as true.

Logical Operators

JavaScript uses the following logical or boolean operators. C/C++ programmers will recognize them as being the same as those used with that language. In contrast to the bitwise operators which used numbers, logical operators use boolean values, although non-boolean values will also generate results.

```
Client Side: YES        Server Side: YES

Math
zero value evaluates to false
non-zero value evaluates to true

String
zero length string "" evaluates to false
non-zero length string e.g., "a" evaluates to true

AND: &&
true && true evaluates to true
true && false evaluates to false
false && false evaluates to false

OR: ||
true || true evaluates to true
true || false evaluates to true
false || false evaluates to false

NOT: !
```

```
!true evaluates to false
!false evaluates to true
```

JavaScript also has a conditional evaluation, similar to C/C++, in which the value of the expression is determined by a conditional evaluation.

Client Side: YES   Server Side: YES

```
(conditional expression) ? value if true : value if false
```

You could probably use some explanation if you haven't seen this before. Let's look at an example.

```
var i = 3;              // define and assign i, j, and k
var j = 4;
var k

k = ( i == j ) ? 10 : 20; // since i != j, the value 20
                          // is assigned to k
```

In this code fragment, the value of k will be determined by the result of the comparison between i and j. In this example, i != j ,so the conditional evaluation will take the "false" value, which is 20, and this will be assigned to the variable k. This is another example of JavaScript incorporating constructs from C/C++ into the language.

String Operators

Client Side: YES   Server Side: YES

```
String Concatenation: +
"abc" + "def" evaluates to "abcdef"

EXAMPLE
var i = "abc"
var j = "def"
var k;

k = i + j;
document.write( k );
```

This results in:

```
abcdef
```

String concatenation takes two strings and merges them into a single string. This also works on numbers and strings, and boolean values and strings. For example,

```
var str = "abc";
var num = 123;

document.write( str + num );
```

results in this output

```
abc123
```

Figure 5-3 and Listing 5-5 show how combinations of strings, numbers, and boolean values behave when concatenated with strings.

In short, the concatenation of a string and any other data type will result in a string. The order of the data types does not matter in this case. One very important note on this is that one of the operands of the concatenation expression must be a string.

It should be pretty clear what happens if you have two numbers and the "concatenation" operator. It looks like addition, and will be treated as such.

```
var i = 3;       // define i, j, and k and assign values
var j = 4;
var k;

k = i + j;       // since both i and j are numeric, the
                 // + operator is addition, not
                 // string concatenation
```

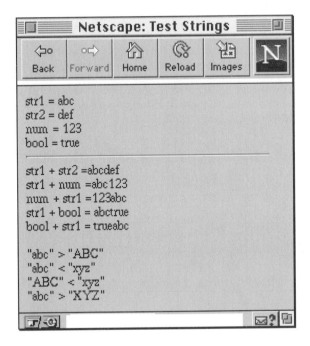

FIGURE 5-3   Results of string concatenation and string comparisons. See Listing 5-5

```
<HTML>
<!-- File: LIST5_05.HTM
     Usage: demonstrate string concatenation
            and compares.
  -->
<HEAD>
<TITLE>Test Strings</TITLE>
</HEAD>

<BODY>
<SCRIPT LANG="JavaScript">
var str1 = "abc";
var str2 = "def";
var str3;
var num = 123;
var bool = true;

var sort1 = "abc";
```

LISTING 5-5   HTML DEMONSTRATING THE SORTING ORDER OF JAVASCRIPT STRINGS.

```
var sort2 = "ABC";
var sort3 = "xyz";
var sort4 = "XYZ";

document.write( "<P>str1 = " + str1 );
document.write( "<BR>str2 = " + str2 );
document.write( "<BR>num = " + num );
document.write( "<BR>bool = " + true );
document.write( "<HR>" );

str3 = str1 + str2;
document.write( "str1 + str2 =" + str3 );

str3 = str1 + num;
document.write( "<BR>str1 + num =" + str3 );

str3 = num + str1;
document.write( "<BR>num + str1 =" + str3 );

str3 = str1 + bool;
document.write( "<BR>str1 + bool = " + str3 );

str3 = bool + str1;
document.write( "<BR>bool + str1 = " + str3 );
// The sorting order of each pair of variables is
// displayed.  Although the order is well known,
// this code demonstrates the order through executing
// comparisons.

document.write( "<P>&QUOT;" + sort1 + "&QUOT;" )
if (sort1 < sort2 )
{
    document.write( " &LT; " );
}
else
{
    document.write( " &GT; " );
}
document.write( "&QUOT;" + sort2 + "&QUOT;" );

document.write( "<BR>&QUOT;" + sort1 + "&QUOT;" )
if (sort1 < sort3 )
{
    document.write( " &LT; " );
}
else
{
    document.write( " &GT; " );
```

LISTING 5-5   (CONTINUED) HTML DEMONSTRATING THE SORTING ORDER OF JAVASCRIPT STRINGS.

```
}
document.write( "&QUOT;" + sort3 + "&QUOT;" );

document.write( "<BR>&QUOT;" + sort2 + "&QUOT;" )
if (sort2 < sort3 )
{
   document.write( " &LT; " );
}
else
{
   document.write( " &GT; " );
}
document.write( "&QUOT;" + sort3 + "&QUOT;" );

document.write( "<BR>&QUOT;" + sort1 + "&QUOT;" )
if (sort1 < sort4 )
{
   document.write( " &LT; " );
}
else
{
   document.write( " &GT; " );
}
document.write( "&QUOT;" + sort4 + "&QUOT;" );

</SCRIPT>
</BODY>
</HTML>
```

LISTING 5-5   (CONTINUED) HTML DEMONSTRATING THE SORTING ORDER OF JAVASCRIPT STRINGS.

What isn't clear is what happens if you have a boolean value ("true" or "false") and a string or numeric value. Remember one important point when dealing with this situation:

 The boolean values "true" and "false" are treated as the numeric quantities 1 and 0 respectively.

Keeping this in mind, let's look at what happens when we concatenate boolean and numeric data types.

```
var bool_T = true;
var bool_F = false;
```

```
var num = 123;
var result;

result = bool_T + bool_T;   // Treat boolean values as
                            // numeric and assign the
                            // numeric value 2 to result.

result = bool_T + num;      // Assign value 1 + 123 or 124
                            // to result.

result = bool_T + bool_F    // Assign value 1 + 0 or 1 to
                            // result.
```

In short, if the concatenation has no string, the boolean quantities are converted to their numeric equivalents and addition is performed.

Strings also support comparison operators, where they use the sorting order of the ISO Latin-1 character set. The most important thing to remember about this sorting is that upper- and lower-case characters are two different characters to the language with the lower- case characters having a "higher" sort value than the upper-case characters. For example:

```
"A" < "Z"
"A" < "a"
"Z" < "a"

"Bob" < "bob"
"ZZZ" < "bob"
```

Think of it this way; the sorting order begins with the numeric characters 0, 1, …, 9, then the upper-case characters A, B, C, …, Z, and then the lower-case characters a, b, c, …, z. We'll cover the functions or String object methods to do this in Chapter 6.

Operator Precedence

Most languages have a precedence for operators. What this means is, if you don't use parentheses to explicitly define which operation is to occur first, what should the language do first? For example,

```
k = 2 * 3 + 4;
```

If you do the addition first, 3 + 4, and then the multiplication 2 * 7, the result of the expression is 14. On the other hand, if you do the multiplication first, 2 * 3, then the addition, 6 + 4, the result is 10.

Defining an order of operator precedence gives the language definition so that you can anticipate which operators will be executed first. For example, in JavaScript, addition is evaluated before multiplication. So, we'd end up with the following order of execution from our expression above.

```
k = 2 * 3 + 4
    2 * ( 3 + 4 )
    2 * 7
    14
```

Clearly, you could change the order of execution by explicitly using parentheses to force execution in the order you wanted.

```
k = ( 2 * 3 ) + 4
      6 + 4
      10
```

Table 5-3 gives the order in which JavaScript will execute operators when parentheses do not explicitly define the order.

TABLE 5-3. *JavaScript operator order of precedence.*

comma ,
assignment = += -= *= /= %= <<= >>= >>>=&= ^= | =
conditional ?:
logical-or ||
logical-and &&
bitwise-or |
bitwise-xor ^
bitwise-and &
equality == !=
relational < <= > >=
shift << >> >>>
addition/subtraction + -
multiply/divide * / %
negation/increment ! ~ - ++ --
call, member () [] .

Frankly, I find that it is error-prone to rely on a language's order of precedence when determining the value of an expression. My recommendation is to make liberal use of parentheses to force the execution of an expression in a particular order.

Conditionals

Up to this point, we haven't discussed any way for JavaScript to conditionally execute statements or to control looping of code to execute statements repeatedly. Before we begin that discussion, two points need to be raised: the lack of a "goto" statement and "partial evaluation" of a condition expression.

GOTO Missing in Action

For anyone who has read FORTRAN code written before the advent of structured programming practices, the GOTO statement is not missed. JavaScript does not support the use of the GOTO statement, which is a major contributor to unreadable code.

Partial Evaluation

Partial evaluation is the practice of short circuiting a condition expression evaluation once you know the outcome of the evaluation. Let's take a look at an example:

```
var i = 3;
var j = 4;
var k = 5;

if ( ( i < j ) || ( j > k ) )
{
    do_something();
}
else
{
    do_something_else();
}
```

In the conditional expression

```
if ( ( i < j ) || ( j > k ) )
```

the first part of the statement is true (i < j). The entire statement will now have the value "TRUE" because the first part (i < j) is "or'ed" with the second part of the statement (j > k). The result of a true statement "or'ed" with any other statement will be a true statement.

JavaScript saves itself the trouble of executing the (j < k) part of the conditional expression because it knows that the result of the entire conditional expression will be true.

So, what does this mean to the programmer? Well, in our example above, it doesn't mean much because the expression (j < k) didn't affect the value of any variable. However, what would happen in Listing 5-6?

```
<HTML>
<HEAD>
<SCRIPT>

function write_it()
{
    parent.other_frame.some_form.input_field.value =
        "some text";
    return true;
}

</SCRIPT>
</HEAD>

<BODY>
<SCRIPT>

var i = 3;
var j = 4;

if ( ( i < j ) || write_it() ) // partial evaluation
{
    // execute if true
}
else
{
    // execute if false
}
</SCRIPT>
</BODY>
</HTML>
```

LISTING 5-6   WHAT HAPPENS TO THE FUNCTION WRITE_IT() WHEN THE "IF" STATEMENT IS PARTIALLY EVALUATED?

We've included a couple of constructs we haven't covered in detail yet, but let's run though the code.

In the <HEAD> section, a script and a function are defined. The function write_it() is going to change the value of a form's input field in another frame of the window. It will then return a value of true to the script that called it.

```
function write_it()
{
    parent.other_frame.some_form.input_field.value =
        "some text";
    return true;
}
```

The script that is going to call write_it() is found in the <BODY> of the document.

```
var i = 3;
var j = 4;

if ( ( i < j ) || write_it() )
```

Unless you aware of JavaScript's partial evaluation of conditional expressions, you might tear your hair out trying to figure out why write_it() doesn't work! The problem is that the first part of the conditional statement (i < j) evaluates true, so JavaScript never gets around to calling write_it() at all.

This behavior is very different from many other programming languages and the programmer needs to be aware of the problem. Figures 5-4 and 5-5, and Listing 5-7 demonstrate an example of partial evaluation.

The following conditional control structures all behave the same in this way. Keep in mind that partial evaluation of any condition expression can cause some portion of the expression to be ignored. The safest route is to put only comparisons and no function calls in a conditional expression.

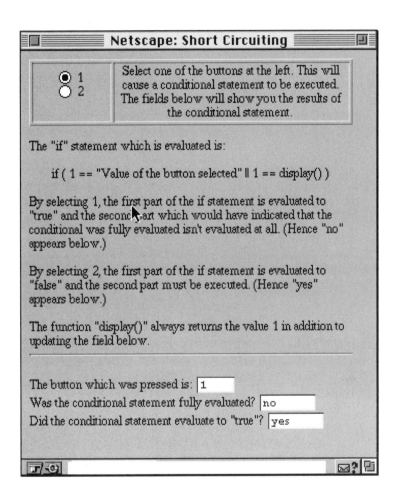

FIGURE 5-4   Conditional expressions are partially evaluated until the value of the entire statement can be determined without any additional evaluation.

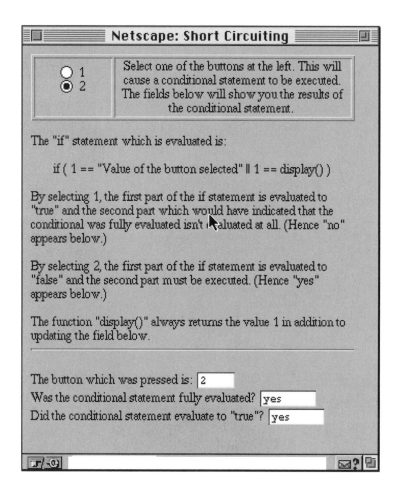

FIGURE 5-5   Partial evaluation of a conditional expression.

```
<html>

<!-- File: LIST5_07.HTM
     Usage: a demonstration that JavaScript short
            circuits evaluation of conditionals.
   -->

<head>
<title>
Short Circuiting
</title>

<script lang="JavaScript">

function display()
{
   // if this function is called at all it will place the
   // text "yes" in the form text field "in_disp2" of form
   // "fo_display" and return the value 1

   document.fo_display.in_disp2.value = "yes";
   return 1;
}

function processAction( btn_value )
{

   // Put the value passed to it into the form
   // text field "in_disp1" of form "fo_display"

   document.fo_display.in_disp1.value = btn_value;

   // Preset the value of form text field "in_disp2" to the
   // text "no"

   document.fo_display.in_disp2.value = "no";
```

LISTING 5-7   HTML AND JAVASCRIPT WHICH GENERATE THE PAGES IN FIGURE 5-4 AND FIGURE 5-5
DEMONSTRATING SHORT CIRCUITED EVALUATION OF CONDITIONALS.

```
// In the following conditional statement, the first part
// 1 == 1 always evaluates to "true".  Since we are
// "or-ing" this with the second part, evaluation short
// circuiting says that the second part will never be
// evaluated, hence display() will never be called.
//
// If you want to test this, change "||" to "&&" which
// will force the second part of the conditional to be
// evaluated, calling display()

   if ( 1 == btn_value || 1 == display() )
   {

      // Demonstrate that a "true" evaluation occured by
      // placing the text "yes" into the text field
      // "in_disp3" of form "fo_display"

      document.fo_display.in_disp3.value = "yes";
   }
   else
   {

      // If the conditional statement had evaluated "false"
      // the text "no" would have been put into the text
      // field "in_disp3"

      document.fo_display.in_disp3.value = "no";
   }

   return;
}

</script>
</head>
```

LISTING 5-7   (CONTINUED) HTML AND JAVASCRIPT WHICH GENERATE THE PAGES IN FIGURE 5-4 AND FIGURE 5-5 DEMONSTRATING SHORT CIRCUITED EVALUATION OF CONDITIONALS.

```
<body>
<table border=1>
    <td ALIGN="middle" VALIGN="middle" WIDTH=25%>
        <form name="fo_selection">
            <input type=radio name="btn_" onClick=
                "processAction(fo_selection.btn_.value='1')">
            1
            <br>
            <input type=radio name="btn_" onClick=
                "processAction(fo_selection.btn_.value='2')">
            2
        </form>
    </td>
    <td>
        <p>Select one of the buttons at the left.  This will
            cause a conditional statement to be executed.  The
            fields below will show you the results of the
            conditional statement.
    </td>
</table>

<p>The &quot;if&quot; statement which is evaluated is:
<p><center>if ( 1 == &quot;Value of the button
    selected&quot; || 1 == display() )</center>
<p>By selecting 1, the first part of the if statement is
    evaluated to &quot;true&quot; and the second part which
    would have indicated that the conditional was fully
    evaluated isn't evaluated at all. (Hence &quot;no&quot;
    appears below.)
<p>By selecting 2, the first part of the if statement is
    evaluated to &quot;false&quot; and the second part must
    be executed.  (Hence &quot;yes&quot; appears below.)
<p>The function &quot;display()&quot; always returns the
    value 1 in addition to updating the field below.

<HR>
```

LISTING 5-7   (CONTINUED) HTML AND JAVASCRIPT WHICH GENERATE THE PAGES IN FIGURE 5-4 AND FIGURE 5-5 DEMONSTRATING SHORT CIRCUITED EVALUATION OF CONDITIONALS.

```
<form name="fo_display">
   The button which was pressed is:
   <input name="in_disp1" size=5 type=text value=" ">
   <br>
   Was the conditional statement fully evaluated?
   <input name="in_disp2" size=8 type=text value=" ">
   <br>
   Did the conditional statement evaluate to
   &quot;true&quot;?
   <input name="in_disp3" size=8 type=text value=" ">
</form>
</body>
</html>
```

LISTING 5-7   (CONTINUED) HTML AND JAVASCRIPT WHICH GENERATE THE PAGES IN FIGURE 5-4 AND FIGURE 5-5 DEMONSTRATING SHORT CIRCUITED EVALUATION OF CONDITIONALS.

JavaScript Conditional Expressions

JavaScript supports the following conditional and control expressions:

```
while ( logical statement )
{
   // Execute these statements until the logical
   // statement is false.
}

for ( initial condition; test condition; loop condition )
{
   // Execute these statements until the test condition
   // is false.
}

if ( logical statement )
{
   // Execute these statements once if the logical
   // statement is true.
}
else
{
   // Execute these statements once if the logical
   // statement is false.
}
```

Whereas these are familiar to a C/C++ programmer, there are probably several you're not used to seeing. Where's switch, do-while, and goto? At this point, these control structures are not included in JavaScript, but there's no telling what Netscape will do in the future. With the possible exception of the switch statement, the other control statements are not really needed to make the language complete and useful.

Let's go over those statements which are part of the language.

while

Client Side: YES   Server Side: YES

```
while (logical statement)
{
    statements
}
```

The while statement is a loop that repeatedly executes the statements within the brackets until the logical statement with the while evaluates to false. For example,

```
var response_ok = false;
while ( !response_ok ) // Loop until !response_ok ==
                       //    false.
                       // Remember !response_ok negates
                       //    the value of response_ok.
{
    do_something_useful(); // Call a procedure to do
                           //    something.

    response_ok =
       document.confirm( "Do you want to quit?" );

                           // Prompt user whether she wants
                           //    to quit.  Answering "OK"
                           //    returns true, "Cancel"
                           //    returns false, which does
                           //    another loop.
}
```

The logical statement in the while statement can be any expression which will evaluate to a logical value. This could be a logical expression, variable, or function call.

for

The `for` statement has two forms, the C/C++ form:

```
for ( initial; condition; update ) { … }
```

and a form unique to JavaScript:

```
for ( variable in object ) { … }
```

for (...;...;...) {}

Client Side: YES   Server Side: YES

```
for ([initial expression]; [condition];
     [update expression]) {statements}
```

As in C/C++, this form of a `for` loop has three expressions: the initial expression, which tells you where the `for` loop starts; the condition, which tells the `for` loop when to stop; and, the update expression, which tells the `for` loop what to change in each iteration of the loop. A common use of the `for` loop is to count through some number of items, although it isn't limited to this. Here are two examples:

```
var str = "My String";    // Define a string.
var i;

for ( i = 0; i < str.length; i++ )
                          // Initial: i = 0
                          // Stop when i is greater than
                          //    8.  (Note that str.length
                          //    retrieves the "length"
                          //    property of the variable
                          //    named "str".)
                          // Increment i each loop.
{
    document.write( str.charAt( i ) );
}
```

This would write the following on the document:

```
My String
```

The value of i was 0 during the first iteration of the loop. At the end of the loop, the condition was tested to see if i < str.length. The condition was found to be true, so the loop incremented by executing the loop statement i++ which increments the value of i.

This isn't very interesting because you could have done the same thing by writing

```
document.write( str );
```

which is much simpler. However, let's look at another example, that shows the flexibility of the for loop.

```
var str = "My String";    // Define a string.
var i;
for ( i = (str.length - 1); i < 0; i-- )
                          // Initial, i = 8
                          // Stop when i is less than 0
                          // Decrement i each loop
{
    document.write( str.charAt( i ) );
}
```

This writes the following on the document:

```
gnirtS yM
```

You can argue that this isn't a whole lot more interesting than the first example, but we've seen that we don't have to increment the value of the initial and condition statements. We have the flexibility to do other things.

for (var in obj) {}

Client Side: YES   Server Side: YES

```
for (variable in object) {statements }
```

We have to get a little ahead of ourselves here to discuss this version of the for loop. As mentioned earlier, JavaScript is an object-oriented language, which means that you can assign properties to an object. In the for example above, we saw that a string object, "My String", had a property called "length" which gave us the length or number of characters in the string.

Whereas an object has more than one property, the `for (variable in object)` statement will loop through all of the properties of the object, assigning them to the variable so that you can operate on them.

Let's look at the following example (Listing 5-8 and Figure 5-6) where the `for` loop will step through all of the properties of the document and display them in the document window:

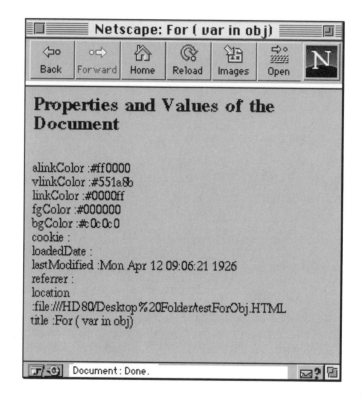

FIGURE 5-6   The document which is created by the HTML in Listing 5-8

In the HTML in Listing 5-8, the variable `obj` received a string which contained the name of a property of the document. We'll discuss this later in Chapter 6, but the `eval()` function was needed to view the contents of the property because `obj` only contained a string with the name of the property. The way to use that string and display the contents is to build a command using the string.

```
eval( "document.write( document." + obj + ")" );
```

```
<HTML>

<!-- File: LIST5_08.HTM
     Usage: Demonstrate the use of
            for ( var in obj )form
  -->

<HEAD>
<TITLE>For ( var in obj )</TITLE>
</HEAD>

<BODY>
<H2>Properties and Values of the Document</H2>

<SCRIPT>

var target_object = document;
                    // Define a variable and assign
                    //   the current document as its
                    //   value.
var obj;

for ( obj in target_object )
                    // For all properties of
                    //   target_object (the document),
                    //   loop.
{
   document.write( "<BR>" + obj + " :" );
                    // Write the name of the object

   eval( "document.write( document." + obj + ")" );
                    // eval() is needed to display the
                    //   contents of the obj variable.
                    //   Build a document.write() using
                    //   the document and property
                    //   currently pointed at by obj.
}

</SCRIPT>
</BODY>
</HTML>
```

LISTING 5-8   THE HTML TO DISPLAY ALL OF THE PROPERTIES OF A DOCUMENT.

Looking at the contents of the `eval()`,

```
"document.write( document." + obj + ")"
```

and assuming that `obj` is "title", one of the properties of the document, the string would be evaluated as

```
"document.write( document." + obj + ")"
"document.write( document." + "title" + ")"
"document.write( document.title)
```

This ends up as

```
eval( "document.write( document.title)" );
```

which is executed as if

```
document.write( document.title)
```

were executed by itself. More on this in Chapter 6 when we talk about built-in methods of the language.

continue

Client Side: YES   Server Side: YES

```
continue
```

The `continue` statement should be familiar to C/C++ programmers. This statement will cause the execution of a loop to end and jump to the next iteration, if another iteration is possible. The following example shows the use of `continue`.

```
var i;
for ( i = 0; i < 20; i++ )
{
   if ( i%10 != 0 )
   {
     document.write( i ); // Executed whenever i is not
                          //    a multiple of ten.
     continue;            // Jump to end of loop
   }

   document.write( "<BR>" );  // This statement only
```

```
//    executed when i is a
//    multiple of ten.

//  end of loop
}
```

The script would write this on the document window.

```
123456789
111213141516171819
```

The continue statement works in the

- for
- while

statements.

break

Client Side: YES   Server Side: YES

```
break
```

The break statement is similar to the continue statement in that execution of the loop is interrupted, but instead of jumping to the next increment, the loop itself is terminated. Execution of the script will pick up with the first statement after the loop. The following example will terminate the while loop execution when i equals 10, rather than at 100:

```
var i = 0;

while ( i < 100 )
{
    i++;
    if ( i == 10 )
    {
        break;
    }
}
```

The break statement works in the

- for
- while

statements.

if ... then ... else

Client Side: YES   Server Side: YES

```
if (condition) {statements} [else {statements}]
```

The JavaScript if...then...else statement is the same as you'd find in other languages. The condition statement is evaluated as a logical expression. If the expression evaluates to true, the statements in the block directly following the condition statement are executed. If the condition statement evaluates to false, and if an else statement follows, the statements in that block are executed, otherwise, if no else block exists, the execution continues after the if statement. The following code gives an example:

```
var i = 2;
var j = 3;

if ( i < j )
{
   // These statements will be executed.
}
else
{
   // These statements are not executed.
}
```

Note that the condition statement can be any variable, expression, or function which returns a boolean value.

function Statement

Client Side: YES   Server Side: YES

```
function name([param] [, param] [..., param])
   {statements…}
```

The function statement provides a way to group together statements which will be executed whenever the function name is used in JavaScript. You can pass parameters into the function which are used by the code inside the function to do its job. The function can return a single value through the return statement inside the function. There can be more than one return statement, but the first statement executed will exit the function.

info	Make sure that all function statements are defined before they are used in JavaScript.

An important note is to make sure that all function statements are defined before they are used in JavaScript. For instance, the code in Listing 5-9 will generate an error when loaded because the function expiration_date() isn't defined at the point when it is used:

```
<HTML>
<BODY>

<SCRIPT LANG="JavaScript">
document.write( expiration_date() );

var publish_date = new Date("3/5/99");

function expiration_date()
{
   var calculated_date;

   // Code to take a defined variable called
   // publish_date and add a week to show when the
   // information displayed expires.  The variable
   // calculated_date contains that date.

   return calculated_date;
}
</SCRIPT>
</BODY>
</HTML>
```

LISTING 5-9   A FUNCTION DEFINED AFTER IT IS CALLED WILL GENERATE AN ERROR.

The correct way to structure this script is shown in Listing 5-10.

```
<HTML>

<HEAD>
<SCRIPT LANG="JavaScript">
var publish_date = new Date("3/5/99");

function expiration_date()
{
    var calculated_date;

    // Calculate expiration date.

    return calculated_date;
}
</SCRIPT>
</HEAD>

<BODY>
<SCRIPT>
document.write( expiration_date() );
</SCRIPT>
</BODY>

</HTML>
```

LISTING 5-10   DEFINING FUNCTIONS BEFORE THE ARE CALLED.

In Listing 5-10 we've defined the function `expiration_date()` and the global variable `publish_date` in the `<HEAD>` section so that they are loaded and available to the rest of the document when needed during the load.

Note also that the script has some JavaScript code that is executed on load ,

```
document.write( expiration_date() );
var publish_date = "3/5/99";
```

and JavaScript which is only executed when invoked,

```
function expiration_date()
{ … }
```

return Statement

Client Side: YES   Server Side: YES

```
return expression
```

The `return` statement is used to return a value from a function. If no return statement is specified, then the function returns the `<undefined>` value. Table 5-4 illustrates what happens in different situations where return values are expected from functions.

TABLE 5-4. *How JavaScript handles function return values*

Function Returns a Value to the Calling Statement	Calling Statement Expects a Value	Result

Yes
 	
Example:
`function myFunc1()`
`{ return a_value }`
	Yes
	
	Example:
	`a = myFunc1();`
		The content of `a_value` is assigned to the variable "a".

Yes	No Example: `myFunc1();`	The content of `a_value` is discarded.

No
 	
Example:
`function myFunc2()`
`{ return // no value}`
	Yes	The value "`<undefined>`" is assigned to the variable "a".

No	No	No value is sent or received.

A function can have more than one `return` statement, but the first one executed will exit the function and return the value (if any) to the calling program. The following example has four `return` statements, however, only one of them will ever be executed. Whenever a `return` statement is found, the browser takes the value associated with `return`, if any, exits back to the calling script, and delivers the return value or `<undefined>` if no return value is present.

```
function myFunc( aVar )
{
    if ( aVar == 1 )
```

```
{
    return 10;
}
else
    if ( aVar == 2 )
    {
        return 20;
    }

return 30;

return 40;    // This statement will never be reached!
}
```

This script also has a problem. The statements following

```
return 30;
```

will never be executed because the script fails to provide a way to get there. As soon as the return 30 statement is executed, the function myFunc returns to the calling script and no other statements are used.

The value assigned during the return statement can be a literal, variable, expression, or function call. All of the following return statements are legal:

```
return 30;         // Return a numeric literal
return aVar;       // Return the value contained in the
                   //   variable aVar
return aVar * 3;   // Return the value of the expression
                   //   Avar * 3
return myFunc();   // Call another function myFunc() and
                   //   return the value that it returns
```

Scope of Variables, Defining Global and Local Variables

Up to now we've been declaring variables with the var statement more or less wherever we needed a variable to store information, and then we accessed those variables within the function or script where they were needed.

• Local Variables: Variables defined within a function that are only accessible from within the function

• Global Variables: Variables defined outside of a function that are accessible globally unless overridden by a local variable declaration within a function.

Take a look at Listing 5-11 and Figure 5-7 to see how this works.

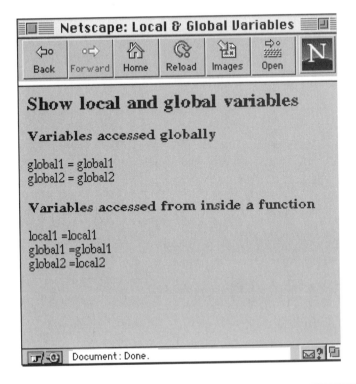

FIGURE 5-7   Demonstration of local and global variable declarations. See Listing 5-11 for an explanation of the code.

Passing Parameters

When you pass parameters into a function, the parameters are passed by value, not by reference. This means that a copy of the value of a parameter is passed into the function and any changes made to the parameter inside the function will not affect the value of the parameter used to pass into the function. Let's look at an example to clarify this in Listing 5-12.

Looking at the definition for myFunc(), notice that it is passed a value in the variable name aVar, and that the contents of aVar are modified during the execution of myFunc(). The value of aVar is then passed back to the calling script.

```
<HTML>

<!-- File: LIST5_11.HTM
     Usage: Demonstrate local and global
            variable scope.
  -->

<HEAD>
<TITLE>Local & Global Variables</TITLE>
</HEAD>

<BODY>

<SCRIPT>

  // Define two global variables

var global1 = "global1";
var global2 = "global2";

  // Define a function

function show_it()
{

    // Define two local variables
    // Overlay the global variable "global2"
    //   with a local variable of the same name.

  var local1 = "local1";
  var global2 = "local2";

    // Write out the contents of the local and global
    // variables.  Note that the local variable "global2"
    // has overlaid the global variable of the same name.

  document.write( "<H3>Variables accessed from inside a " +
                  "function</H3>" );
  document.write( "<p>local1 =" + local1 );
  document.write( "<br>global1 =" + global1 );
  document.write( "<br>global2 =" + global2 );

  return;
```

LISTING 5-11 USING LOCAL AND GLOBAL VARIABLES AND OVERRIDING THE DEFINITION OF A GLOBAL VARIABLE WITH A LOCAL VARIABLE.

```
}
// Print out the global variables
document.write( "<H2>Show local and global " +
                "variables</H2>" );
document.write( "<H3>Variables accessed globally</H3>" );
document.write( "<p>global1 = " + global1 );
document.write( "<br>global2 = " + global2 );

    // Call the function to print out its
    // variables.

show_it();
</SCRIPT>
</BODY>
</HTML>
```

LISTING 5-11   (CONTINUED) USING LOCAL AND GLOBAL VARIABLES AND OVERRIDING THE DEFINITION OF A GLOBAL VARIABLE WITH A LOCAL VARIABLE.

```
<HTML>
<!-- File: LIST5_12.HTM
     Usage: Demonstrate that parameters are
            passed by value, not reference.
   -->
<HEAD>
<SCRIPT LANG="JavaScript">
function myFunc( aVar )
{
    aVar = aVar * 10;
    return aVar;
}
</SCRIPT>
</HEAD>
<BODY>
<SCRIPT>
var myVar = 5;
var yourVar = myFunc( myVar );
document.write( myVar + ":" + yourVar );
</SCRIPT>
</BODY>
</HTML>
```

LISTING 5-12   PASSING PARAMETERS TO JAVASCRIPT FUNCTIONS IS BY VALUE.

In the <BODY> section, we define a variable called myVar, assign it a value, and use myVar to call myFunc(myVar). The question is, what happens to the value of myVar? Since JavaScript passes parameters by value, the value of myVar is unchanged by the execution of myFunc() and yourVar is assigned the value 50, using the script. This code would result in this document output.

```
5:50
```

The only information passed back by the function is through the return statement, which sends back a single value to the calling script.

So, how do you modify more than one variable with a single function call? Good question, and unfortunately, JavaScript doesn't have the flexibility of C/C++ in being able to call by both value and reference. (Calling by reference allows a function to modify the contents of the variables used as parameters in calling the function.)

One, slightly dangerous method (from the perspective of structured programming) is available to modify more than one variable, and that is to use globally defined variables in the function. As we showed in the last section, globally defined variables are accessible to functions. If you make a change to a global variable, that change is global. The danger is that you are circumventing a structure of the language to keep things straight. How will you remember that a function changes a global variable? You may, at some point, forget that the global variable was changed in your function and introduce a defect into your code.

HTML and JavaScript Comments

As is always the case in a book on programming languages, you have to use some language constructs before they are formally defined or else you end up trying to define everything at once. This section concerns comments in HTML and JavaScript, but you've already see a lot of them before this.

You will have noticed that two different types of comments have been used in the scripts so far. HTML comments which look like the following:

```
<!-- This is an HTML comment. -->
```

and JavaScript comments which look like this,

```
// This is a JavaScript comment.
```

We should probably let you know that JavaScript also supports comments which look like the following:

```
/* This is also a JavaScript comment. */
```

Once again, C programmers will find the `/* comments */` familiar, while C++ programmers will be used to `//` comments. JavaScript owes a lot to C/C++ and Java (probably because Java took much of the C/C++ languages as its base).

The use of comments is important in all programming to remind the programmer what he or she did when a piece of code is six months old and he or she can't remember why the code was programmed a certain way. Comments are also critical for other people who are looking at your code.

At this point, we need to discuss several issues:

- What is the definition of the HTML and JavaScript comments?
- When do you use HTML vs. JavaScript comments?
- Can you use HTML comments to hide JavaScript from browsers which don't support JavaScript?

Definition of HTML and JavaScript Comments

HTML Comments

```
<!-- HTML Comments -->
```

Any number of lines can occur between the beginning and ending brackets. HTML comments should be used anywhere in HTML, but should not be used in a JavaScript.

Although the definition we use here for an HTML comment is very common among browsers, the reality is that no definition of an HTML comment exists. The definition for `<!--` and `-->` is actually two-part. First, `<!` and `>` define a meta-command to the HTML interpreter. Within the `<!` and `>` pair you can define a comment by placing it between `--` and `--`. The following HTML comments are all legal:

```
<!-- This is a comment on one line. -->
<!-- This is a comment
     on two lines.                    -->
<!
  -- This is a comment on several    --
  -- lines.                          --
                                       >
```

Notice that the last comment opened the meta-command mode, put two comments inside the command mode, and then closed it with a single ">". This will be important later.

JavaScript Comments

```
// Comments which extend to the end of the line.
/* Comments which are opened and closed */
/* either within one line or across
   several lines.                            */
```

The single line form of a JavaScript comment "//" blocks out everything to the right of it on the line. JavaScript statements can exist to the left of the comment designator.

The open and close form of a JavaScript comment "/* ... */" can exist within Java-Script on a line or across several lines. Once a JavaScript comment has been opened with "/*", it must be closed with "*/".

All JavaScript comments must appear between opening <SCRIPT> and closing </SCRIPT> tags. JavaScript comments used outside of the SCRIPT section will appear as text on the browser window.

Comments To Hide Javascript From Non-Javascript Capable Browsers

One of the problems in using JavaScript is that few browsers have implemented the capability to interpret JavaScript. What happens if a non-JavaScript-capable browser gets your beautiful Web page full of JavaScript? The answer is that the page looks like trash. To make HTML browsers robust, if they get a tag which they don't understand, the browser just ignores the tag and keeps going. Let's consider the affect of a JavaScript page (see Listing 5-13).

```
<HTML>
<BODY>
Today:
<SCRIPT LANG="JavaScript">
var today = new Date();
document.write( today.getMonth() + "/" + today.getDate() +
                "/" + today.getYear() );
</SCRIPT>
</BODY>
</HTML>
```

LISTING 5-13   JAVASCRIPT INTERPRETED BY A JAVASCRIPT-AWARE BROWSER.

A JavaScript-capable browser would display the following:

```
Today: 4/15/99
```

A non-JavaScript-capable browser would display something akin to the following:

```
Today: var today = new Date(); document.write( today.get-
Month() + "/" + today.getDate() + "/" + today.getYear() );
```

Which is messy. It's clear that what happened is that the browser got the <SCRIPT> tag and didn't know what to do with it, so it was ignored. The next thing the browser saw was your JavaScript code which it is now interpreting as text to be displayed as a part of the document. Leaving your customer with this mess is not a good practice, assuming that you want to communicate something to people who access your Web site. We can use a combination of HTML and JavaScript comments to attempt to hide JavaScript from browsers that don't interpret JavaScript. Let's look at our example again (see Listing 5-14).

```
<HTML>
<!-- File: LIST5_14.HTM
     Usage: Demonstrate hiding JavaScript from browsers
            which can not use it.
  -->
<BODY>
Today:
<SCRIPT LANG="JavaScript">
<!--
var today = new Date();
document.write( today.getMonth() + "/" + today.getDate() +
                "/" + today.getYear() );
// -->
</SCRIPT>
</BODY>
</HTML>
```

LISTING 5-14   THE SAME HTML AND JAVASCRIPT AS LISTING 5-13, BUT THIS TIME INCLUDING COMMENTS.

This time, the non-JavaScript browser will display

```
Today:
```

Which is better. But, what if our script had been as shown in Listing 5-15?

```
<HTML>
<!-- File: LIST5_15.HTM
     Usage: A demonstration of a script which does not
            successfully hide from a browser which
            is not capable of understanding JavaScript.
  -->
<BODY>
Today:
<SCRIPT LANG="JavaScript">
<!--
var today = new Date();
document.write( today.getMonth() + "/" + today.getDate() +
               "/" + today.getYear() );
if (today.getYear() > 99 )
   { document.write( "<BR>Happy New Millennium!" ); }
// -->
</SCRIPT>
</BODY>
</HTML>
```

LISTING 5-15 ESSENTIALLY THE SAME HTML AND JAVASCRIPT AS LISTING 5-13, WITH A ">" CHARACTER INCLUDED IN THE SCRIPT.

We'd end up with the following:

```
Today: 99 ) { document.write( "<BR>Happy New Millennium!"
); }
```

What happened? Remember we said that the HTML comments `<!--` and `-->` were really a SGML meta-command "`<!...>`" with a meta-command comment "`--...--`" inside? When we got to the line

```
if (today.getYear() > 99 )
```

the "greater than" boolean operator looked to the non-JavaScript browser like a termination of the comment. Next came the "99)" and the rest of the script which, since you were out of the meta-command mode, was interpreted as text to be displayed.

If you want to avoid this kind of mess you need to follow these rules:

1. Never use the "greater than" symbol "`>`" in JavaScript being hidden from non-JavaScript browsers.

2. Rewrite your boolean comparisons to avoid "`>`".

3. Never embed HTML tags in your `document.write()` statements. Use string methods to invoke the same effects. (See Chapter 6.)

4. Never embed "`--`" in your JavaScript, as it will terminate the meta-command comment string.

5. Warn browsers that a JavaScript-capable browser is required to view the page.

Although at this writing the current version of Microsoft's Internet Explorer does not support JavaScript, it is "JavaScript-friendly" in that it does not display any of the text found between the `<SCRIPT>` tags.

Using Server-side JavaScript to Redirect non-JavaScript-Capable Browsers

All of the solutions offered above for hiding JavaScript suffer from a common problem. You really want to let people see your page, and including JavaScript in it is an attempt to improve the usefulness of your production. Just removing the JavaScript from the data stream may keep the page clean, but some of the content will surely be lost.

A much better solution is found in server-side JavaScript, which is covered in Chapter 7 and beyond. Simply put, server-side JavaScript executes on the HTTP server itself, without necessarily sending any JavaScript code to the client. We will show an example of how to use server-side JavaScript to capture the type of browser on an incoming connection, and re-route the request to a HTML document which is consistent with the capabilities of that browser. This way, a single URL can serve both types of browsers. Figure 5-8 shows the server-side JavaScript HTTP server directing the connection to the right page, all without CGI programming on the server!

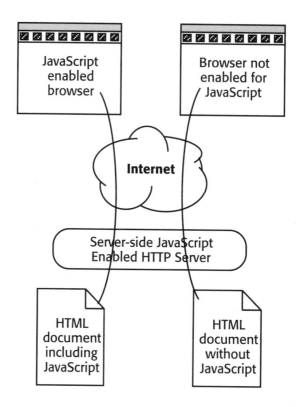

FIGURE 5-8   Using Server-side JavaScript to direct incoming requests to pages which are appropriate to the browser in use.

Objects, Methods, and Properties

- Navigator Object
- Windows
- Frames
- Text Objects
- Object Methods
- Built-in Objects
- Built-in Methods

JavaScript Compared

JavaScript relies heavily on the Java language for much of its structure and form. It attempts to become an object-oriented language, and to some extent succeeds. In many respects, JavaScript reminds us of a cross between Apple Computer's HyperTalk and C++. Like HyperTalk, JavaScript has objects which are pre-defined, variables which contain any data type, and events which cause actions on objects. Like C++, objects are referred to by the hierarchy which leads to them. Functions which operate on data within objects are called methods and access to objects is through their properties and methods. Let's discuss this in more detail before we move on to the JavaScript specifics.

Objects and Methods and Props, Oh My!

Any discussion of JavaScript must begin with a clear understanding of objects and their associated methods, properties, and events. Let's start with objects.

Objects and Properties

The object at the highest level is the navigator itself (see Figure 6-1). In some respects this seems like an unfortunate choice of term by Netscape since their product is called the Netscape Navigator. Any other vendor who implements JavaScript, may feel uncomfortable implementing an object which seems to imply their competitors product.

```
Navigator Object
Properties
    appName
    appCodeName
    appVersion
    userAgent
Methods
    -none-
```

FIGURE 6-1   The Navigator object with its properties and methods.

The Navigator object includes properties which relate to the Navigator itself, at a very high level. For instance, one of the properties of the Navigator is called "appName" which is the name of the browser. In the case of the Netscape Navigator, the appName is "Netscape". You access this property by first giving the name of the object, "navigator", then appending a period and the name of the property.

```
var var_appName = navigator.appName;
```

This complies with common object-oriented structure, in particular, C++ syntax for accessing an object and its properties. Just using the structure appName without the reference to its object won't work. JavaScript will assume that you're defining a variable.

Another example of accessing an object is accessing an input text field in a form in a frame from another frame (see Figure 6-2). To access a form field in another frame, the complete path to that object must be specified. First, we use the keyword "parent" to take us to the document which loaded the frames in the first place. This is where all of the frames are defined and known. Then we go to the correct frame. In this example we're just using the numeric designation for objects since they are all numbered as they are created. You can also specify names for objects, which can be a two-edged sword. Although it is nice to use names, you can forget what kind of an object you're dealing with. Next, we reference the form object within the frame, then the input field, and finally the property of that field called "value". As you might expect, changing the value property of an input field changes what the user sees in that field on the screen.

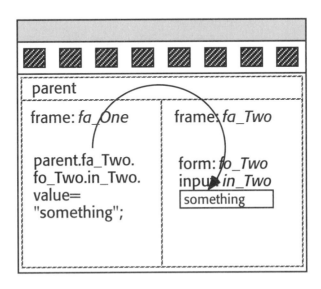

FIGURE 6-2   You must use the complete hierarchy to access an object in another frame.

One of the biggest problems you'll encounter in writing JavaScript is in making sure that you've accessed the objects in the right order, and that you have gone deep enough into the object tree to access an object. More than once, you'll see the dreaded

```
Object has no properties
```

error message. Most of the time, this means that you haven't accessed the object through the tree of objects with sufficient depth to uniquely identify what you're after. Because JavaScript will create variables on-the-fly for you (a mixed blessing at best), accessing an object incorrectly usually results in a variable being created for you without the property you're after. We'll discuss how to access objects correctly, particularly when we're accessing frames.

At the higher levels, JavaScript has these objects:

- navigator - the application program running the browser. window - the visible window in which documents are displayed. A window can contain more than one document in frames. A navigator can contain more than one window.
- frame - a window can be divided up into as many as 6 frames, each with its own document.
- document - an HTML page downloaded from the server.
- form - an HTML form with its objects, properties, and methods.

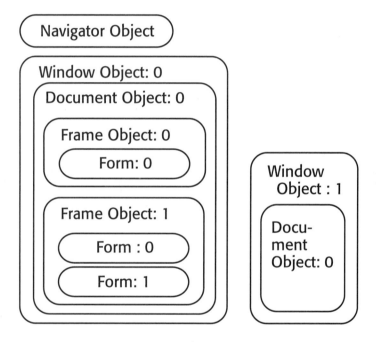

FIGURE 6-3   A hierarch of JavaScript objects. Forms are contained in Documents, which are contained in Windows.

Notice that Figure 6-3 shows more than one frame[0]: one in window[0], and one in window[1]. To uniquely identify an object, you must specify the path to that object. For example, to access form[0] from a script within frame[1], you just have to reference

```
forms[0].someProperty
```

To access forms[0] in frames[1] from a script running in frames[0], you have to reference

```
parent.frames[1].forms[0].someProperty
```

Lastly, to access forms[0] in frames[1] in window[0] from a script running in window[1] you must reference

```
window[0].frames[1].forms[0].someProperty
```

Keeping this all straight can be troublesome, but you'll get the hang of it.

Using names for objects instead of their array reference, as in frame[1], helps you to be sure that you're getting the object you want, but, since getting the right level of hierarchy is so important in JavaScript it is easy to forget whether the named object is an element of a form or the form itself. We recommend that you spend the time to create a naming convention such as "fo_..." for a form, and "fa_..." for a frame.

One last point on properties is that some properties are read-only and others may be written to. For example, the title property of a document is read-only. We might like to be able to change the title on-the-fly, but the structure of HTML specifies that once a document is loaded, including the document title as shown at the top of the window, nothing can be changed without reloading the entire document. (Note that forms have fields which can be changed by JavaScript and the user, but from the perspective of the browser, this doesn't count as a change because the structure of the form doesn't change.) For example, if you attempt to write to document.title, you will get an error.

```
var docTitle = document.title; // get the document's title
document.title = "Something New"; // THIS WON'T WORK!
```

An example of a read/write property is the value of a text input field of a form. This property may both be written to and read from.

```
var myInput = forms[0].text[0].value;
                 // get the contents of the input field
forms[0].text[0].value = "Something New";
                 // JavaScript changes the contents of
                 // the input field of the form.
```

Methods

Methods are a way to refer to functions which only work on a given object. You've already seen the `document.write()` method, which is used frequently in this book. In this case, `write()` is defined as a function which only works on document data types. If you attempt to use `write()` without referencing its object, JavaScript will assume that you defined a function of your own called `write()` and go looking for it. This will result in an error when it doesn't find it. Objects which have methods defined for them always operate on themselves.

For example, the `window.alert()` method allows the script to send a message to the user, such as for an error condition. The following code fragment could be used within a script to let the user know that an input was incorrect.

```
        // retrieve user input from a form text field
var user_input = form.textName.value;
        // test the input, if good, return true
        //   if not, return false
if ( testUserInput( user_input ) )
{
   do_something_with_the_input();
}
else
{
   window.alert( "Illegal user input!" );
}
```

The alert is displayed in Figure 6-4

FIGURE 6-4   A JavaScript alert by the user's script.

What would happen if you tried to use the `alert()` method on a document object like this?

```
document.alert( "This won't work! );
```

First, you will get an error from JavaScript, like the one shown in Figure 6-5.

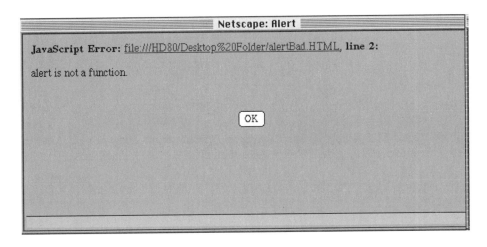

FIGURE 6-5   JavaScript alert generated by the navigator itself.

The reason for this is that the document object does not have an `alert()` method, only the `window` object. You must use methods on the objects which support them. This chapter will review all of the available objects and their associated methods.

Events

The last component of the object-oriented technology employed by JavaScript are events. Events are actions, usually associated with a user, which occur on an object. If you are familiar with HyperTalk, events are familiar to you. Examples of events are:

- `onClick`
- `onSelect`
- `onFocus`
- `onBlur`

Unlike methods and properties which occur inside of the JavaScript code, events are associated with the Navigator objects themselves and are defined in the HTML code rather than in the JavaScript code. For example, in Listing 2-6, we saw the following HTML defining a user input form which used the onChange event:

```
<FORM NAME="foLang">
   Select a language:
   <SELECT NAME="seLang" ONCHANGE="sayHi(this.form)">
      <OPTION SELECTED>English
      <OPTION>French
      <OPTION>German
      <OPTION>Italian
      <OPTION>Spanish
   </SELECT>
   <BR><BR>
   <INPUT TYPE="TEXT" NAME="inHello" VALUE="Hello World!"
SIZE=40>
</FORM>
```

The form describes a select menu which contains five options. The select menu itself is given the name "seLang" and the onChange event is defined. Events execute JavaScript code inside the quotation marks. In this case, the code which is executed is a call to a JavaScript function "sayHi()". Any Java-Script statements separated by semi-colons are possible. This example has only a single JavaScript statement, but more could have been possible.

Javascript Objects With Their Associated Properties, Methods, and Events

When describing the components of an object, literal text which needs to appear just as it is written will be in normal type. For example,

```
navigator.appName
```

needs to be written exactly as indicated here. Text which needs to be replaced with an expression or object name will appear in italic type. For example,

```
formName.text.value
```

needs to have "*formName*" replaced by an actual name of a form, as defined by the <FORM> tag and NAME attribute. The rest of the statement, "...text.value", needs to be written exactly as it appears.

navigator Object

JavaScript has only one `navigator` object. This corresponds to the browser which the user is running and in which the JavaScript is executing. The `navigator` object holds information about the browser. The object has no methods or events. Table 6-1 contains information about the properties of the navigator object.

Client-side: YES   Server-side: NO

```
navigator
```

Properties:

- `navigator.appCodeName`
- `navigator.appName`
- `navigator.appVersion`
- `navigator.userAgent`

TABLE 6-1. *Properties of the navigator object.*

Property	Access	Usage
appCodeName	read-only	A string with the code name of the browser. For Netscape, this is "Mozilla"
appName	read-only	A string with the name of the browser. For Netscape, this is "Netscape". When other browsers support JavaScript, you can use this to differentiate between them if the feature sets are different.

TABLE 6-1. (Continued) Properties of the navigator object.

Property	Access	Usage
appVersion	read-only	A string with the version number of the browser. For example, "2.0 (Macintosh; I; 68K)" for Netscape 2.0 running on a Macintosh 68K system.
		The general form is *releaseNumber* (*platform*; *country*)
		releaseNumber is the release number of the product.
		platform is the client platform where the browser is running. Legal values include "Win16" for Windows 3.11 (the 16-bit version of Windows), "Macintosh", "Win32" for Windows 95, and XWIN for the UNIX versions of XWindows.
		country is "I" for international and "U" for US domestic release.
		In some cases, an additional field is provided as in the example above. "68K" indicates that
userAgent	read-only	A string with the user agent. For example, "Mozilla/2.0 (Macintosh; I;68K)" for Netscape 2.0 running on a Macintosh 68K system.
		This is the string provided by the client to the HTTP server to identify itself.

Methods:

```
None.
```

The navigator object does not have any methods associated with it.

Event handlers:

```
None.
```

The navigator object does not have any event handlers associated with it.

Property of:

```
None.
```

The navigator object is not a property of any other object in the hierarchy of Java-Script objects.

Example

An interesting use of the `navigator.appVersion` or `navigator.userAgent` properties would be to direct a user to information appropriate to the platform he or she is running on. For example, the following code fragment would exist in a document defining the frames of a window. The frames are named "fa_control" and "fa_output". The control frame is preloaded with a document which presumably gives the user some controls with which to manipulate the windows. The second frame, called "fa_output" doesn't get loaded at this point.

```
<FRAMESET COLS="50%,50%">
   <FRAME NAME="fa_control" SRC=somedoc.HTML>
   <FRAME NAME="fa_output">
</FRAMESET>

<SCRIPT lang="JavaScript">

if ( navigator.appVersion.indexOf( "Macintosh" ) != -1 )
{
   fa_output.document.open( "text/HTML" );
                                         //open for output
   output_Macintosh_information();    //output
   fa_output.document.close();        //close and force
}                                     //display

if (navigator.appVersion.indexOf( "WIN" ) != -1 )
{
   fa_output.document.open( "text/HTML" );
   output_Windows_information();
   fa_output.document.close();
}

</SCRIPT>
```

Inside the `<SCRIPT>` tag, the `appVersion` property of the `navigator` object is accessed with the string method `indexOf()`. This method returns the index number of the character which matches the start of the string specified. In the first case, the string "Macintosh" is sought. If this string is found, `indexOf()` returns the number of the character which begins the string; if the string is not found, `indexOf()` returns -1.

The `if` statement returns true only if -1 is not returned, which means that the string was found in `appVersion`. The if statement then passes control to the script which opens the frame document for output, calls a routine to fill the frame, and then closes the frame, forcing the new frame content to appear.

window Object

Client-side: YES   Server-side: NO

`window`

The `window` object is the visible window on the screen when your browser is executing. Each browser window has an associated JavaScript `window` object. The browser can open more than one window at a time. For example, when you first open the Netscape Navigator browser, a window is opened and the home document is loaded into this window. The user has the option of creating additional windows using the New Web Browser command under the File menu. Windows can also be created by JavaScript. The only windows that JavaScript can access are those which are created by JavaScript using the `window.open()` method. Tables 6-2 through 6-5 contain comprehensive information about the window object.

Frames are an extension of the `window` object and possess the same properties, methods, and events as a `window` object. All `window` object definitions listed in this section apply to both frames and windows. Frames are covered in more detail in the next section.

<u>Synonyms:</u>

You can refer to a window using the following methods of reference (see Table 6-2):

- `window`
- `self`
- `top`
- *`windowVariable`*

TABLE 6-2. *Synonyms for the window object.*

Synonym	Usage
window	The object "window" is used to refer to the current window in which JavaScript is executing.
self	The object "self" refers to the current window.

TABLE 6-2. (Continued) Synonyms for the `window` object.

Synonym	Usage
top	The object "top" refers to the top-most browser window.
windowvariable	A variable which contains the value returned by the `window.open()` method. JavaScript can only access those windows which have been created by JavaScript using the `open()` method. *windowvariable* = window.open("*URL*", "*windowName*", ["*windowFeatures*"])

Properties:

- `window.defaultStatus`
- `window.name`
- `window.status`

TABLE 6-3. Properties of the Window Object

Property	Access	Usage
defaultStatus	read/write	A string with the default message displayed in the menu bar at the bottom of the browser window.
name	read-only	An object name, the name associated with a window when the window.open() method is called. (See window.open() under the window methods in this section.)
status	read/write	A string with a temporary message for the menu bar.

Methods:

- `alert( "message text" )`
- `close()`
- *variable* = `confirm( "message text" )`
- *windowvariable* = `open("URL", "windowName", ["windowFeatures"])`
- *variable* = `prompt( "message text", ["default input"] )`
- *timeoutID* = `setTimeout(expression, msec)`
- `clearTimeout(timeoutID)`

TABLE 6-4. *Methods of the window object.*

Method	Returns	Usage
alert()	\<undefined\>	alert(*"message text"*) Display "*message text*" in a user dialog box with an OK button. Nothing is returned to JavaScript
close()	\<undefined\>	close() Close the current window. The window disappears from the user's screen and is unavailable for any access. close(*newWindow*) Close the window pointed at by newWindow. newWindow is the pointer to a window returned by open().
confirm()	boolean	response = confirm(*"message text"*) Display "*message text*" in a user dialog box with OK and Cancel buttons. Returns true if the user presses OK. Returns false if the user presses Cancel.
open()	pointer to new window object	newWindow = open("*URL*", "*windowName*", ["*windowFeatures*"]) Create a new browser window. Return a pointer to that window. URL is the URL to load when the window is created *windowName* is the name of the window used to reference its objects *windowFeatures* are configuration parameters for the window, such as whether to display the location field and directory buttons.

TABLE 6-4. (Continued) Methods of the window object.

Method	Returns	Usage
prompt()	a string with the user's input	*userInput* = prompt(*"message text"*, [*"default input"*]) Display a dialog box with *"message text"* and a user text input field with the optional *"default input"* displayed. An OK button is displayed. Return the contents of the user text input field when OK is clicked. default input may be any JavaScript data type.
setTimeout()	timeout ID	*timeoutID* = setTimeout(*expression, msec*) *timeoutID* is used to cancel the timer with clearTimeout(). *expression* is a JavaScript statement to be executed when the timer expires *msec* is a number, the number of milliseconds (thousandths of a second) until the timer expires and expression is executed.
clearTimeout()	\<undefined\>	clearTimeout(*timeoutID*) *timeoutID* is the value returned by setTimeout() to identify the timer.

Event handlers:

```
onLoad="JavaScript statement(s)"
onUnload="JavaScript statement(s)"

used within
<BODY … [onLoad="…"] [onUnload="…"]>
<FRAMESET … [onLoad="…"] [onUnload="…"]>
```

Property of:

```
None.
```

window is not a property of any other object.

window Synonyms

TABLE 6-5. Built in synonyms for windows.

window Object Synonyms
• window
• self
• top
Logical window references:
• *windowreference*

The window object is at the top of the object hierarchy in JavaScript. The navigator object is separate from the rest of the object hierarchy (see Figure 6-6). All JavaScript objects are referenced under their window and, if no window reference is given, JavaScript assumes that the current window in which the JavaScript code is executing is the window referenced.

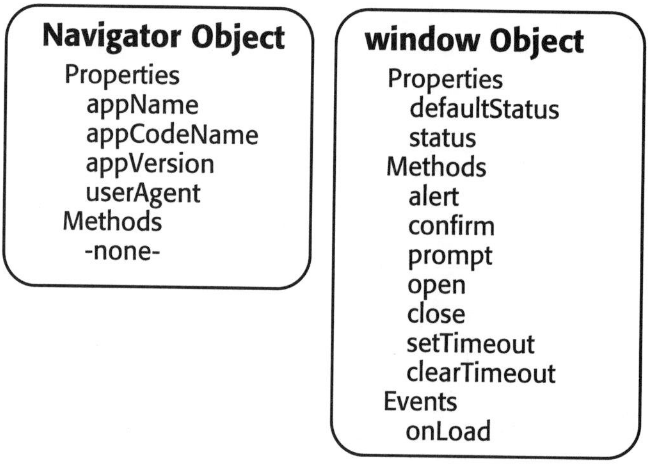

Navigator Object
Properties
    appName
    appCodeName
    appVersion
    userAgent
Methods
    -none-

window Object
Properties
    defaultStatus
    status
Methods
    alert
    confirm
    prompt
    open
    close
    setTimeout
    clearTimeout
Events
    onLoad

FIGURE 6-6   Navigator and window object properties and methods.

window

- `window.propertyName`
- `window.methodName`

`window` refers to the current window or frame from which the Java-Script code is executing. All of the properties and methods associated with a window can be accessed from this object.

self

- `self.propertyName`
- `self.methodName`

`self` is a synonym which refers to the current `window` or `frame` and is a property of a `window` or `frame`. All of the properties and methods of a `window` apply to `self`. You can use `self` to indicate a window if you have named a form the same as a window. In general, this is a very poor programming practice and we recommend using some type of naming convention such as the one we have used in this book to indicate a form, frame, and window. For example, a window could be named `wn_somename`; a form, `fo_somename`; and a frame, `fa_somename`. This type of convention allows you to use the same name in several places. It also permits you to use a name which is meaningful to you.

top

- `top.propertyName`
- `top.methodName`

`top` is a synonym for the window which is the "top-most" from the perspective of the hierarchy of JavaScript. For example, the JavaScript of a window can open another browser window, which in turn could open another browser window. Referring to top would reference the window which started it all. Figure 6-7 demonstrates this.

`top.propertyName` will refer to the first window of the chain, even though the window referred to as top may not be physically viewed on top of the other two.

windowReference

- `windowvariable = open("URL", "windowName", ["windowFeatures"])`

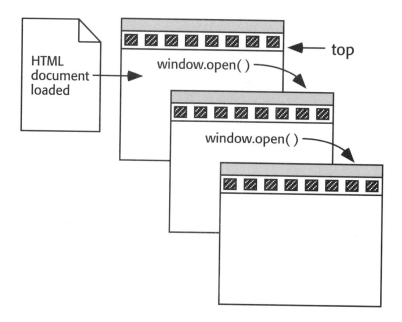

FIGURE 6-7   Three browser windows are opened showing the heirarchy of windows as referenced by JavaScript.

- *windowvariable.property*
- *windowvariable.method()*

The last way to refer to a window is through a variable initialized by the `window.open()` method. This will create a new window and load the specified URL.

window Properties

defaultStatus

windowReference`.defaultStatus`

The `defaultStatus` message is what the browser displays at the bottom of the screen when nothing else is going on. An action, such as passing over a link, will cause the `defaultStatus` message to be replaced with another message, in this case the URL pointed at by the link. The difference between `defaultStatus` and status is that the status message is temporary and will be replaced with the `defaultStatus` message. For example,

1. Set `defaultStatus` message. It appears in the status message bar, replacing the existing or system status message.

2. An event, such as passing over a link, replaces the status message with the message of the event, such as the URL of the link passed over.

3. The event is completed and the status bar receives the new default status message again.

status

- *windowReference*.`status`

The `status` property updates the status message bar at the bottom of the browser window. This should not be confused with the `defaultStatus` property of the window which was discussed earlier. The `status` property can be set at any time, but, will be overwritten with the first event which updates the status message bar. The following outlines the course of events in placing a status message in the status message bar;

1. Set status message to some text. It appears in the status bar in the window replacing the defaultStatus message.

2. An event ,such as passing over a link, replaces the status message with the message of the event, such as the URL of the link passed over

3. The event is over and the status bar receives the defaultStatus message.

One of the most frequent uses of the status message bar (or so it seems) is to display scrolling messages to the user. However, this consumes a lot of your browser's bandwidth and many times the value of the message is hidden on the small message bar at the bottom of the screen. Although this appears to be an interesting use of a scrolling message, a better application would be to use the status message bar for what it was designed, transient messages to the user. Other more interesting ways to catch the user's eye are available.

window Methods

Because of the scope of methods and properties, all window methods are default to the current window if you call them without the window or *window-*

variable objects. The only exceptions to this are the `open()` and `close()` methods, which are common to the document object. For example, the following code fragments are equivalent when referencing the current window:

```
window.alert( "This is an alert!" );
alert( "This is an alert!" );
```

However, if you were going to access a variable, method or property of another window, you'd need to reference that window directly as in the following:

```
var newWindow = open( "myURL.HTML", "myWindow" );
newWindow.alert( "This is an alert from " +
    newWindow.name );
```

To make code more readable, we recommend using the window object to specifically reference the window from which you are executing.

alert

```
alert("message")
```

"message" may be any literal string, an object which contains a string, or an expression which evaluates to a string.

returns: <undefined>

The `alert()` method will display a user alert as demonstrated in Figure 6-8. This differs from the JavaScript or Browser error message as found in Figure 6-5. The `alert()` method does not return any value to the user and the user has only the option of pressing the button labeled "OK". Use the `alert()` method to give the user information of which he or she needs to be aware, but for which no action is required.

confirm

Displays a Confirm dialog box with the specified message and OK and Cancel buttons.

```
variable = confirm("message")
```

"message" may be any literal string, an expression which evaluates to a string, or any property which evaluates to a string.

FIGURE 6-8   A JavaScript alert as displayed by the statement `window.alert("Illegal user input!")`.

`confirm()` returns a boolean value: true if the user selects "OK", false if the user selects "Cancel".

The `confirm()` method displays a message with two buttons labeled "Yes" and "No". See Figure 6-9 for an example. The results of the `confirm()` method can be used to affect JavaScript execution.

FIGURE 6-9   The confirm box generated by the following JavaScript statement: `myVar = window.confirm( "This is a message from confirm!" )`.

prompt

```
variable = prompt(message, [inputDefault])
```

The *message* may be any literal string, any expression which evaluates to a string, or any object property which is a string.

inputDefault is any string or expression which can evaluate to a string, and is used to fill the user input field with a default value.

returns: `prompt()` returns the string the user input to the dialog box.

The `prompt()` method displays a dialog box with the message text displayed, a field for user input, and a button labeled "OK" (see Figure 6-10). The user is prompted for input which is returned to JavaScript.

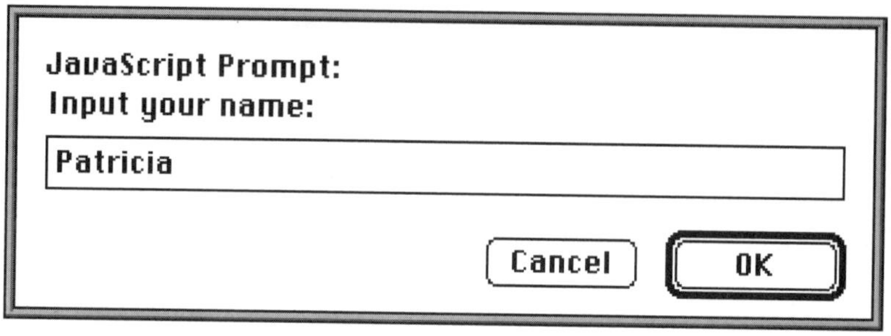

```
JavaScript Prompt:
Input your name:

Patricia

                                    Cancel      OK
```

FIGURE 6-10   Dialog box created by the following JavaScript statement: `myVar =
window.prompt("Input your name:", "Joe");`

open

* *windowvariable* = window.open("*URL*", "*windowName*",
["*windowFeatures*"])

"*URL*" specifies the location to use when opening the window. If *URL* is an empty string "", an empty window is created.

windowName specifies a name for this object. The window name can only contain alphanumeric characters or the underscore "_" character.

windowFeatures is an optional string parameter to specify display options for the window. The string should be a comma-separated list of options as shown in Table 6-6.

The window.open() method opens a new browser window, which is the same as if the user had specified the File New Web Browser commands from the menu. Because of the potential conflict with the document.open() method, JavaScripts should always fully specify window.open() when creating a new window.

TABLE 6-6. Options available to the window.open() method.

Option Name	Values	Action if "yes" or "1" (Note: "toolbar" is equivalent to specifying "toolbar=yes")
toolbar	=yes|no =1|0	Display the toolbar at the top of the window. This is the bar with "Back" and "Home" on it.
location	=yes|no =1|0	Display the location entry field.
directories	=yes|no =1|0	Display the directories tool bar. This is the bar with "What's New" and "What's Cool" on it.
status	=yes|no =1|0	Display the status bar at the bottom of the window. This is the message bar where the browser, window.defaultStatus, and window.status display their messages.
menubar	=yes|no =1|0	Display the menu at the top of the window.
scrollbars	=yes|no =1|0	Display horizontal and vertical scroll bars to view the document in the window if it is physically larger than the window itself.
resizable	=yes|no =1|0	Allow the user to resize the window.
width	=pixels (positive integer)	The width of the window in pixels.
height	=pixels	The height of the window in pixels.

The list of options is a string separated by commas and containing no spaces. You may specify any number of options, leaving out those options you don't want to specify. Options left out of the list will take the false value. If you leave out the options list altogether, the default will be for all options to be true.

Examples

```
myWin = window.open( "myURL.HTML", "myWindow" );
        // create a window called "myWindow", store the
        // reference in the variable myWin, load the
        // URL: myURL.HTML, and set all options to true
```

```
yourWin1 = window.open( "yourWin.HMTL", "yourWindow1",
    "toolbar" );
yourWin2 = window.open( "yourWin.HMTL", "yourWindow2",
    "toolbar=yes" );
yourWin3 = window.open( "yourWin.HMTL", "yourWindow3",
    "toolbar=1" );
    // all three calls do the same thing: create three
    // windows respectively called "yourWindow1",
    // "yourWindow2", and "yourWindow3"; store the
    // references
    // respectively in yourWin1, yourWin2, yourWin3;
    // load the same URL, "yourWin.HTML", into
    // all three window; and ,display the toolbar.
    // Note the three ways to specify that the tool
    // bar is on.  All other options are off.

VAR winOptions = "toolbar,menubar=1,
                  scrollbars=yes,status"
theirWin = window.open( "theirWin.HTML", "theirWindow",
    winOptions );
    // put the window.open options in a variable and
    // use the variable in the open() method.
```

close

```
window.close()
```

The `window.close()` method closes the current window.

setTimeout

```
timeoutID = setTimeout(expression, msec)
```

expression is a string expression.

msec is a numeric value or numeric string in millisecond units.

returns: an identifier that is used only to cancel the evaluation with the clearTimeout method.

The `setTimeout()` method waits the number of milliseconds (thousands of a second) specified by *msec* and then evaluates the string in expression once as a JavaScript statement. The expression will expect to be a fully complete JavaScript statement. This is similar to the `eval()` method. Note that a five second wait would be specified as 5000 milliseconds.

clearTimeout

```
clearTimeout(timeoutID)
```

timeoutID is the timeout setting that was returned by a previous call to the setTimeout method.

returns: <undefined>

`clearTimeout()` will cancel a `setTimeout()` which was executed previously and has not expired yet.

window Events

The methods and properties we've covered so far for the window object have all been directly tied to that object. For instance, `window.alert()` sends an alert from the window, and `window.close()` closes the window. Window events are tied to the window, but are defined in the HTML, which results in actual objects being created on the screen. The window object has two events defined for it, the onLoad and onUnload events. These are defined in the `<BODY>` and `<FRAMESET>` tags of the HTML in the document being loaded.

Event handlers execute JavaScript code found in their definition. For example, the following code fragment would execute the `alert()` method with the message "Loading a document!" when the document was being loaded by the user:

```
<BODY onLoad="window.alert( 'Loading a document! )' >
```

The important point is that the contents of the `onLoad="…"` statement is any legal JavaScript statement. In other listings we saw event handlers which called a JavaScript function such as the following:

```
<SELECT onChange="doSomething()" >
```

The string which is pointed at by the event can also contain multiple JavaScript statements. The rules are:

- All JavaScript statements must be terminated with a semi-colon ";".
- All strings must use the single quotes "''".

An example of this would be

```
<BODY onLoad= "var msg ='Loading a document on a ';
```

```
if ( navigator.appVersion.indexOf(
    'Macintosh' ) != -1 )
{
   msg = msg + 'Macintosh!';
}
else
{
   if ( navigator.appVersion.indexOf(
       'Win' ) != -1 )
   {
      msg = msg + 'Windows PC!';
   }
   else
   {
      msg = msg + 'another machine!';
   }
}
window.alert( msg );" >
```

This rather drawn-out example puts several lines of JavaScript code into the onLoad event handler. Because we are already inside a pair of double quotation marks, we must use single quotation marks for all string literals in the code. Likewise, the event handler requires that all JavaScript statements end with the semi-colon. This is one way to sneak JavaScript code into your document outside of the <SCRIPT> tag.

All legal event handlers may be specified within a tag. A window will not have any event handlers until the <BODY> tag has completed loading into the window.

onLoad

```
<BODY onLoad="...">
<FRAMESET onLoad="...">
```

The onLoad event handler is called whenever the browser completes the loading of a window.

onUnload

```
<BODY onUnload="...">
<FRAMESET onUnload="...">
```

The `onUnload` event handler is called whenever the browser is exiting a document, which means that the document is leaving the top-most or visible document in a browser window.

Frames Are Windows Within Windows

Frames are an extension to HTML which Netscape proposed and implemented in their browsers. As you'll see in the rest of this chapter, frames are an exception to the hierarchy of objects. Within all other JavaScript objects, you expect to find an order progression from one to the next, without skipping objects. For example, a text field object is within a form object, which is within a document object, within a window object (see Figure 6-11).

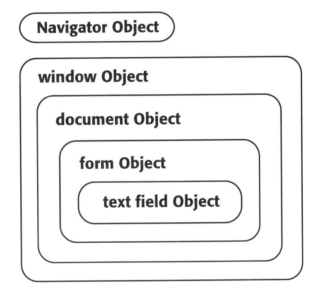

FIGURE 6-11   Hierarchy of objects from text field to document.

Frames are an extension of window objects in that they all have the same characteristics of a window object (properties, methods, and events), but frames are not required objects in the hierarchy of objects (see Figure 6-12). What is meant by this is that frames may or may not appear within a window. When they do, they behave like windows within windows; but when they don't appear, you don't have to reference them.

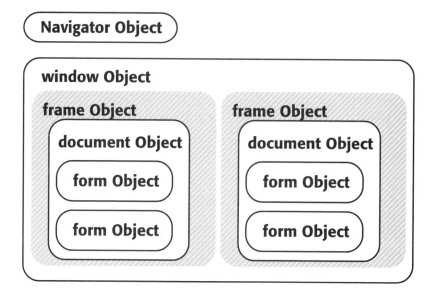

FIGURE 6-12   The hierarchy from text field to window.

Frames are a hybrid of sorts on a window object. Although frames are contained within a window, they contain many of the properties, methods, and events associated with a window. A window will either contain frames or documents, but not both at the same time. A window will always contains properties and methods.

Figure 6-13 shows a simple window. The window contains a document provided by the HTML in Listing 6-1. The properties of the windows are defined by the HTML, including the existence of an onLoad event which calls a JavaScript function. The onUnload event is undefined and does not exist for this example.

Listing 6-2 and Figure 6-14 show a little more complex arrangement where the initial document defines two frames, "fa_control" and "fa_output". The top-most window document does not have a body section, so no events are available for this object. The example has two frames within the window, and each frame has its own set of properties, methods, and events which are those defined for window objects.

When frames are defined by the HTML, some additional properties are available to JavaScript.

```
<HTML>
<HEAD>
<TITLE>Window Title</TITLE>
<SCRIPT>
doSomething()
{
  // JavaScript to do something when the
  // document is loaded
}
</SCRIPT>
</HEAD>

<BODY onLoad="doSomething()">
<P> HTML for the body of the window
</BODY>
</HTML>
```

LISTING 6-1   HTML REFERENCED IN FIGURE 6-12.

frame Object

A window can consist of multiple frames, each with its own document loaded from a separate URL. Each frame consists of a single document which can be loaded either by direct reference in the <FRAME> tag or by being written with JavaScript using the document.write() method.

Client-side: YES   Server-side: NO

```
frame
```

```
<FRAMESET>
```

A frame is defined from within the <HEAD> tag of a document. When frames are defined within a window, all text within the document where <FRAMESET> appears is ignored; however, JavaScript functions, variables, and handlers are active.

```
<FRAMESET
   ROWS="rowHeightList"
   COLS="columnWidthList"
   [onLoad="handlerText"]
   [onUnload="handlerText"]>
   [<FRAME SRC="locationOrURL" NAME="frameName">]
</FRAMESET>
```

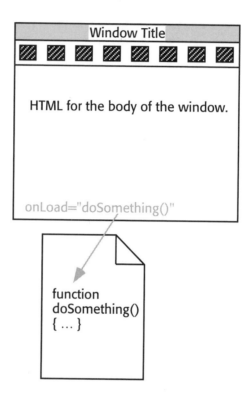

FIGURE 6-13 Content of the window created by Listing 6-1.

ROWS defines the row height within the window using either a percentage of the available window (e.g., ROWS="25%,25%,50%" to define three frames in rows) or as a number specifying the number of pixels (e.g., ROWS="50,50,100"). Separate the units with commas.

COLS defines the column width within the window using either a percentage of the available window (e.g., COLS="67%,33%" to define two frames in columns) or as a number specifying the number of pixels (e.g., COLS="100,100"). Separate the units with commas.

<FRAME> defines a frame.

SRC is the location, or URL which should be used to load the document for the frame. The SRC cannot be an anchor name. If no SRC is specified, the document is empty.

```
<HTML>
<!-- File: LIST6_02A.HTM
     Usage: Parent document to set up frames and
            demonstrate load and unload
     Calls: LIST6_02B.HTM, LIST6_02C.HTM
  -->
<HEAD>
<TITLE>Load and Unload</TITLE>

<FRAMESET COLS="50%,50%">
   <FRAME NAME="fa_control" SRC=LIST6_02B.HTM>
   <FRAME NAME="fa_output" SRC=LIST6_02C.HTM>
</FRAMESET>
</HEAD>
</HTML>
```

```
<HTML>
<!-- File: LIST6_02B.HTM
     Usage: demonstrate onLoad event
     Called by: LIST6_02A.HTM
  -->

<HEAD>
<SCRIPT LANG="JavaScript">

// declare global variables
var today = new Date();
var onLoadExecuted = false;
var userName;

function doSomethingOnLoad()
{
   userName = window.prompt( "What is your name?", " ");
   document.fo_hello.in_hello.value = userName;
   onLoadExecuted = true;
}
</SCRIPT>
</HEAD>

       File LIST6_02B.HTM continues on the next page.
```

LISTING 6-2   DEMONSTRATION OF A PARENT DOCUMENT LOADING FRAMES.

```
                   Continuation of LIST6_02B.HTM.

<BODY onLoad="doSomethingOnLoad()" >

<SCRIPT LANG="JavaScript">
document.write( "<P>Frame: " + window.name );
document.write( "<P>Today's Date:" +
                today.toLocaleString() );
</SCRIPT>

<FORM NAME="fo_hello">
   <P>How are you today,
   <INPUT TYPE=text NAME="in_hello" SIZE=10>
   ?
</FORM>

</BODY>
</HTML>
```
```
<HTML>
<!-- File:LIST6_02C.HTM
     Usage:
     Called by: LIST6_02A
  -->

<HEAD>
<SCRIPT>
function doSomethingOnUnload()
{
   // alert the user that the frame is going away
   window.alert( "Goodbye " );
}
</SCRIPT>
</HEAD>

       File LIST6_02C.HTM continues on the next page.
```

LISTING 6-2   (CONTINUED) DEMONSTRATION OF A PARENT DOCUMENT LOADING FRAMES.

```
                    Continuation of LIST6_02B.HTM.

<BODY onUnload="doSomethingOnUnload()" >

<SCRIPT LANG="JavaScript">
document.write( "<P>Frame: " + window.name );
document.write( "<P>Today's Date:" +
            parent.fa_control.today.toLocaleString() );
if ( parent.fa_control.onLoadExecuted )
{
   document.write( "<P>The onLoad event of frame " +
                   "fa_control has executed." );
}
else
{
   document.write( "<P>The onLoad event of frame " +
                   "fa_control has not executed." );
}

</SCRIPT>

<P>This frame will trigger a JavaScript alert when it is
   unloaded.
</BODY>
</HTML>
```

LISTING 6-2   (CONTINUED) DEMONSTRATION OF A PARENT DOCUMENT LOADING FRAMES.

NAME is the name by which the frame will be referred to in JavaScript. The frames[index].name property returns this value.

Frame Synonyms:

You can refer to a frame using the following methods of reference.

```
[windowReference.]frames[index]
[windowReference.]frameName
parent.frameName
parent.frames[index]
frameName
frames[index]
```

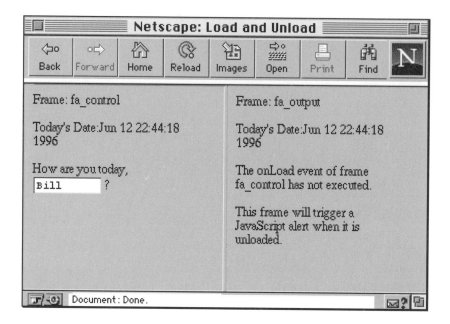

FIGURE 6-14   The onLoad event retrieves the user's name and places it in the form. However, the onLoad event of the first frame "fa_control" does not execute before the second frame "fa_output" is loaded!

TABLE 6-7. Frame synonyms.

Synonym	Usage
frames[]	An array which represents all of the frames within a window. The minimum value is 0 and the maximum value is window.frames.length - 1.
parent	The object "parent" is used in frames to refer to the window from which the <FRAMESET> was defined. Use parent to refer to another frame in the same window.

Properties:

```
frameReference.name
frameReference.length
```

TABLE 6-8. Properties of the frame object.

Property	Access	Usage

length	read-only	`windowReference.length`
		`windowReference.frames[index].`
		    `length`
		A number, which is the number of frames within the window.

name	read-only	A string which was associated with the frame in the `<FRAME NAME="frameName">` tag.

<u>Methods</u>

```
timeoutID = setTimeout(expression, msec)
clearTimeout(timeoutID)
```

TABLE 6-9. Methods of the frame object.

Method	Returns	Usage

setTimeout()	timeout ID	`timeoutID =`
		`setTimeout(expression, msec)`
		timeoutID is used to cancel the timer with clearTimeout().
		expression is a JavaScript statement to be executed when the timer expires.
		msec is a number, the number of milliseconds (thousandths of a second), until the timer expires and expression is executed.

clearTimeout()	\<undefined\>	`clearTimeout(timeoutID)` *timeoutID* is the value returned by setTimeout() to identify the timer.

<u>Event handlers:</u>

```
None.
```

Although the onLoad and onUnload events are defined within the `<FRAMESET>` tag, they are a part of the window object.

<u>Property of:</u>

```
window
```

Frames are a property of a window object.

frames Array

```
frames[]
```

The frames array contains a reference to every frame defined within a window. The length of the array can be determined by accessing the frames.length property. The frames are numbered beginning at zero and the last frame is numbered `frames.length - 1`. The following code fragment would retrieve the name of each frame within the current window and place the names in a variable.

```
var frameNames = "";
var i;
for ( i = 0; i < parent.frames.length - 1; i++ )
{
    frameNames = frameNames + parent.frames[i].name + " ";
}
```

parent Synonym

```
parent.property
parent.method()
```

`parent` is a way to refer to the window which contains the frame in which a JavaScript is executing. `parent`, is not a property of a window, but a way to refer to the window from which the `<FRAMESET>` tag was executed. `window.parent` is not a legal reference. Use parent as you would the window property itself.

For example, in Figure 6-15, the reference `parent.title` would give you the title of the window which contained the two frames, "fa_one" and "fa_two". Likewise, a global variable created and stored in the parent window could be accessed from the child frames as `parent.glo_var`. Further, a method or object contained in "fa_two" could be accessed from the frame "fa_one" as `parent.fa_two.document.open()` opened and replaced the contents of the frame "fa_two".

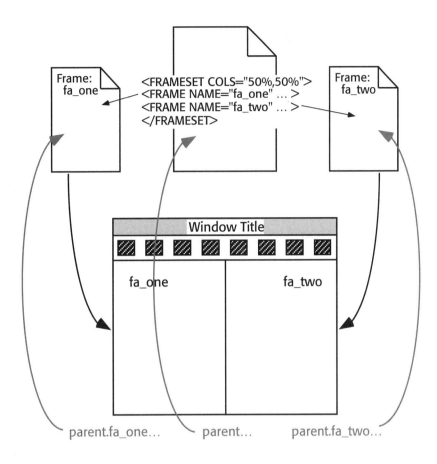

FIGURE 6-15   This parent window has no content except two frames.

document Object

Client-side: YES   Server-side: NO

```
document
```

The document object contains all of the visible components of a window or frame. (From here on, we'll refer to window objects only, knowing that frames contain all properties, objects, methods, and events of window objects. All *windowReference* statements will include *frameReference* statements, such as window.frames[*index*].)

It is very important to remember that documents are static objects which cannot be changed once they are loaded. All of the characteristics of a document, the colors used to represent links or text, the anchors, the background, etc. are determined at the time of the document's loading and cannot be changed. The only way to change these characteristics is to reload the document with the changes implemented. As we'll see with the `document.open()` and `document.write()` methods, JavaScript can define the content of a document, but only as it is being written to the window. None of the document properties can be changed once the document has been loaded.

The document object has no synonyms since a window or frame contains only a single document.

<BODY> and <HEAD> tags

The document object is defined using the <BODY> and <HEAD> tags.

```
<HEAD>
<TITLE>Document Title</TITLE>
</HEAD>

<BODY
   BACKGROUND="backgroundImage"
   BGCOLOR="backgroundColor"
   TEXT="foregroundColor"
   LINK="unfollowedLinkColor"
   ALINK="activatedLinkColor"
   VLINK="followedLinkColor"
   [onLoad="handlerText"]
   [onUnload="handlerText"]>

<!-- place HTML for document here -->

</BODY>
```

BACKGROUND points at the URL of an image that fills the background of the document.

BGCOLOR, TEXT, LINK, ALINK, and VLINK are color specifications expressed as a hexadecimal RGB triplet (in the format "rrggbb" or "#rrggbb"), or as a string literal representing a color.

Properties:

```
document.alinkColor
```

```
document.bgColor
document.cookie
document.fgColor
document.lastModified
document.linkColor
document.referrer
document.title
document.vlinkColor
```

TABLE 6-10. Properties of the document object.

Property	Access	Usage
alinkColor	read-only	A string reflecting the ALINK attribute of the <BODY> tag. Format is "rrggbb" or "#rrggbb".
bgColor	read/write	A string reflecting the BGCOLOR attribute of the <BODY> tag. Can be set any time, but will only take effect after a new document is loaded. Format is "rrggbb" or "#rrggbb".
cookie	read/write	A string specifying a "cookie".
fgColor	read-only	A string reflecting the TEXT attribute of the <BODY> tag. Format is "rrggbb" or "#rrggbb".
lastModified	read-only	A string reflecting the date a document was last modified on the server.
linkColor	read-only	A string reflecting the LINK attribute of the <BODY>. Format is "rrggbb" or "#rrggbb".
referrer	read-only	A string reflecting the URL of the calling document.
title	read-only	A string reflecting the contents of the <TITLE> tag in the <HEAD> section.
vlinkColor	read-only	A string reflecting the VLINK attribute of the <BODY> tag. Format is "rrggbb" or "#rrggbb".

<u>Methods:</u>

```
document.clear()
document.close()
document.open()
document.write()
document.writeln()
```

TABLE 6-11. *Methods of the document object.*

Method	Returns	Usage
clear()	\<undefined\>	`document.clear()` Clears the document window so that nothing is displayed.
close()	\<undefined\>	`document.close()` Closes an output stream to a document which was previously opened with document.open(). This forces the output to the window. No more writing to the document is possible. A subsequent call to document.open() will replace the document in the window.
open()	\<undefined\>	`document.open([`"*mimeType*"`])` Open a window's document for output. The existing document in the window will be replaced by the document being provided. *mimeType* specifies any of the following document types: text/html, text/plain, image/gif, image/jpeg, image/xbm, plugIn. `plugIn` is any two-part plug-in MIME type that Netscape supports.

TABLE 6-11. (Continued) Methods of the document object.

Method	Returns	Usage
write()	\<undefined\>	`document.write(`*`expression1`*`[,`*`expression2`*`], ...[,`*`expressionN`*`])` After a document has been opened with `document.open()`, `document.write(…)` writes any JavaScript expression, such as a string literal or a number to the document. Multiple `document.write()` statements may be executed between `document.open()` and `document.close()` `expression1` through `expressionN` are any JavaScript expressions.
writeln()	\<undefined\>	`document.writeln(`*`expression1`*`[,`*`expression2`*`], ...[,`*`expressionN`*`])` The same as `document.write()` except that a `newLine` character is appended to the end. This will have no effect on the image displayed in the document's window, unless the `<PRE>` tag has been invoked to turn off HTML formatting.

Event handlers

```
None.
```

Although the onLoad and onUnload event handlers are found in the `<BODY>` tag, they are considered event handlers for the window object.

Objects of document and their properties, objects, events, and methods

```
document.anchors[]
document.anchors.length
document.anchors[].propertiesAndMethods
document.forms[].propertiesObjectsAndMethods
document.forms.length
document.history.propertiesAndMethods
document.links[].properties
document.links.length
(links) <A MouseOver="…">
document.location.propertiesAndMethods
```

TABLE 6-12. *Objects and Properties of the Document Object*

Objects	Access	Usage
anchors[*index*]	read-only	An array of strings reflecting all the anchors in a document as defined by the `<A>` tags.
anchors.length	read-only	A number indicating the number of entries in the `anchors[]` array.
forms[*index*]	read-only	An array of form references reflecting all the forms in a document as defined by the `<FORM>` tags
forms.length	read-only	A number indicating the number of entries in the `forms[]` array.
formReference. formProperties ObjectsAnd Methods		Refer to the section on forms in this chapter for more information on the forms properties, methods, and objects.
history	object	An object which refers to the history of a browser's window. document.history by itself does not refer to any value which can be used by JavaScript. The URLs in the history list cannot be retrieved.
history.length	read-only	A number reflecting the length of the history list.
history.go()	method	`document.history.go( delta or URL)` A method to load the URL specified where delta is a positive or negative number and URL is a URL from the history list.
history.back()	method	`document.history.back()` A method to load the URL, which is one back in the list from the current position.
history. forward()	method	`document.history.forward()` A method to load the URL, which is one forward in the list from the current position.
links[*index*]	read-only	An array of strings reflecting all the links in a document by the `<A>` tags.
links.length	read-only	A number indicating the number of entries in the `links[]` array.
linkName.location property	read-only	Links have the properties of a location object. See the location object definition in this chapter.

TABLE 6-12. (Continued) Objects and Properties of the Document Object

Objects	Access	Usage
(links) <A MouseOver=" ...">	event	An event of the link object Execute JavaScript when the cursor passes over the link defined by the anchor <A> tag.
(links) <A onClick="...">	event	An event of the link object Execute JavaScript when the user clicks on the link defined by the anchor <A> tag.
location	read-only	A string reflecting the complete URL of a document.
other location properties and methods	read-only	Refer to the section on the location object in this chapter for more information on location properties and methods.

Property of:

```
window
```

Figure 6-16 shows the structure of the JavaScript objects we've covered so far. Remember that the frame object is identical to the window object in properties and methods, but that it is optional and does not necessarily appear between the document and window objects. Further, recall that multiple window objects are possible and within each window object, multiple frame objects are possible. However, within a single frame or window, only one document object is present.

document Properties

Some of the properties of a document could be used to filter users, but this isn't a good idea because all you need is a browser which does not support JavaScript to get around this. A better solution would be to use Server-side JavaScript. See Chapters 9 and 10 for more on Server-side JavaScript.

alinkColor

```
document.alinkColor
```

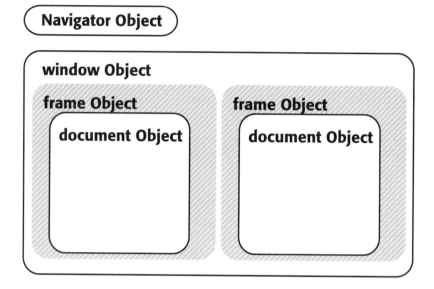

FIGURE 6-16 Hierarchy from document to window.

This property is determined by the ALINK attribute of the <BODY> tag and specifies the color of an active link (after the mouse button has been pressed over a link, but before the mouse button is released). The value is a hexadecimal RGB triplet or a literal color. This property is read-only. The format of the RGB triplet is "rrggbb".

bgColor

```
document.bgColor
```

This property is determined by the BGCOLOR attribute of the <BODY> tag and specifies the background color of the document. The value is a hexadecimal RGB triplet or a literal color. The default value can be set by the user in the preferences of the browser. This property can be set at any time, but will only take effect when a document is loaded. The format of the RGB triplet is "rrggbb".

cookie

```
document.cookie
```

A string which is available between executions of the browser. The cookie is a string stored in the preferences file of the browser and contains information that the JavaScript or CGI interface wants to save between accesses to the document. String methods can pull apart the cookie looking for specific information. You can set the cookie property at any time.

fgColor

```
document.fgColor
```

The fgColor property is determined by the FGCOLOR attribute of the <BODY> tag and represents the color of text which is not a link. The value is a hexadecimal RGB triplet or a literal color. The format of the RGB triplet is "rrggbb". This property is read-only.

lastModified

```
document.lastModified
```

This is a string representing information from the document server indicating the date that the document was last modified. This is a read-only property.

linkColor

```
document.linkColor
```

This property is determined by the LINK attribute of the <BODY> tag and specifies the color of a link. The value is a hexadecimal RGB triplet or a literal color. This property is read-only. The format of the RGB triplet is "rrggbb". The default value is chosen by the user in the browser preferences.

referrer

```
document.referrer
```

When a document includes a link to a second document, the first document is preserved as the "referrer". This information, in the form of a URL string, is available through this property. This is a read-only property.

An interesting use of this property is to take actions based on the source of the referral to the current document. The following code fragment searches to see if a referral came from another document at BYU. If it does, then one document is provided; if not, a different document is used.

```
if ( document.referrer.indexOf( "byu" ) != -1 )
{
    // referral comes from a document at BYU

    // open a document in a frame for output
    parent.myFrame.document.open( "text/HTML" );
    writeDocFromBYU();
    parent.myFrame.document.close();
}
else
{
    // referral did not come from BYU
    parent.myFrame.document.open( "text/HTML" );
    writeDocFromElsewhere();
    parent.myFrame.document.close();
}
```

Another interesting use of this is to lock out certain referrals. Using the referrer property, you can limit access to a document. The following code fragment attempts to do this:

```
if ( document.referrer == someURL )
{
    // don't display a document, just gripe at it!
    window.alert( "I won't load this document!" );
}
else
{
    // display the document
    document.open( "text/HTML" );
    writeDocFromElsewhere();
    document.close();
}
```

Of course, the limitation in this is that you are depending on the browser having JavaScript capabilities for you to enforce this. A non-Java-Script-capable browser would just fly right by this. Using server-side Java-Script would solve this problem by executing the limiting code on the server instead of on the client, which you cannot control.

title

```
document.title
```

This property represents the content of the `<TITLE>` tag within the `<HEAD>` section. If the document has not defined the title, the value is `<undefined>`. This is a read-only property.

vlinkColor

```
document.vlinkColor
```

This property is determined by the `VLINK` attribute of the `<BODY>` tag and specifies the color of a link. The value is a hexadecimal RGB triplet or a literal color. This property is read-only. The format of the RGB triplet is "rrggbb". The default value is chosen by the user in the browser preferences.

document Methods

Documents are considered total static objects by the browser. Once the document has been written, no changes (except to the contents of forms) can be made. This means that you cannot change the contents of a document, you must replace it. Each time you want to write to a document, you need to follow this order:

1. document.open("text/HTML")

2. document.write(...); document.write(...); ...

3. document.close();

The first statement clears the old document and prepares the window or frame to receive a new document. (Be sure you don't overwrite the document containing your script!)

 document.write() will overwrite any document which already exists in your browser window. This includes an and all JavaScript functions and objects.

The second statement can be repeated as often as you like to build the contents of the document. As we'll see in the section on string objects, calls can be used to create HTML formatting, but you can also include your own formatting, such as

```
document.write( "<H1>A Heading in the document" );
document.write( "<P>A new paragraph with text" );
```

The third statement closes the document and forces the content to be displayed on the window.

clear

```
document.clear()
```

This method empties the document being pointed at.

close

```
document.close()
```

The close method closes a stream which was opened with the open() method and was written to with the write() or writeln() methods. The contents of the stream are forced to be displayed in the window.

open

```
document.open(["mimeType"])
```

mimeType can be any of the following document types:

- text/html
- text/plain
- image/gif
- image/jpeg
- image/xbm
- plugIn

The open() method clears out a document and prepares to display a new document of the specified type. The write() and writeln() methods are used to write data to the document. Whether there is any difference between write() and writeln() depends on the document type and the mode it is in. The stream is ended with the close() method, which forces all output to be displayed in the document window. Issuing another open() will cause the existing document to be cleared and a new document to be written.

The mimeType parameter is optional and specifies the type of the document. If you don't specify a *mimeType*, "text/html" is assumed. Table 6-13 explains the different mimeType parameter values.

TABLE 6-13. Values and usage for mimeTypes in the open() method.

mimeType Value	Usage
text/html	Indicates that the document will contain ASCII text with HTML formatting. `writeln()` has no effect on the formatting unless the `<PRE>` tag is used.
text/plain	Indicates that the document will contain plain ASCII text with end-of-line characters to delimit displayed lines. `writeln()` has the effect of starting a new line.
image/gif	Indicates a document encoded with a GIF header and pixel information.
image/jpeg	Indicates a document encoded with a JPEG header and pixel information.
image/xbm	Indicates a document encoded with an XBM header and pixel information.
plugIn	Load the indicated plug-in and use it as the destination for `write()` and `writeln()` methods.

write

```
write(expression1 [,expression2], ...[,expressionN])
```

The `write()` method writes output to a document stream which has been initiated with the `open()` method. The parameters expression1 through expressionN can be any valid JavaScript expressions, including string literals.

writeln

```
writeln(expression1 [,expression2], ...[,expressionN])
```

The `writeln()` method is the same as the write() method except that a newLine character is appended to the end of the output.

document Objects

The document object includes more than just text; it includes objects which are always present, such as the history and location objects, and objects which must be defined by the HTML creating the document, such as the form, anchor, and link objects. Figure 6-17 shows the hierarchy of JavaScript objects from document objects through the window.

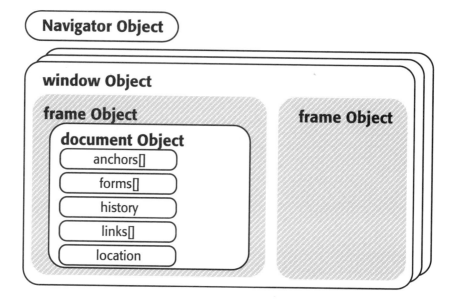

FIGURE 6-17   Hierarchy from document objects to window.

anchors Array Object

```
document.anchors[index]
document.anchors.length
```

The `anchors[]` array contains all of the references to anchor tags `<A>` which have been defined in the document with HTML, or with the `anchor()` method of the string object. The length property of the anchors object indicates the number of elements in the array.

<u><A> Tag</u>

```
<A [HREF=locationOrURL
    NAME="anchorName"
    [TARGET="windowName"]>
    anchorText
</A>
```

HREF defines the *locationOrURL*, which if specified, will be a hot link in the document with the *locationOrURL* as the destination. Specifying this attribute makes this a member of the links[] array.

NAME defines the *anchorName* to which a <A HREF> can link as a hot link destination. Specifying this attribute makes this a member of the anchors[] array.

TARGET defines the window into which the link was loaded. This can only be used if the HREF attribute is present. For more information, see the section on link.

anchorText defines the text to display at the anchor.

See also the anchor() method in the string object as an alternate way to define an anchor programmatically when writing a document with the document.write() method. See the anchor() method under the string object in this chapter.

The <A> tag can server two purposes:

1.It can be a link to an anchor or document.

2.It can define an anchor to which another <A> tag can link.

Including the NAME attribute of the <A> tag makes the tag a member of the anchors[] array. The *anchorName* will appear in the array as an element. Specifying the HREF attribute also makes the tag a member of the links[] array. More on links in that section of this chapter.

An anchor can be a member of both the links[] and anchors[] arrays. The order of anchor references in the anchors[] array is the order in which they appear in the document. As with other JavaScript arrays, the first element is referenced as anchors[0] and the last member as anchors[anchors.length - 1].

Methods of the anchors[] array and anchors object:

None

Event handlers:

None

Property of:

document

forms Array and Object

The forms array and forms object are created by the <FORM> tag in the document HTML. The form object itself has a section devoted to it in this chapter. Here we will cover only a few basics.

<u>forms array:</u>

```
document.forms[index]
document.forms.length
```

<u>forms object:</u>

```
document.forms[index].propertyOrMethod
document.formName.propertyOrMethod
```

<u>Property of:</u>

```
document
```

<u><FORM> tag:</u>

```
<FORM
    NAME="formName"
    TARGET="windowName"
    ACTION="serverURL"
    METHOD=GET | POST
    ENCTYPE="encodingType"
    [onSubmit="handlerText"]>
    formElements
</FORM>
```

NAME defines the *formName* by which the form can be referenced in JavaScript. Use document.*formName* instead of document.forms[]. For example,

```
<FORM NAME="myForm">
```

can be referenced in JavaScript as

```
document.myForm.propertyOrMethod
```

TARGET defines a window that form responses go to when the server returns the result. The *windowName* can be a literal frame or window expression, such as top, parent, or self; but, cannot be a JavaScript expression, such as parent.*frameName* or windowName.*frameName*. This value can be accessed through the target property of the form.

ACTION defines the URL of the server where the form information is sent. This can either be a CGI application or a Server-side JavaScript application. You could also specify a mailto: URL if you wanted to send the form via the email interface.

METHOD can be either GET or POST and defines how the information is conveyed to the server. GET will append the information in the screen to the URL, which is retrieved through the server-side environment variable QUERT_STRING. POST sends the information which is made available on the server via stdin.

ENCTYPE defines a MIME encoding for the data using the format "application/x-www-form-urlencoded" (the default) or "multipart/form-data". You can access this value through the encoding property of form.

formElements refers to the individual elements of a form. This will be discussed in more detail in the section on the form object in this chapter.

Since the HTML of a document can specify more than one form, each form object is separate from the others. You can refer to a form either by its index in the forms[] array, or by its name as defined in the NAME attribute. For example, if the following HTML defined three forms:

```
<FORM NAME="fo_one" …>
    formElements
</FORM>

<FORM NAME="fo_two" …>
    formElements
</FORM>

<FORM NAME="fo_three" …>
    formElements
</FORM>
```

Then you could reference them in JavaScript as follows:

```
document.fo_one.propertyOrMethod
document.fo_two.propertyOrMethod
document.fo_three.propertyOrMethod
```

```
document.forms[0].propertyOrMethod // same as fo_one
document.forms[1].propertyOrMethod // same as fo_two
document.forms[2].propertyOrMethod // same as fo_three
```

and the value of document.forms.length would be 3.

The value of each element in the forms array is `<object nameAt-tribute>`, where nameAttribute is the `NAME` attribute of the form. The `forms[]` array is read-only and any attempts to write information into the array will be ignored by JavaScript.

history Object

The history object gives access to the history list of URLs. However, for security reasons, the actual values of the list or the URLs in the list are not available to JavaScript. It is important to note that for security reasons, the actual value of the URLs in the history list are not available to JavaScript. This means that if you go back into the history list to a URL which is not a part of your programming, your JavaScript will have lost control of the execution until the user returns to a document with your JavaScript in it.

Property:

```
document.history.length
```

The length property provides the length of the history list itself.

Methods:

```
document.history.go( delta or URL )
document.history.back( )
document.history.forward( )
```

Event handlers:

```
None.
```

Property of:

```
document
```

history.back() Method

```
document.history.back()
```

The `history.back()` method does not take any parameters and loads the URL of the position one back from the current position in the list. This is the same as the "Back" button on the browser. Using the statement `document.history.go(-1)` is the same as `document.history.back()`.

history.forward() Method

```
document.history.forward()
```

The `history.forward()` method does not take any parameters and loads the URL of the position one forward from the current position in the list. This is the same as the "Forward" button on the browser. Using the statement `document.history.go(1)` is the same as `document.history.forward()`.

history.go() Method

```
history.go(delta or "URL")
```

`delta` defines the number of steps forward or backward in the history list. A positive integer gives you steps forward; negative gives steps backward.

`URL` is a string which represents all or part of a URL in the history list.

The `history.go()` method moves forward and backward in the history list. If the parameter is an integer, `go()` moves the number of steps in the history forward or backward based on whether the number is positive or negative. If the argument of `go()` is a string, the first location which contains the location string as a substring will be loaded. The match between the location string and history list is case-sensitive.

links array Object

Client-side: YES   Server-side: NO

```
document.links[index]
```

The `links[]` array contains all of the references to anchor tags <A> which have been defined in the document with HTML or with the `link()` method of the string object which have the HREF attribute. The length property of the links object indicates the number of elements in the array.

<A> Tag

```
<A HREF=locationOrURL
   [NAME="anchorName"]
   [TARGET="windowName"]>
   linkText
</A>
```

HREF defines the *locationOrURL*, which if specified, will be a hot link in the document with the *locationOrURL* as the destination. Specifying this attribute makes this a member of the links[] array.

NAME defines the anchorName to which an <A HREF> can link as a hot link destination. Specifying this attribute makes this a member of the anchors[] array.

TARGET defines the window into which the link was loaded. This can only be used if the HREF attribute is present. For more information, see the section on link.

linkText defines the text to display at the link. The text is interpreted as HTML-formatted text and can include HTML formatting tags.

See also the link() method in the string object as an alternate way to define a link programmatically when writing a document with the document.write() method. See the link() method under the string object in this chapter.

The <A> tag can serve two purposes,

1. It can be a link to an anchor or document.

2. It can define an anchor to which another <A> tag can link.

Specifying the HREF attribute also makes the tag a member of the links[] array. An anchor can be a member of both the links[] and anchors[] arrays. The order of link references in the links[] array is the order in which they appear in the document. As with other JavaScript arrays, the first element is referenced as links[0] and the last member as anchors[links.length - 1].

Properties of the link object:

```
document.links.length
```

Methods of the links[] array and links object:

```
None
```

Event handlers:

```
onClick="JavaScript statement(s)"
MouseOver="JavaScript statement(s)"
```

used within

```
<A HREF=locationOrURL [onClick="…"] [MouseOver="…"]>
```

Property of

```
document
```

A link is text or an image which is defined as a hypertext link. Normally, two browser behaviors are associated with a link:

1. A hypertext jump to a new document or location within a document when the user clicks on the linkText (or image) defined between the <A> and </A> tags.

2. A display of the link location in the status bar when the user passes the cursor over the linkText.

The link is defined when the document is loaded and once defined, the link-Text cannot be changed without changing the entire document. Text can also be defined as a link using the `link()` method of the string object in conjunction with `document.write()` when creating a document.

Because link is a location, all of the properties of the location object are available to the link object. (See Table 6-14.) The link object and its properties comprise a read-only object and cannot be changed by JavaScript.

When a link is taken by a user, the URL of the originating document will become the referrer property of the new destination document when it is loaded.

TABLE 6-14. Location Properties Of The Links Object.

link Property	Usage
linkname.hash	An anchor name in the URL.
linkname.host	The hostname:port portion of the URL .

TABLE 6-14. (Continued) Location Properties Of The Links Object.

link Property	Usage
linkname.hostname	The host and domain name, or IP address, of a network host.
linkname.href	The entire URL.
linkname.pathname	The URL-path portion of the URL.
linkname.port	the communications port that the server uses for communications.
linkname.protocol	The beginning of the URL, including the colon.
linkname.search	A query.
linkname.target	Reflects the TARGET attribute of the anchor tag <A TARGET="windowName">.

onClick Event

```
<A HREF="locationOrURL" onClick="JavaScript
    statement(s)">
linkText
</A>
```

The onClick event defines one or more JavaScript statements which are executed when the user clicks on the linkText.

MouseOver Event

```
<A HREF="locationOrURL"
    MouseOver="JavaScript statement(s)">
linkText
</A>
```

The mouseOver event handler is called when the cursor passes over the linkText defined in the anchor tag.

location Object of the document Object

Client-side: YES   Server-side: NO

```
document.location.propertyName
```

The location object of the existing document gives information about the currently loaded URL and any other object which is a location object type, for example, the links object. By itself, location is not an object which will return any useful information. You need to use one of its properties as defined here.

Properties:

```
hash
host
hostname
href
pathname
port
protocol
search
```

TABLE 6-15. Properties of the link Object.

Property	Usage
hash	an anchor name in the URL including the leading hash mark "#"
host	the hostname:port portion of the URL
hostname	the host and domain name, or IP address, of a network host
href	the entire URL
pathname	the URL path portion of the URL
port	the communications port that the server uses for communications
protocol	the beginning of the URL, including the colon
search	a query in the URL including the leading question mark

Methods:

```
None
```

Event handlers:

```
None
```

Property of:

```
document
```

All `document.location` properties are read-only and cannot be changed by the JavaScript. All of the properties are strings. Using the following definitions, the location properties are defined as

```
protocol//hostname:port/pathname?search#hash
```

Examples

The following examples illustrate the use of location properties to access information about the URL of a document. If the following URL were the location, the properties of location would be as follows,

```
http://computer.organization.net:80
    /home/myHTML/myDoc.HTML?query#anchorLocation

location.protocol == "http:"
location.hash == "#anchorLocation"
location.host == "computer.organization.net:80"
location.hostname == "computer.organization.net"
location.href == "http://computer.organization.net:80
    /home/myHTML/myDoc.HTML?query#anchorLocation"
location.pathname == "home/myHTML/myDoc.HTML"
location.port == "80"
location.search == "?query"
```

form Object

Client-side: YES   Server-side: NO

```
formName.propertyName
formName.methodName(parameters)
forms[index].propertyName
forms[index].methodName(parameters)
```

The form object is a property of the document object, but can only be defined using the `<FORM>` tag and the tags which are defined inside the `<FORM>` tag. The `forms[]` array, which is a property of the document object, contains references to all of the form objects within a document. Each form is a distinct entity with its own properties and objects.

```
<FORM
    NAME="formName"
    TARGET="windowName"
    ACTION="serverURL"
```

```
    METHOD=GET | POST
    ENCTYPE="encodingType"
    [onSubmit="handlerText"]>
</FORM>
```

NAME defines the *formName* by which the form can be referenced in JavaScript. Use document.*formName* instead of document.forms[]. For example,

```
<FORM NAME="myForm">
```

can be referenced in JavaScript as

```
document.myForm.propertyOrMethod
```

TARGET defines a window that form responses go to when the server returns the result. *windowName* can be a literal frame or window expression, such as top, parent, or self, but it cannot be a JavaScript expression, such as parent.frameName or windowName.frameName. This value can be accessed through the target property of the form.

ACTION defines the URL of the server where the form information is sent. This can either be a CGI application or a server-side JavaScript application. You could also specify a mailto: URL if you wanted to send the form via the email interface.

METHOD can be either GET or POST and defines how the information is conveyed to the server. GET will append the information in the screen to the URL which is retrieved through the server-side environment variable QUERT_STRING. POST sends the information which is made available on the server via stdin.

ENCTYPE defines a MIME encoding for the data using the format "application/x-www-form-urlencoded" (the default) or "multipart/form-data". You can access this value through the encoding property of form.

formElements refers to the individual elements of a form, which are themselves objects. The objects which are possible are: button, checkbox, hidden, password, radio, reset, select (options array), submit, text, and textarea.

Properties of the form object:

```
    action
    encoding
    method
    target
    elements array
    forms.length
```

TABLE 6-16. Properties of the form Object.

Property	Access	Usage
action	read/write	*formReference*.action The action property is defined by the ACTION attribute of the <FORM> tag. You can set the action property at any time.
encoding	read/write	*formReference*.encoding The encoding property is defined by the ENCTYPE attribute of the <FORM> tag; however, setting encoding overrides the ENCTYPE attribute. You can set the encoding property at any time.
method	read/write	*formReference*.method The method property is defined by the METHOD attribute of the <FORM> tag. The method property should evaluate to either "get" or "post". You can set the method property at any time.
target	read/write	*formReference*.target The target property initially reflects the TARGET attribute of the <FORM> and <A> tags; however, setting target overrides these attributes.
elements[]	read-only	*formReference*.elements[] The elements array contains references to all of the elements within a form. The individual elements are objects within the <FORM> tag. You can also refer to an element by its NAME attribute.
elements[].value	read-only	*formReference*.elements[*index*].value *index* is a number from 0 to elements.length - 1 which refers to an individual element. The value of an elements[] array entry is the HTML used to create the element.
elements.length	read-only	*formReference*.elements.length The length of the elements[] array. The first element is referenced as elements[0] and the last as elements[elements.length - 1].

TABLE 6-16. (Continued) Properties of the form Object.

Property	Access	Usage
forms[]	read-only	*windowReference*.document.forms[*index*] The forms array contains a reference to all forms in a document. You can also refer to a form by its name as defined in the <FORM> tag with the NAME attribute.
forms.length	read-only	*windowReference*.document.forms.length This is the length of the forms[] array. The forms[] array consists of references to all of the forms in the document. The first entry is forms[0] and the last is forms[forms.length - 1].

Methods:

```
submit()
```

TABLE 6-17. Method of the form Object.

Method	Returns	Usage
submit()	<undefined>	*formReference*.submit() The same as pressing the submit button <INPUT TYPE=submit ...> button within a form. The form is submitted to the server for processing by either server-side JavaScript or by a CGI processor.

Events:

```
onSubmit
```

used within

```
<FORM ... onSubmit="JavaScriptStatements"
```

The onSubmit event within the form object will execute JavaScript statements. The code must return true for the submit process to be completed; it must return false for the submit process to be canceled.

Objects:

```
button
checkbox
hidden
password
radio
reset
select (options array)
submit
text
textarea
```

Property of:

```
document
```

elements Array

Client-side: YES   Server-side: NO

```
formReference.elements[index]
formReference.elements.length
```

The `elements[]` array contains a reference to each element within the
`<FORM>` tag. Each form has a separate `elements[]` array. The `elements[]`
array can be used to access each element of the form. Because each type of element within a form can have different properties, methods, and events associated with it, the only way to tell which properties and methods which are
appropriate is to access the value of the `elements[]` entry.

For example, in the following code fragment in which a form is defined:

```
<form name="selectLang">
    <input type=radio name="btn_"
        onClick="processAction(
selectLang.btn_.value='en')">
        English<br>
    <input type=radio name="btn_"
        onClick="processAction(
selectLang.btn_.value='fr')">
        French<br>
    <input type=radio name="btn_"
        onClick="processAction(
selectLang.btn_.value='ge')">
        German<br>
```

```
<input type=radio name="btn_"
    onClick="processAction(
selectLang.btn_.value='it')">
    Italian<br>
<input type=radio name="btn_"
    onClick="processAction(
selectLang.btn_.value='sp')">
    Spanish
</form>
```

the reference to

```
selectLang.elements[0].value
```

would result in the following string:

```
<input type=radio name="btn_"
    onClick="processAction(
selectLang.btn_.value='en')">
```

The only way to tell that the properties and methods associated with a radio object are accessible from `selectLang.elements[0]` is to search for the TYPE attribute and find that the type of object is a radio button.

The best use of this is probably for programmatic access to all of the elements in a form, or as in the example we just went through, accessing individual radio elements. By giving all of the radio elements the same name, we've set them up so that only one of the radio buttons will be "on" at a time. But because we've given them all the same name, the only way to access them individually is through the `elements[]` array.

form Objects

Ten types of objects are defined by HTML and exist within a form:

- button
- checkbox
- hidden
- password
- radio
- reset
- select (options array)
- submit
- text
- textarea

Each object type has its own properties, methods, and events.

button Object

Client-side: YES   Server-side: NO

```
formReference.buttonName.propertyName
formReference.elements[index].propertyName
formReference.buttonName.methodName(parameters)
formReference.elements[index].methodName(parameters)
```

buttonName is the value of the NAME attribute of a button object.

formReference is either the value of the NAME attribute of a form object or an element in the forms array.

index is an integer representing a button object on a form.

propertyName is one of the button properties.

methodName is one of the button methods.

The button object is defined by the `<INPUT TYPE=button>` tag within the `<FORM>` tag section (see Figure 6-18).

```
<INPUT
    TYPE="button"
    NAME="buttonName"
    VALUE="buttonText"
    [onClick="handlerText"]>
```

NAME="*buttonName*" specifies the name of the button object. You can access this value using the name property.

VALUE="*buttonText*" specifies the label to display on the button face. You can access this value using the value property.

The `<INPUT>` tag must appear within the `<FORM>` tag section.

Properties

```
name reflects the NAME attribute.
value reflects the VALUE attribute.
```

TABLE 6-18. Properties of the button Object.

Property	Access	Usage
name	read-only	*formReference*.elements[*index*].name The value of the NAME attribute of the <INPUT NAME="buttonName"> tag. The button may also be referred to by this name as in formReference.buttonName.
value	read/write	*formReference.buttonName*.value *formReference*.elements[*index*].value The value attribute is displayed inside the button on the screen and can be accessed by JavaScript to change what is displayed in the document.

Methods:

```
click
```

TABLE 6-19. Methods of the button Object

Method	Returns	Usage
click()	<undefined>	*formReference.buttonName*.click() Execute the click method on a button to simulate a user click on the button. If an onClick event is defined, that event will be triggered and the JavaScript code associated with the event will be executed.

Event handlers

```
onClick
```

used within

```
<FORM ...>
    <INPUT TYPE=button onClick="JavaScriptStatements">
</FORM>
```

The onClick event occurs when the user clicks on the button defined, or when the click() method is executed on the button object. Each button object has its own onClick event. The onClick event is defined within the <INPUT TYPE=button> tag, which is defined within a <FORM> tag section.

Property of

```
form
```

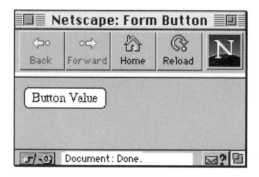

FIGURE 6-18   An example of a button defined with <INPUT TYPE=button>.

Example of onClick

The code in Listing 6-3 will place a single button in a document and attach an `onClick` event to it so that when you click on the event it will change the text in a text field in the same form.

checkbox Object

Client-side: YES   Server-side: NO

```
checkboxName.propertyName
checkboxName.methodName(parameters)
formReference.elements[index].propertyName
formReference.elements[index].methodName(parameters)
```

checkboxName is the value of the NAME attribute of a checkbox object.

formReference is either the value of the NAME attribute of a form object or an element in the forms array.

index is an integer representing a checkbox object on a form.

propertyName is one of the checkbox properties.

methodName is one of the checkbox methods.

```
<HTML>
<!-- File: LIST6_03.HTM
     Usage: Demonstrate the usage of the onClick event
  -->

<HEAD>
<SCRIPT LANG="JavaScript">
function doit()
{
    document.fo_test.in_test.value = "I did it!"
}
</SCRIPT>
</HEAD>

<BODY>
<FORM NAME="fo_test">
   <INPUT TYPE="button" onClick="doit()" VALUE="Click Me!">
   <BR>
   <INPUT TYPE="text" NAME="in_test">
</FORM>
</BODY>
</HTML>
```

LISTING 6-3   DEMONSTRATION OF THE ONCLICK EVENT. THE FORM CONTAINS A BUTTON AND A TEXT FIELD. WHEN THE USER CLICKS ON THE BUTTON, A MESSAGE IS PLACED IN THE TEXT FIELD. SEE FIGURE 6-19.

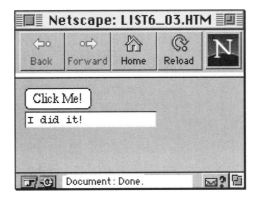

FIGURE 6-19   The browser screen of Listing 6-3 after the user clicks on the button.

A checkbox is defined using the `<INPUT  TYPE=checkbox>` tag within the `<FORM>` tag (see Figure 6-20).

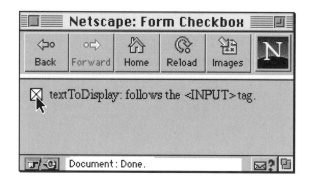

FIGURE 6-20 The checkbox object displayed within a document.

```
<INPUT
   TYPE=checkbox
   NAME="checkboxName"
   VALUE="checkboxValue"
   [CHECKED]
   [onClick="handlerText"]>
   textToDisplay
```

NAME defines the name by which the object can be referenced within the form. checkBoxName can be used in place of the elements[index] reference; for example, formReference.checkBoxName.checkBoxProperty.

VALUE defines a value which is held by the checkbox object. This value can be accessed via the value property of the checkbox object, and will be submitted to the server if the form is submitted to the server. The default value is "on" if the checkbox has been selected.

CHECKED defines whether the checkbox is checked at the time it is loaded into the document. This is accessed via the defaultChecked property.

textToDisplay specifies the label to display beside the checkbox. This label can accept any HTML text formatting tags.

Properties:

```
checked
defaultChecked
```

```
name
value
```

TABLE 6-20. *Properties of the checkbox Object within the form Object.*

Property	Access	Usage
checked	read/ write	*formReference.checkBoxName*.checked *formReference*.elements[*index*].checked The checked property returns true if the box has been selected and is displaying a check mark; it returns false if the box is not selected.
defaultChecked	read/ write	*formReference.checkboxName*.defaultChecked *formReference*.elements[*index*].defaultChecked The defaultChecked property returns true if the box will appear with a check mark when loaded or when the form has been reset; it returns false if the box will not appear checked.
name	read-only	*formReference*.elements[*index*].name The value of the NAME attribute of the <INPUT NAME="checkboxName"> tag. The checkbox may also be referred to by this name as in formReference.checkboxName.
value	read/ write	*formReference.checkboxName*.value *formReference*.elements[*index*].value Unlike the button object, the value property of checkbox is not displayed on the document, but is accessible to JavaScript. The contents of the value property are sent to the server when the form is submitted to server-side JavaScript or to CGI on the server.

Methods:

```
click()
```

Events:

```
onClick
```

TABLE 6-21. Methods of the checkBox Object Within the form Object

Method	Returns	Usage
click()	<undefined>	*formReference.checkboxName*.click() *formReference*.elements[*index*].click() The click() method for the checkbox object is similar to the button object. Use this method to programmatically click on a checkbox.

used within

```
<FORM>
    <INPUT TYPE=checkbox onClick="JavaScriptStatements">
</FORM>
```

The onClick event for checkbox is similar to the button object. Whenever the user clicks on the checkbox or the click() method is executed on the object, the onClick JavaScript statements will be executed.

Property of:

form

hidden Object

Client-side: YES   Server-side: NO

```
hiddenName.propertyName
formName.elements[index].propertyName
```

hiddenName is the value of the NAME attribute of a hidden object.

formName is either the value of the NAME attribute of a form object or an element in the forms array.

index is an integer representing a hidden object on a form in the elements[] array.

propertyName is one of the hidden object's properties.

The hidden object is a text field which is hidden from being displayed on the document. The contents of the hidden object are defined in the <INPUT TYPE=hidden> tag. JavaScript and the server have access to the contents of the hidden field. Note that the hidden object has no methods or events.

```
<INPUT
    TYPE=hidden
    NAME="hiddenName"
    [VALUE="textValue"]>
```

NAME="*hiddenName*" specifies the name of the hidden object. You can access this value using the name property.

VALUE="*textValue*" specifies the initial value of the hidden object.

Properties:

> name
> value

TABLE 6-22. *Properties of the hidden Object.*

Property	Access	Usage
name	**read-only**	*formReference*.elements[*index*].name The value of the NAME attribute of the <INPUT TYPE=hidden NAME="hiddenName"> tag. The hidden field may also be referred to by this name as in formReference.hiddenName.
value	**read/write**	*formReference.hiddenName*.value *formReference*.elements[*index*].value The value of the hidden field is accessible to JavaScript. The contents of the value property are sent to the server when the form is submitted to server-side JavaScript or to CGI on the server.

Methods:

> None

Event handlers:

> None

Property of:

> form

password Object

Client-side: YES   Server-side: NO

passwordName.propertyName
passwordName.methodName(parameters)
formReference.elements[index].propertyName
formReference.elements[index].methodName(parameters)

passwordName is the value of the NAME attribute of a password object.

formReference is either the value of the NAME attribute of a form object or an element in the forms array.

index is an integer representing a password object on a form.

propertyName is one of the password object's properties.

methodName is one of the password object's methods.

The password object displays a text field, similar in concept to the <INPUT TYPE=text> tag; however, instead of displaying text as it is typed into the field by the user, the field displays asterisks "***" to show the number of letters which have been typed (see Figure 6-21). The actual text is available to JavaScript through the value property and to server-side JavaScript and CGI applications. Like the text field (defined later in this chapter), the password field is a single line whose length is defined by the attribute SIZE.

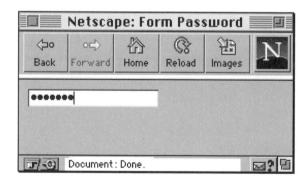

FIGURE 6-21   Example of a password field within a form.

<INPUT

```
TYPE=password
NAME="passwordName"
[VALUE="textValue"]
SIZE=integer>
```

NAME defines the name by which JavaScript can refer to the object. This is accessible via the name property.

VALUE defines the text which is stored in the field. The initial contents of the field when loaded or when the form is reset are accessible via the property defaultValue. The current contents of the field are available in the value property.

SIZE defines the length of the field in number of characters.

Properties:

```
defaultValue
name
value
```

TABLE 6-23. Properties of the password Object.

Property	Access	Usage
defaultValue	read/write	*formReference.passwordName*.defaultValue *formReference*.elements[*index*]. defaultValue The value of the password field which is present when the document is loaded or the form is reset.
name	read-only	*formReference*.elements[*index*].name The value of the NAME attribute of the <INPUT TYPE=password NAME="passwordName"> tag. The password field may also be referred to by this name as in formReference.passwordName.
value	read/write	*formReference.passwordName*.value *formReference*.elements[*index*].value The value of the password field is accessible to JavaScript. The contents of the value property are sent to the server when the form is submitted to Server-side JavaScript or to CGI on the server.

Methods:

```
focus()
blur()
select()
```

The methods for the password object are the same as for the text, textarea, and select objects. A detailed description of the blur, focus, and select states, including the methods and events associated with those states, appears later in this chapter.

TABLE 6-24. Methods of the password Object.

Method	Returns	Usage
blur()	<undefined>	*formReference.passwordName*.blur() *formReference*.elements[*index*].blur() The blur() method removes focus from a form element.
focus()	<undefined>	*formReference.passwordName*.focus() *formReference*.elements[*index*].focus() The focus() method focuses on a form element in preparation of entering data.
select()	<undefined>	*formReference.passwordName*.select() *formReference*.elements[*index*].select() The select() method selects text within a form element in preparation of being changed.

Event handlers:

None.

Property of:

form

radio Object

Client-side: YES   Server-side: NO

```
radioName[index].propertyName
radioName[index].methodName(parameters)
formReference.elements[index].propertyName
```

formReference`.elements[`*index*`].`*methodName*`(`*parameters*`)`

radioName is the value of the NAME attribute of a radio object.

index is an integer.

formReference is either the value of the NAME attribute of a form object or an element in the forms array.

propertyName is one of the radio properties.

methodName is one of the radio methods.

The radio button object is defined by the HTML loaded in a document and is contained within the `<FORM>` tag section for a form. Radio buttons differ from checkboxes in that all of the radio buttons with a common name with a single form are considered a group and only one of their number can be on at any one time. The radio object is defined with the `<INPUT TYPE=radio>` tag. Refer to Figure 6-22 for an example of radio buttons.

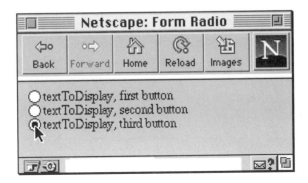

FIGURE 6-22   Example of radio buttons within a form.

```
<INPUT
    TYPE=radio
    NAME="radioName"
    VALUE="buttonValue"
    [CHECKED]
    [onClick="handlerText"]>
    textToDisplay
```

NAME defines the radioName by which JavaScript can refer to the object. All buttons with a single form having the same name property will be considered a group and only one of them can be on at a time. You access the NAME attribute through the name property.

VALUE defines a property which is accessible to JavaScript and is sent to the server when the form is submitted. However, the VALUE attribute is not visible on the document to the user.

CHECKED specifies that the radio button is selected. You can access this value using the defaultChecked property.

textToDisplay specifies the label to display beside the radio button.

Properties:

```
checked
defaultChecked
length
name
value
```

TABLE 6-25. Properties of the radio button Object.

Property	Access	Usage
checked	read/write	*formReference.radioName*.checked *formReference*.elements[*index*].checked The checked property returns true if the radio button has been selected; it returns false if the box is not selected.
defaultChecked	read/write	*formReference.radioName*.defaultChecked *formReference*.elements[*index*]. defaultChecked The defaultChecked property returns true if the radio button will appear selected when loaded or when the form has been reset; it returns false if the box will not appear selected.

TABLE 6-25. (Continued) Properties of the radio button Object.

Property	Access	Usage
length	read-only	*formReference.radioName*.length *formReference*.elements[*index*].length Each group of radio buttons can contain one or more displayed buttons in the group. The number of buttons under a given radioName is retrieved by the length property. The first radio button of the group is referenced as radioName[0] and the last is referenced as radioName[radioName.length - 1]
name	read-only	*formReference*.elements[*index*].name The value of the NAME attribute of the <INPUT TYPE=password NAME="radioName"> tag. The radio button may also be referred to by this name as in formReference.radioName.*propertyOrMethod*
value	read/write	*formReference.radioName*.value *formReference*.elements[*index*].value The value of the radio button object is accessible to JavaScript. The contents of the value property are sent to the server when the form is submitted to server-side JavaScript or to CGI on the server.

Methods:

    click

TABLE 6-26. Method of the radio button Object.

Methods	Returns	Usage
click()	<undefined>	*formReference.radioName*[*index*].click() *formReference*.elements[*index*].click() The click() method for the radio object is similar to the button object. Use this method to programmatically click on a specific radio button indicated by the index value.

Event handlers:

```
onClick
```

used with

```
<FORM>
    <INPUT TYPE=radio onClick="JavaScriptStatements">
</FORM>
```

The `onClick` event for radio button is similar to the button object. Whenever the user clicks on the radio button or the `click()` method is executed on the object, the `onClick` JavaScript statements will be executed.

<u>Property of:</u>

```
form
```

reset Object

Client-side: YES   Server-side: NO

```
resetName.propertyName
resetName.methodName(parameters)
formReference.elements[index].propertyName
formReference.elements[index].methodName(parameters)
```

resetName is the value of the NAME attribute of a reset object.

formReference is either the value of the NAME attribute of a form object or an element in the forms array.

index is an integer representing a reset object on a form.

propertyName is one of the reset object properties.

methodName is one of the reset object methods.

The reset object is a button within a form which resets all of the form elements to their default values (see Figure 6-23). The object is defined using the HTML `<INPUT TYPE=reset>` tag. The reset object must appear within a `<FORM>` tag section. Unlike the submit object, which can be overridden by return false from the onClick event handler code, the reset process cannot be stopped once the reset button has been clicked.

```
<INPUT
```

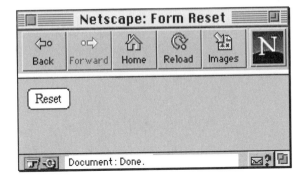

FIGURE 6-23   Example of a reset button within a form.

```
TYPE="reset"
NAME="resetName"
VALUE="buttonText"
[onClick="handlerText"]>
```

NAME defines the name of the reset object which can be used by JavaScript to access it directly. The NAME attribute is accessible via the name property.

VALUE defines the text which will be displayed in the reset button. You can access this using the value property.

<u>Properties:</u>

```
name
value
```

<u>Methods:</u>

```
click
```

<u>Event handlers:</u>

```
onClick
```

used with

```
<FORM ...>
   <INPUT TYPE=reset onClick="JavaScriptStatements">
</FORM>
```

TABLE 6-27. Properties of the reset button Object.

Property	Access	Usage
name	read-only	*formReference*.elements[*index*].name The value of the NAME attribute of the <INPUT NAME="resetName"> tag. The reset button may also be referred to by this name, as in formReference.resetName.
value	read/write	*formReference.resetName*.value *formReference*.elements[*index*].value The value attribute is displayed inside the reset button on the screen and can be accessed by JavaScript to change what is displayed in the document.

TABLE 6-28. Method of the reset button Object.

Method	Returns	Usage
click()	<undefined>	*formReference.resetName*.click() Execute the click method on a reset button to simulate a user click on the button. If an onClick event is defined, that event will be triggered and the JavaScript code associated with the event will be executed.

The onClick event occurs when the user clicks on the reset button defined, or when the click() method is executed on the reset button object. Each reset button object has its own onClick event. The onClick event is defined within the <INPUT TYPE=reset> tag, which is defined within a <FORM> tag section.

Property of:

form

select Object (Options Array)

Client-side: YES   Server-side: NO

```
selectName.propertyName
selectName.methodName(parameters)
selectName.options[index].propertyName
```

selectName is either the value of the NAME attribute of a select object or an element in the elements array.

index is an integer representing an option in a select object.

propertyName is one of the properties listed below.

methodName is one of the methods listed below.

The select object is a scrolling list of items which can be selected (see Figure 6-24). The select objecct is defined by HTML in the <FORM> tag section.

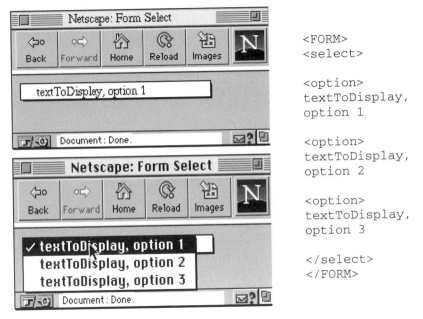

```
<FORM>
<select>

<option>
textToDisplay,
option 1

<option>
textToDisplay,
option 2

<option>
textToDisplay,
option 3

</select>
</FORM>
```

FIGURE 6-24   Examples of <select> objects with options.

```
<FORM>
<select size=5>
<option>
textToDisplay,
option 1
<option>
textToDisplay,
option 2
<option>
textToDisplay,
option 3
</select>
</FORM>
```

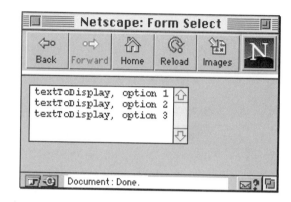

FIGURE 6-24   (Continued) Examples of <select> objects with options.

```
<SELECT
   NAME="selectName"
   [SIZE="integer"]
   [MULTIPLE]
   [onBlur="handlerText"]
   [onChange="handlerText"]
   [onFocus="handlerText"]>
   <OPTION VALUE="optionValue" [SELECTED]> textToDisplay
   [ ... <OPTION> textToDisplay]
</SELECT>
```

NAME defines the JavaScript object name. It can be accessed via the name property.

SIZE defines the number of options which are available before the user clicks on the select object.

MULTIPLE specifies that the select object is a scrolling list (not a selection list).

OPTION specifies a selection element in the list. You can access the options using the options array.

VALUE defines a value which is assigned to the object. This value is not visible to the user. The VALUE attribute is accessed through the value property.

SELECTED specifies that the option is selected by default. You can access this value using the defaultSelected property.

textToDisplay specifies the text to display in the list. You can access this value using the text property.

Properties of select object:

```
length
name
options
selectedIndex
```

TABLE 6-29. Properties of the select Object.

Property	Access	Usage
length	read-only	*selectName*.length *selectName*.options.length *formReference.selectName*.length *formReference*.options.length *formReference*.elements[*index*].length *formReference*.elements[*index*].options. length The length property of the select object provides the number of <OPTION> tags defined for the object. You can either access the length of the select object or the length of the options object within the select object. The result will be the same.
name	read-only	*formReference*.elements[*index*].name The NAME attribute of the select object is accessed via the name property. This is the name by which JavaScript can access the object.
options	read-only	*formReference.selectName*.options *formReference*.elements[*index*].options The options array contains object information regarding the <OPTION> tags within the select object. The options property itself is read-only. The value of selectName.options is the full HTML of the <SELECT> tag. The value of selectName.options[index] is always null.

TABLE 6-29. (Continued) Properties of the select Object.

Property	Access	Usage
selectedIndex	read/write	*formReference.selectName.*selectedIndex *formReference.*elements[*index*]. selectedIndex The selectedIndex property is the index of the option which has been selected. This option may be set programmatically, which results in the index chosen as being selected. If multiple selected options are permitted, selectedIndex represents the first such index.

Properties of options object:

```
defaultSelected
index
length
selected
selectedIndex
text
value
```

The options objects correspond to the <OPTION> tags within the select object. Each <OPTION> tag has one option object and they are arranged in the same order as they were loaded into the document.

The first option object is referenced as selectName.options[0] and the last as selectName.options[selectName.length - 1].

Methods:

```
blur()
focus()
```

Events:

```
onBlur
onChange
onFocus
```

used with

```
<SELECT onBlur="…" onChange="…" onFocus="…">
```

*TABLE 6-30. **Properties of the option objects within select.***

Property	Access	Usage
defaultSelected	read/write	*formReference.selectName*.options[*index*].defaultSelected defaultSelected is a boolean value, with true indicating that the option is the default, and false indicating that it is not. The defaultSelected property determines which <OPTION> is selected when the document loads, or when a form reset occurs.
index	read-only	*formReference.selectName*.options[*index*].index *formReference*.elements[*index*].options[*index*].index The index property gives the index number of an option object.
length	read-only	*formReference.selectName*.options.length *formReference*.elements[*index*].options.length The length property of the options array gives the number of option objects (one for each <OPTION> tag) in the select object. The options objects are in the same order as the <OPTION> tags.
selected	read/write	*formReference.selectName*.options[*index*].selected *formReference*.elements[*index*].options[*index*].selected selected is a boolean value representing whether an <OPTION> is selected with true indicating that it is selected and false indicating that it is not. The selected property can be set programmatically. The document is updated immediately when the selected property is updated. This is more useful than the selectedIndex property of the select object when the MULTIPLE attribute has been chosen.

TABLE 6-30. (Continued) Properties of the option objects within select.

Property	Access	Usage
selectedIndex	read/write	*formReference.selectName*.options. selectedIndex *formReference*.elements[*index*].options. selectedIndex selectedIndex is a number representing the option which has been selected. This property can be updated programmatically to select an option.
text	read/write	*formReference.selectName*.options[*index*]. text *formReference*.elements[*index*]. options[*index*].text text is a string which represents the *textToDisplay,* which follows the <OPTION> tag. Note that text can be updated, but this will not update the form as displayed to the user; however, the value attribute will be updated. In other words, the display on the form will not match the contents of the form object.
value	read/write	*formReference.selectName*.options[*index*]. value *formReference*.elements[*index*]. options[*index*].value value is a string representing the value or text assigned to the option. The value property is not displayed on the document.

For details on using the onFocus and onBlur event handlers, see the section later in this chapter.

```
<SELECT onChange="JavaScriptStatements">
```

The onChange event is used to capture changes in the select object. The following code fragment from Hello World 2 in Chapter 2 uses the onChange event of the select object. Whenever there is a change in the form, the onChange event handler is called to update the rest of the form.

TABLE 6-31. Methods of the select Object.

Method	Returns	Usage
blur()	\<undefined\>	*formReference.passwordName*.blur() *formReference*.elements[*index*].blur() The blur() method removes focus from a form element.
focus()	\<undefined\>	*formReference.passwordName*.focus() *formReference*.elements[*index*].focus() The focus() method focuses on a form element in preparation of entering data.

```
<FORM NAME="foLang">
   Select a language:
   <SELECT NAME="seLang" ONCHANGE="sayHi(this.form)">
      <OPTION SELECTED>English
      <OPTION>French
      <OPTION>German
      <OPTION>Italian
      <OPTION>Spanish
   </SELECT>
   <BR><BR>
   <INPUT TYPE="TEXT" NAME="inHello" VALUE="Hello World!"
     SIZE=40>
</FORM>
```

Property of:

```
select is a property of form
options is a property of select
```

submit Object

Client-side: YES   Server-side: NO

submitName.propertyName
submitName.methodName(parameters)
formReference.elements[index].propertyName
formReference.elements[index].methodName(parameters)

submitName is the value of the NAME attribute of a submit object.

formReference is either the value of the NAME attribute of a form object or an element in the forms array.

index is an integer representing a submit object on a form.

propertyName is one of the submit properties.

methodName is one of the submit methods.

The submit button is used to submit a form to the server for processing (see Figure 6-25). The contents of the form, including any hidden fields, will be sent to the server where either server-side JavaScript or a CGI program can manipulate the data before returning a response. The <INPUT TYPE=submit> tag must appear within a <FORM> tag section.

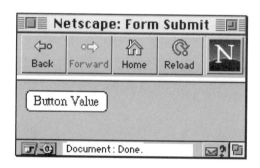

FIGURE 6-25   Example of a submit button.

```
<INPUT
    TYPE="submit"
    NAME="submitName"
    VALUE="buttonText"
    [onClick="handlerText"]>
```

NAME defines the name of the submit object which JavaScript can use to access the object. The NAME attribute is accessible in the name property of the submit object.

VALUE defines the label in the submit button. This can be accessed via the value property.

The submit button is either clicked on by the user or programmatically invoked with the click() method. When this happens, the form is submitted using the ACTION attribute of the <FORM> tag to determine how to submit the form to the server. Once the submit button has been clicked, the form will be submitted to the server; however, additional processing may be accomplished using the onClick event handler. If you want to have control over whether a form is submitted or not, do not use the submit object. Instead use another object, such as a button object, and use the submit() method of the <FORM> to determine whether you want the form submitted to the server.

Properties:

```
name reflects the NAME attribute
value reflects the VALUE attribute
```

TABLE 6-32. Properties of the submit button object.

Property	Access	Usage
name	read-only	*formReference*.elements[*index*].name The value of the NAME attribute of the <INPUT NAME="resetName"> tag. The submit button may also be referred to by this name as in formReference.resetName.
value	read/write	*formReference.submitName*.value *formReference*.elements[*index*].value The value attribute is displayed inside the submit button on the screen and can be accessed by JavaScript to change what is displayed in the document.

Methods:

```
click
```

TABLE 6-33. Methods of the submit button object.

Method	Returns	Usage
click()	<undefined>	*formReference.submitName*.click() Execute the click method on a submit button to simulate a user click on the button. If an onClick event is defined, that event will be triggered and the JavaScript code associated with the event will be executed.

Event handlers:

```
onClick
```

used with

```
<FORM ...>
   <INPUT TYPE=submit onClick="JavaScriptStatements">
</FORM>
```

The onClick event occurs when the user clicks on the submit button defined, or when the click() method is executed on the submit button object. Each submit button object has its own onClick event. The onClick event is defined within the <INPUT TYPE=submit> tag, which is defined within a <FORM> tag section.

<u>Property of:</u>

```
form
```

text Object

Client-side: YES   Server-side: NO

```
textName.propertyName
textName.methodName(parameters)
formReference.elements[index].propertyName
formReference.elements[index].methodName(parameters)
```

textName is the value of the NAME attribute of a text object.

formReference is either the value of the NAME attribute of a form object or an element in the forms array.

index is an integer representing a text object on a form.

propertyName is one of the text properties.

methodName is one of the text methods.

The text input field is a single line field on the document into which the user can type or JavaScript can use to display information (see Figure 6-26). If the text is longer than the field, the text scrolls within the field.

info   Note that text within a text object or a textarea object can not be formatted using HTML tags.

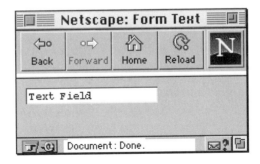

FIGURE 6-26   Example of a text field.

```
<INPUT
    TYPE="text"
    NAME="textName"
    VALUE="textValue"
    SIZE=integer
    [onBlur="handlerText"]
    [onChange="handlerText"]
    [onFocus="handlerText"]
    [onSelect="handlerText"]>
```

NAME defines the name of the text object. JavaScript can refer to the object using textName. The NAME attribute is available through the name property of the object.

VALUE defines the initial content of the text field. This can be accessed through the defaultValue property.

SIZE defines the number of characters in the text field.

Properties:

```
defaultValue
name
value
```

Methods:

```
focus()
blur()
select()
```

TABLE 6-34. *Properties of the text Object*

Property	Access	Usage
defaultValue	read/write	*formReference.textName*.defaultValue *formReference*.elements[*index*]. defaultValue The value of the text field which is present when the document is loaded or the form is reset.
name	read-only	*formReference*.elements[*index*].name The value of the NAME attribute of the <INPUT TYPE=text NAME="textName"> tag. The text field may also be referred to by this name as in formReference.textName.
value	read/write	*formReference.textName*.value *formReference*.elements[*index*].value The value of the text field is accessible to JavaScript and can be changed at any time. The changed contents will appear as the value is changed. The contents of the value property are sent to the server when the form is submitted to server-side JavaScript or to CGI on the server.

The methods for the text field object are the same as for the password, textarea, and select objects. A detailed description of the blur, focus, and select states, including the methods and events associated with those states, appears later in this chapter.

TABLE 6-35. *Methods of the text Object.*

Method	Returns	Usage
blur()	<undefined>	*formReference.textName*.blur() *formReference*.elements[*index*].blur() The blur() method removes focus from a form element.
focus()	<undefined>	*formReference.textName*.focus() *formReference*.elements[*index*].focus() The focus() method focuses on a form element in preparation of entering data.

TABLE 6-35. (Continued) Methods of the text Object.

Method	Returns	Usage
select()	\<undefined\>	*formReference.textName*.select() *formReference*.elements[*index*].select() The select() method selects text within a form element in preparation of being changed.

Event handlers:

```
onBlur
onChange
onFocus
onSelect
```

used with

```
<FORM>
    <INPUT TYPE=text … onBlur="…" onChange="…"
        onFocus="…" onSelect="…" >
</FORM>
```

For details on using the onFocus, onBlur, and onSelect event handlers, see the section later in this chapter.

```
<INPUT TYPE=text onChange="JavaScriptStatements">
```

The onChange event is used to capture changes in the contents of a text field. When the user selects and changes the contents of a text field, the onChange event handler is called.

Property of:

```
form
```

textarea Object

Client-side: YES   Server-side: NO

```
textareaName.propertyName
textareaName.methodName(parameters)
formReference.elements[index].propertyName
formReference.elements[index].methodName(parameters)
```

textareaName is the value of the NAME attribute of a textarea object.

formReference is either the value of the NAME attribute of a form object or an element in the forms array.

index is an integer representing a textarea object on a form.

propertyName is one of the textarea properties.

methodName is one of the textarea methods.

The textarea object is a multi-line, scrollable text field (see Figure 6-27). The textarea object is defined within the <FORM> tag section. Unlike the <TEXT> tag, the <TEXTAREA> tag has an end tag, </TEXTAREA>, between which the default contents of the textarea object are stored.

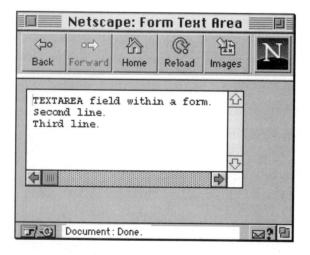

FIGURE 6-27   Example of a textarea field.

```
<TEXTAREA
    NAME="textareaName"
    ROWS="integer"
    COLS="integer"
    [onBlur="handlerText"]
    [onChange="handlerText"]
    [onFocus="handlerText"]
    [onSelect="handlerText"]>
    textToDisplay
```

```
</TEXTAREA>
```

NAME defines the name of the textarea object which JavaScript can use to access the object's properties and methods. The NAME attribute can be accessed via the name property.

ROWS and COLS define the number of characters vertically and horizontally on the document for the textarea.

textToDisplay specifies the initial value of the textarea object. A textarea allows only ASCII text. To break text between two lines, insert the newline character between lines. You can access this value using the defaultValue property. The textarea does not allow HTML formatting of the text inside the object.

 Note that text within a text object or a textarea object can not be formatted using HTML tags.

The textarea object is updated when the contents are changed via the value property. To programmatically update the textarea, you'll need to use the newline character which is appropriate to your platform. Table 6-36 indicates the newline character(s) for common client platforms.

TABLE 6-36. Appropriate newline characters for different platforms.

Platform	Newline Characters(s)
DOS, Windows	<carriage return><line feed>
Macintosh	<carriage return>
UNIX	<line feed>

This means that to separate lines in a textarea field, you will need to look at the platform on which the JavaScript is executing (most likely via the userAgent property of the navigator object, and update the newline character appropriately).

Properties:

```
defaultValue
name
value
```

TABLE 6-37. Properties of the textarea Object.

Property	Access	Usage
defaultValue	read/write	*formReference.textareaName*.defaultValue *formReference*.elements[*index*]. defaultValue The value of the textarea field which is present when the document is loaded or the form is reset.
name	read-only	*formReference*.elements[*index*].name The value of the NAME attribute of the <INPUT TYPE=textarea NAME="textareaName"> tag. The text area field may also be referred to by this name, as in formReference.textareaName.
value	read/write	*formReference.textareaName*.value *formReference*.elements[*index*].value The value of the textarea field is accessible to JavaScript and can be changed at any time. The changed contents will appear as the value is changed. The contents of the value property are sent to the server when the form is submitted to server-side JavaScript or to CGI on the server.

Methods:

```
focus()
blur()
select()
```

The methods for the textarea field object are the same as those for the password, text, and select objects. A detailed description of the blur, focus, and select states, including the methods and events associated with those states, appears later in this chapter.

Event handlers:

```
onBlur
onChange
onFocus
onSelect
```

TABLE 6-38. Methods for the textarea Object.

Method	Returns	Usage
blur()	<undefined>	*formReference.textName*.blur() *formReference*.elements[*index*].blur() The blur() method removes focus from a form element.
focus()	<undefined>	*formReference.textName*.focus() *formReference*.elements[*index*].focus() The focus() method focuses on a form element in preparation of entering data.
select()	<undefined>	*formReference.textName*.select() *formReference*.elements[*index*].select() The select() method selects text within a form element in preparation of being changed.

used with

```
<INPUT TYPE=textarea onBlur="…" onChange="…"
onFocus="…" onSelect="…">
```

For details on using the onFocus, onBlur, and onSelect event handlers see the section later in this chapter.

```
<INPUT TYPE=textarea onChange="JavaScriptStatements">
```

The onChange event is used to capture changes in the contents of a textarea field. When the user selects and changes the contents of a text field, the onChange event handler is called.

Property of:

```
form
```

focus, select, and blur Methods and Events

The text field objects of the form object have three methods and objects which we haven't discussed thoroughly yet. They are as follows:

```
focus        onFocus
select       onSelect
             onChange
```

```
blur        onBlur
```

These methods and events give the programmer control over what to do when a user views and manipulates document text fields. The fields affected are password, text, textarea, and select. See the specific sections for details on which of these events is applicable. Also, Table 6-39 summarizes how various user-initiated actions affect these methods and events.

TABLE 6-39. User Actions and Resulting text and textarea Object Events.

User Action	Result
• User tabs or clicks on a text input field.	• The field receives "focus" and the onFocus event handler is invoked, if present.
• User selects text within the text input field, or types in the text input field.	• The field receives "select" and the onSelect event handler is invoked if present.
• User clicks outside the field.	• If the field has changed content, the onChange event handler is invoked if present. • The field receives "blur" and the onBlur event handler is invoked.

Any object which supports the focus(), select(), or blur() methods can programmatically invoke these events on the object concerned.

Listings 6-4 through 6-6 and Figures 6-28 through 6-30 demonstrate the application of the onFocus, onSelect, onChange, and onBlur events. Listing 6-4 is the frame layout document which divides the screen into two pieces. Listing 6-5 creates a form with a text field. As changes are made to the text field, the events trigger messages in the second frame of the window. Listing 6-6 is the initial contents of the second frame which are overwritten as soon as any event occurs on the text field. Figures 6-28 through 6-30 demonstrate the use of this code and the events it is demonstrating.

Built-in Objects

JavaScript defines three objects which are built into the browser itself and are available to any level of object and script:

- Math
- String
- Date

```
<HTML>
<!-- File: LIST6_04.HTM
     Calls: LIST6_05.HTM, LIST6_06.HTM
     Usage: This document demonstrates the concepts
        of "focus", "blur", "change" and "select"
        as developed in JavaScript.

        The first frame "fa_control" will have a text
        field which the user can make changes in.  The
        second frame will change messages based on the
        the focus of the text field.
  -->

<HEAD>
<TITLE>Focus, Select, Blur</TITLE>
</HEAD>

<FRAMESET ROWS="67%,33%">
   <FRAME SRC=LIST6_05.HTM name="fa_control"
         scrolling="auto">
   <FRAME SRC=LIST6_06.HTM name="fa_output"
         scrolling="auto">
</FRAMESET>

</HTML>
```

LISTING 6-4   FRAME DEFINITION DOCUMENT FOR LISTINGS 6-5 AND 6-6.

The Math object defines common mathematical constants and functions. The string object defines string functions which can be applied to any variable or property which evaluates to a string in JavaScript. The Date object is technically not an object, but a formatting of a string object.

Math Object

Client-side: YES   Server-side: YES

```
Math.propertyName
Math.methodName(parameters)
```

Properties:

E

```
<HTML>

<!-- File: LIST6_05.HTM
     Called by: LIST6_04.HTM
     Usage: This document will send messages to the
         frame named "fa_output" indicating the different
         stages of the text field's focus.
  -->

<HEAD>
<SCRIPT LANG="JavaScript">
function testIntNaN( vTest )
{

// Name: testIntNaN()
// Usage: test a value to see if it is a number
// Parameters: vTest, the value to be tested
// Returns: true or false based on whether vTest is an
//          integer number
// Problems: "-0" (negative zero) evaluates as not a number
//           and returns false mixed text which begins with
//            a number returns true (e.g., "1xyz")
//

   var vResult = parseInt( vTest );

   if ( ( vResult < 0 ) && ( ( -vResult ) < 0 ) )
   {
      // Using the trick, we found that vTest is not a
      // number
      return false;
   }

   if ( vResult == 0 )
   {
      // Look for "0" in vTest
      var vIdx = vTest.indexOf( "0" )

      if ( ( vIdx == -1 ) || ( vIdx > 0 ) )
      {
          return false;
      }
```

LISTING 6-5   THE FRAME WHICH DEMONSTRATES THE ONFOCUS, ONCHANGE, ONSELECT, AND ONBLUR EVENTS.

```
      }
   return true;
}

function pause( vPause )
{
   if ( !testIntNaN( vPause ) )
   {
      alert( "pause() error" );
      return;
   }

   var vTime = new Date();
   var vStart = Date.parse( vTime );
   var vNow;

   var i = 0;
   var vTest = true;

   while ( vTest )
   {
      vTime = new Date();
      vNow = Date.parse( vTime );

      if ( (vNow - vStart) >= ( vPause ) )
      {
         vTest = false;
      }

      i++;
      if ( i > 3000 )
      {
         vTest = false;
         alert( "aborting pause()" );
      }
   }
}

function fo_change()
{
   parent.fa_output.document.open( "text/html");
   parent.fa_output.document.write( "<p>Change" );
```

LISTING 6-5   (CONTINUED) THE FRAME WHICH DEMONSTRATES THE ONFOCUS, ONCHANGE, ONSELECT, AND ONBLUR EVENTS.

```
      parent.fa_output.document.close();
      pause( 500 );
      return;
}

function fo_focus()
{
      parent.fa_output.document.open( "text/html");
      parent.fa_output.document.write( "<p>Focus" );
      parent.fa_output.document.close();
      pause( 500 );
      return;
}

function fo_select()
{
      parent.fa_output.document.open( "text/html");
      parent.fa_output.document.write( "<p>Select" );
      parent.fa_output.document.close();
      pause( 500 );
      return;
}

function fo_blur()
{
      parent.fa_output.document.open( "text/html");
      parent.fa_output.document.write( "<p>Blur" );
      parent.fa_output.document.close();
      pause( 500 );
      return;
}
</SCRIPT>
</HEAD>

<BODY>
<P>To experiment with focus, blur, and select, place
   the cursor over the text field below and click in
   the field.  Type some text and click outside of the
   field. Select the text within the field and click
   outside of the field again.
```

LISTING 6-5 (CONTINUED) THE FRAME WHICH DEMONSTRATES THE ONFOCUS, ONCHANGE, ONSELECT, AND ONBLUR EVENTS.

```
<P>As you do all of this, note how the different states
   of &quot;focus&quot;, &quot;blur&quot;,
   &quot;select&quot;, and &quot;change&quot occur as
   displayed in the bottom frame.
<BR>

<FORM NAME=fo_control>
   Test field
   <input type="text"
      onChange="fo_change()"
      onFocus ="fo_focus()"
      onSelect="fo_select()"
      onBlur  ="fo_blur()">
</FORM>
</BODY>
</HTML>
```

LISTING 6-5   (CONTINUED) THE FRAME WHICH DEMONSTRATES THE ONFOCUS, ONCHANGE, ONSELECT, AND ONBLUR EVENTS.

```
<HTML>
<!-- File: LIST6_06.HTM
     Called by: LIST6_04.HTM
     Usage: This document will be replaced by
        messages from focus1.html as the user
        experiments with the concepts of "focus",
        "blur", "select", and "change".
  -->

<BODY>
<P>This frame will contain messages regarding the
   focus of the text field in the frame above.
</BODY>
</HTML>
```

LISTING 6-6   INITIAL CONTENT OF THE SECOND FRAME FROM LISTING 6-4.

```
LN2
LN10
LOG2E
LOG10E
PI
```

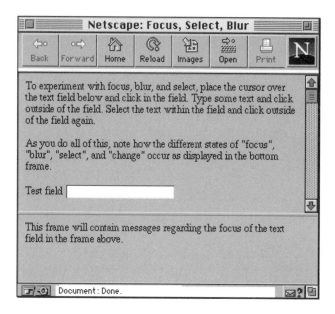

FIGURE 6-28 The initial state of the two frames before the user has done anything to the text field.

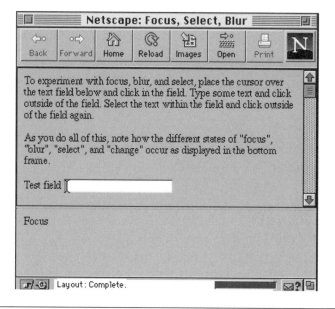

FIGURE 6-29 The text field has received the focus event because the cursor is inside the field and the user has clicked the mouse.

FIGURE 6-30   The text field object has received the blur event since the cursor is outside the text field and the user has clicked the mouse.

```
SQRT1_2
SQRT2
```

TABLE 6-40. Properties of the Math Object.

Property	Usage
E	Math.E Euler's constant and the base of natural logarithms, about 2.718.
LN2	Math.LN2 The natural logarithm of 2, about 0.693.
LN10	Math.LN10 The natural logarithm of 10, about 2.302.
PI	Math.PI The value π, about 3.1415.
SQRT1_2	Math.SQRT1_2 The square root of one-half, about 0.707.

TABLE 6-40. (Continued) Properties of the Math Object.

Property	Usage
SQRT2	Math.SQRT2
	The square root of two, about 1.414.
LOG2E	Math.LOG2E
LOG10E	Math.LOG10E

Methods:

```
abs()
acos()
asin()
atan()
ceil()
cos()
exp()
floor()
log()
max()
min()
parsefloat()
parseint()
pow()
random()
round()
sin()
sqrt()
tan()
```

The Math methods can be divided into four categories:

- Trigonometric Functions
- Rounding Functions
- Logarithmic Functions
- General Math Functions

Events:

```
None.
```

TABLE 6-41. Trigonometric Functions of the Math Object.

Method	Returns	Usage
acos()	a number between 0 and pi radians	Math.acos(*argument*) The argument is a numeric expression whose value is between -1 and 1. Returns the arc cosine of the argument. If the argument is outside this range, the method returns 0.
asin()	a number between -pi/2 and pi/2 radians	Math.asin(*argument*) The argument is a numeric expression whose value is between -1 and 1. Returns the arc sine of the argument. If the argument is outside this range, the method returns 0.
atan()	a number between -pi/2 and pi/2 radians	Math.atan(*argument*) Returns the arc tangent of the argument. The argument is any numeric expression.
cos()	a number between -1 and 1	Math.cos(*argument*) Returns the cosine of the argument. The argument is any numeric expression.
sin()	a number between -1 and 1	Math.sin(*argument*) Returns the sine of the argument. The argument is any numeric expression.
tan()	a number	Math.tan(*argument*) Returns the tangent of the argument. The argument is any numeric expression.

TABLE 6-42. Rounding Functions of the Math Object.

Method	Returns	Usage
ceil()	a number	Math.ceil(*argument*) Returns the smallest integer greater than or equal to the argument. The argument is any numeric expression. Math.ceil(3.44) == 4
floor()	a number	Math.floor(*argument*) Returns the largest integer less than or equal to the argument. The argument is any numeric expression. Math.floor(3.44) == 3

TABLE 6-42. (Continued) Rounding Functions of the Math Object.

Method	Returns	Usage
round()	a number	Math.round(*argument*) Returns the argument rounded to the nearest integer. Arguments whose fractional part is .5 are rounded up. Math.round(3.44) == 3 Math.round(3.54) == 4
abs()	a non-negative number	Math.abs(*argument*) Returns the absolute value of the argument. Math.abs(-3.44) == 3.44
max()	a number	Math.max(*arg1, arg2*) Returns the larger of arg1 and arg2. Math.max(3.44, 2.44) == 3.44
min()	a number	Math.min(*arg1, arg2*) Returns the smaller of arg1 and arg2. Math.min(3.44, 2.44) == 2.44

TABLE 6-43. Logarithmic and Power Functions of the Math Object.

Method	Returns	Usage
exp()	a positive number	Math.exp(*argument*) Returns e raised to the power of argument.
log()	a number	Math.log(*argument*) Returns the natural log of the argument. The argument is any positive numeric expression. If the argument is zero or negative, the return value is -1.797693134862316e+308
pow()	a number	Math.pow(*base, argument*) Returns the base raised to the power of the exponent. Math.pow(2, 3) == 2 * 2 * 2

Property of:

```
Built into the language.
```

TABLE 6-44. General Functions of the Math Object.

Method	Returns	Usage
random()	a number	Math.random() Returns a random number. This method is being implemented on all platforms and may not have been implemented on the platform you are interested in.
sqrt()	a positive number	Math.sqrt(*argument*) Returns the square root of the argument. The argument should be zero or positive. If the argument is negative the value 0 will be returned.
parsefloat()	a number	parsefloat(*stringArg*) Convert a string to a floating point number. See built-in methods later in this chapter
parseint()	a number	parseint(*stringArg, radix*) Convert a string to an integer. See built-in methods later in this chapter.

To use a Math object, you need to reference it directly using the Math reserved word. For example, to reference a Math constant use the following statement:

```
Math.PI
```

to refer to the value PI. Constants have the full precision of the math available to JavaScript. The trigonometric function sin() is referenced as

```
Math.sin( argument )
```

Regarding the continuity between platforms and implementations of JavaScript, there is a difference here between Java and JavaScript. Java defines not only a language, but a virtual hardware implementation, which means that the result of a built-in numeric operation in Java will always be the same regardless of the platform and implementation of the language. This is not true of JavaScript. If absolute continuity between platforms is needed in your JavaScript code, you will need to be careful about how the implementations return values to your code.

Because referencing the Math object can be tedious, you can use the "with (Math)" statement so you don't have to continuously repeat "Math." For example, the following code fragments are equivalent:

```
var radius = 5;
var area = Math.PI * radius * radius;

with (Math)
{
   var radius = 5;
   var area = PI * radius * radius;
}
```

string Object

Client-side: YES   Server-side: YES

```
stringName.propertyName
stringName.methodName(parameters)
```

Any variable or property which is evaluated as a string can use the string methods and properties. A string is simply a series of characters. Sometimes the string can be evaluated as a number expression, as in "123.4". As a string, this can be scanned to find the first occurrence of the decimal point. As a number, it can be a part of any numeric expression, so this JavaScript fragment will result in the value 127.4.

```
var num1 = "123.4";
var num2 = num1 + 4;
```

To use the string properties and methods append the property or method to the reference or literal string. For example,

```
var str1 = "abcdefg";
var str2 = str1.toUpperCase();
```

results in str2 containing the string "ABCDEFG".

<u>string Object Properties:</u>

```
length
```

The length property applies to any object which evaluates to a string. The following examples show the use of the length property:

```
"abcdef".length == 6

var str1 = "abcdefg";
```

```
str1.length == 6

<HEAD>
<TITLE>This is a title</TITLE>
</HEAD>

document.title.length == 14
```

Methods:

```
anchor()
big()
blink()
bold()
charAt()
fixed()
fontcolor()
fontsize()
indexOf()
italics()
lastIndexOf()
link()
small()
strike()
sub()
substring()
sup()
toLowerCase()
toUpperCase()
```

Associated Methods:

```
escape(), a built-in method
unescape(), a built-in method
```

We're going to divide up the string methods into three groups,

- Methods with HTML tag equivalents, both text formatting and hypertext links.
- Methods which find sub-strings or index a string.
- Methods which manipulate strings.

Each of these methods will surround the string with the respective tags. These should be used with the document.write() and document.writeln() methods to display formatted text in an HTML document. The string itself is unchanged. For example, the code

```
var str1 = "abcdef";
var str2 = str1.toUpperCase();
document.write( "<P>", str1 );
document.write( "<P>", str2 );
```

does nothing to the contents of str1 itself and results in the following output:

```
abcdef
ABCDEF
```

TABLE 6-45. *String methods which have HTML tag equivalents.*

Method	Tag Equivalent	Usage
big()	\<BIG>...\</BIG>	*stringReference*.big() Surround stringReference with the big font \<BIG> tags.
blink()	\<BLINK>... \</BLINK>	*stringReference*.blink() Surround stringReference with the blinking font \<BLINK> tags.
bold()	\<B>...\</B>	*stringReference*.bold() Surround stringReference with the bold font \<B> tags.
fixed()	\<TT>...\</TT>	*stringReference*.fixed() Surround stringReference with the fixed pitch font \<TT> tags
fontcolor()	\<FONT COLOR = color>...\</FONT>	*stringReference*.fontcolor(*color*) Surround the string reference with the font \<FONT> tags, with the color attribute set to the value of the color argument. The color argument is of the form rrggbb.

TABLE 6-45. (Continued) String methods which have HTML tag equivalents.

Method	Tag Equivalent	Usage
fontsize()	<FONTSIZE = size>... </FONTSIZE>	*stringReference*.fontsize(*size*) Surround the string reference with the font size <FONTSIZE> tags with the size set to the value in the size argument. The size argument is a value from 1 to 7. Specifying a size argument as a string with a sign, such as "+1" or "-2" results in the font size incrementing or decrementing appropriately from the <BASEFONT> size as set in the HTML.
italics()	<I>...</I>	*stringReference*.italics() Surround the string reference with the italic <I> tags.
small()	<SMALL>... </SMALL>	*stringReference*.small() Surround the string reference with the small font <SMALL> tags.
strike()	<STRIKE>... </STRIKE>	*stringReference*.strike() Surround the string reference with the strike out font <STRIKE> tags.
sub()	_{...}	*stringReference*.sub() Surround the string reference with the subscript font <SUB> tags.
sup()	^{...}	*stringReference*.sup() Surround the string reference with the superscript font <SUP> tags.
anchor()	<A ... NAME= "anchorName">	*stringReference*.anchor(*anchorName*) Surround the string reference with the anchor <A> tag with the NAME attribute specified as the anchorName. The attribute anchorName should be a string.
link()	<A ... HREF= locationOrURL>	*stringReference*.link(*locationOrURL*) Surround the string reference with the anchor <A> tag with the HREF attribute specified as a location or URL.

The most useful purpose for the string methods in Table 6-45 are in conjunction with the document.write() and document.writeln() methods when creating a document. For example, the following code fragments are equivalent. Whether the first or second is more readable is up to the reader.

```
var str = "This is a line of text for my document.";
document.write( "<B>" + str + "</B>" );

var str = "This is a line of text for my document.";
document.write( str.bold() );
```

TABLE 6-46. *String object methods for indexing and finding sub-strings.*

Method	Returns	Usage
charAt()	a character	*stringReference*.charAt(*index*) Returns the character at the location pointed at by the value of index. The index argument is a number. The characters in a string are numbered beginning with 0 and continuing until stringReference.length - 1. "abcdef".charAt(3) == "d"
indexOf()	a number	*stringReference*.indexOf(*searchValue*, [*fromIndex*]) Returns the character position inside the string reference of the first occurrence of the searchValue string. If the fromIndex argument is present, the search will begin from the left at that character position. If no match is found, the value -1 is returned. The searchValue argument is a string. The fromIndex argument is a number. "abcdef".indexOf("def") == 3 "abcdefabc".indexOf("abc", 2) == 6

TABLE 6-46. (Continued) String object methods for indexing and finding sub-

Method	Returns	Usage
lastIndexOf()	a number	*stringReference*.lastIndexOf(*searchValue*, [*fromIndex*])
		Returns the index number of the last occurrence of the searchValue string. If the fromIndex argument is present, the search will begin from the right at that character position. If no match is found, the value -1 is returned. The searchValue argument is a string. The fromIndex argument is a number.
		"abcdefabc".lastIndexOf("abc") == 6 "abcdefabc".lastIndexOf("abc",7) == 0
substring()	a string	*stringReference*.substring(*arg1, arg2*)
		Return a portion of the string reference. The arguments arg1 and arg2 are numbers.
		If arg1 < arg2, return the string starting at arg1 and ending with the character before arg2.
		If arg2 < arg1, return the string starting at arg2 and ending with the character before arg1.
		If arg1 == arg2, return the null string.
		"abcdefg".substring(2, 4) == "cd" "abcdefg".substring(5, 3) == "de"

TABLE 6-47. String Methods to convert alphabetic strings

Method	Returns	Usage
toLowerCase()	a string	*stringReference*.toLowerCase()
		Returns the string reference with all alphabetic characters shifted to lower-case. All non-alphabetic characters remain the same.
toUpperCase()	a string	*stringReference*.toUpperCase()
		Returns a string with all alphabetic characters shifted to upper-case.

TABLE 6-47. (Continued) String Methods to convert alphabetic strings

Method	Returns	Usage
escape()	a number	escape("char") Returns the number associated with a character in the ASCII format. See the built-in methods later in this chapter.
unescape()	a string	unescape("number") Returns the character associated with a number in the ASCII format. See the built-in methods later in this chapter.

<u>Event handlers:</u>

```
None
```

<u>Property of:</u>

```
Built into the language
```

Date Object

JavaScript has no formal Date object; however, a correctly formatted string containing date and time information can be manipulated using built-in methods for this purpose.

Date

Client-side: YES   Server-side: YES

```
dateObjectName = new Date()
dateObjectName = new Date("month day, year
                          hours:minutes:seconds")
dateObjectName = new Date(yearInt, monthInt, dayInt)
dateObjectName = new Date(yearInt, monthInt, dayInt,
                          [hoursInt, minutesInt, secondsInt])
```

Two forms can be used to set the date in the Date object: using a string to specify the month, day, and year; or using integer expressions. The arguments ending in "Int" must be integer expressions.

<u>Properties:</u>

> None.

<u>Methods:</u>

```
getDate()
getDay()
getHours()
getMinutes()
getMonth()
getSeconds()
getTime()
getTimeZoneoffset()
getYear()
parse()
setDate()
setHours()
setMinutes()
setMonth()
setSeconds()
setTime()
setYear()
toGMTString()
toLocaleString()
UTC()
```

We've divided the Date methods into four groups:

- Getting date subfields
- Setting date subfields
- Date conversion
- Date object manipulation

To access Date object methods, use the form

```
DateReference.DateMethod()
```

For example, we could get the current date and then retrieve the current year as follows:

```
var v_date = new Date();
var v_year = v_date.getYear();
```

Assuming the current date is April 6, 1999, v_date will contain a reference to 4/6/99 and v_year will contain the number 99.

As with the string methods, calling the following methods for getting sub-fields on an object does not change the value of the object, but the changed value can be assigned to a different variable.

TABLE 6-48. *Methods for Getting Date Information from a Date Reference.*

Method	Returns	Usage
getDate()	a number from 1 to 31	*DateReference*.getDate() Returns the day of the month of the date found in the Date reference. Date("4/6/1999 9:23:45").getDate == 6
getDay()	a number from 0 to 6	*DateReference*.getDay() Returns the day of the week of the date found in the Date reference: 0 == Sunday, 1 == Monday, 2 == Tuesday, 3 == Wednesday, 4 == Thursday, 5 == Friday, and 6 == Saturday. Date("4/6/1999 9:23:45").getDay == 2
getHours()	a number from 0 to 23	*DateReference*.getHours() Returns the hour of the date/time in the Date reference. AM hours are 0 to 11, PM hours are 12 to 23. Date("4/6/1999 9:23:45").getHours == 9
getMinutes()	a number from 0 to 59	*DateReference*.getMinutes() Returns the minutes of the date/time in the Date reference. Date("4/6/1999 9:23:45").getMinutes == 23
getMonth()	a number from 0 to 11	*DateReference*.getMonth() Returns the month of the date in the Date reference: 0 == January, 1 == February, 2 == March, 3 == April, 4 == May, 5 == June, 6 == July, 7 == August, 8 == September, 9 == October, 10 == November, and 11 == December. Date("4/6/1999 9:23:45").getMonth == 4
getSeconds()	a number from 0 to 59	*DateReference*.getSeconds() Returns the seconds of the date/time in the Date Rrference. Date("4/6/1999 9:23:45").getSeconds == 45

TABLE 6-48. (Continued) Methods for Getting Date Information from a Date

Method	Returns	Usage
getYear()	a number	*DateReference*.getYear() Returns the year of the date in the Date reference. Only the last two digits of the year are returned. Date("4/6/1999 9:23:45").getYear == 99

TABLE 6-49. Date Methods for Setting Date Values.

Method	Returns	Usage
new Date()	Date-formatted object into a variable	*dateObject* = new Date() *dateObject* = new Date("month day, year hours:minutes:seconds") *dateObject* = new Date(yearInt, monthInt, dayInt, [hoursInt, minutesInt, secondsInt]) Date() returns the current date and time according to the browser. Date("...") sets a date according to the string. Date(yearInt, ...) sets a date according to the numeric expressions.
setDate()	\<undefined\>	*DateReference*.setDate(*dayArg*) dayArg is a number from 1 to 31. Changes the day in the Date reference to the value in dayArg.
setHours()	\<undefined\>	*DateReference*.setHours(*hoursArg*) hoursArg is a number from 0 to 23. Changes the hour in the Date reference to the value in hoursArg: AM hours are from 0 to 11, PM hours are from 12 to 23.
setMinutes()	\<undefined\>	*DateReference*.setMinutes(*minutesArg*) minutesArg is a number from 0 to 59. Changes the minutes in the Date reference to the value in minutesArg.
setMonth()	\<undefined\>	*DateReference*.setMonth(*monthArg*) monthArg is a number from 0 to 11. Changes the months in the Date reference to the value in monthArg. See the definition of getMonth() for the assignment of numbers to months: For example, 0 == January...

TABLE 6-49. (Continued) Date Methods for Setting Date Values.

Method	Returns	Usage
setSeconds()	<undefined>	*DateReference*.setSeconds(*secondsArg*) secondsArg is a number from 0 to 59. Set the seconds in the Date reference to the value in secondsArg.
setYear()	<undefined>	*DateReference*.setYear(*yearArg*) yearArg is a number greater than 1970. Changes the year value of the Date reference to the value of yearArg.

TABLE 6-50. Date Methods for Date Conversion

Method	Returns	Usage
getTimeZoneoffset()	a number	*DateReference*.getTimeZoneoffest() Returns the difference in hours between the local time and GMT. Note that although you are executing this method in conjunction with a date reference, you are retrieving a system value from the browser. There is no effect on the date reference.
toGMTString()	a string in date format	*DateReference*.toGMTString() Return a string formatted to GMT in the date/time format.
toLocaleString()	a string in date format	*DateReference*.toLocaleString() Return a string formatted to local date/time format standards.

Event handlers:

```
None
```

Property of:

```
Built into JavaScript language.
```

Getting the current date and time is as simple as declaring a variable and creating an instance of Date without any parameters. By calling new with the Date object without providing any additional information you get a date object for the current date and time according to the browser.

TABLE 6-51. Methods for Date Object Manipulation.

Method	Returns	Usage
getTime()	a number	*DateReference*.getTime() Returns the number of milliseconds from January 1, 1970 to the time represented in the Date reference. Use this method to pass a date object from one variable to another.
parse()	a number	Date.parse(*dateString*) The dateString format is "month day, year hours:minutes:seconds". Returns the number of milliseconds since January 1, 1970 to the date specified in the dateString. parse() is a method of the Date object itself. You do not specify a data reference.
setTime()	<undefined>	*DateReference*.setTime(*timeArg*) timeArg is a number which represents the number of milliseconds since 1/1/1970 which is assigned to the Date reference directly. No value is returned.
UTC()	a number	Date.UTC(*year, month, day* [,*hrs* [,*min* [,*sec*]]]) year, month, day, hrs, min, and sec are numbers representing their appropriate quantities. The year is after 1970. Returns the number of milliseconds since 1/1/1970 and the date specified in Universal Coordinated Time (or GMT). Note that UTC() is not called with a Date reference, but directly from the Date object itself.

```
var v_date = new Date() // puts the current date
                        // and time into v_date
```

Internally, JavaScript stores the date as the number of milliseconds since January 1, 1970. Dates prior to 1970 are not supported in JavaScript.

getYear

A comment on getYear() is called for here. As close as we are to the year 2000, it is surprising and a little upsetting that the designers of JavaScript haven't incorporated a full four-digit year into their work. Using just the last two digits, it is possible to assume that a year of "00" is talking about the year 2000, especially since dates prior to 1970 aren't supported (yet). All of the problems associated with sorting dates and keeping code which deals with dates clean would be solved if the designers of JavaScript would abandon the old practices of using two digits for a date.

Write the developers of JavaScript at Netscape and let them know that if they expect their product to be around for the next couple of years, they need to accommodate the pending change at the year 2000.

Built-in Methods

Up to this point, all methods have been associated with some type of object, either built into the JavaScript language like the Math, String, or Date objects, or attached to a window hierarchy. There is another class of methods which are not associated with any object and can be called without reference to an object. These are called the built-in methods, and they are not called with any objects.

Methods

Client-side: YES   Server-side: YES

```
escape()
eval()
parsefloat()
parseint()
unescape()
```

TABLE 6-52. Built-in Methods of JavaScript Itself.

Method	Returns	Usage
escape()	a string representation of a number in the form "%xx"	escape(*oneCharacterString*) *oneCharacterString* is a single character in a string, such as "a". Returns the ASCII encoding of the character in string form.

TABLE 6-52. (Continued) Built-in Methods of JavaScript Itself.

Method	Returns	Usage
isNaN()	boolean	isNaN(*argument*) *argument* is the value you want to test to see if it is "Not a Number". Returns true if the argument is a number; returns false if not. NOTE: At this writing, this function is only available on UNIX browsers!
eval()	a value based on the evaluation	eval(*stringToEvaluate*) *stringToEvaluate* is any legal JavaScript statement. If the statement is a numeric expression, the eval() returns that number.
parsefloat()	a number	parsefloat(*stringToEvaluate*) stringToEvaluate must begin with numeric characters which can be evaluated as a floating point number. Returns the number evaluated as *stringToEvaluate*. parsefloat("12.34") == 12.34 parsefloat("12.34zzzz") == 12.34
parseint()	a number	parseint(*stringToEvaluate*, *radix*) *stringtoEvaluate* must begin with numeric characters, which can be evaluated as an integer. *radix* is the base to use when evaluating the string. If radix is absent, base 10 is assumed. Returns the number evaluated. parseint("12") == 12 parseint("12.34") == 12 parseint("12.34zzz") == 12
unescape()	a single character	unescape("*%xxx*") "*%xxx*" is a string where "*xxx*" is a number from 0 to 255. Returns a single character, which is the ISO Latin-1 equivalent of the numeric value.

escape() and unescape()

```
escape("oneCharacterString")
unescape("numberString")
```

oneCharacterString is a non-alphanumeric character in the ISO Latin-1 character set.

numberString is a string containing numbers in one of two forms: "%xxx", where *xxx* is a number from 0 to 255; or, as a hexadecimal number from "0x00" to "0xFF".

Including characters outside of the "a" to "z" or "A" to "Z" range in an HTML document or a JavaScript-created document can be difficult. For instance, a Macintosh has access to a large array of characters from many European languages. However, if you were to create a document using those characters and place it on a Web server, you wouldn't end up with what you expected. Take, for example, the following heading:

```
<H1>Die Münchner Bibliotek</H1>
```

You'd expect the browser to display the "ü" character as you typed it. In fact, as you look at the document on the Web server from your editor (not a browser!), you'd see the "ü". But, what do you see from a browser's point of view? In an attempt to meet the lowest common denominator for all platforms, the browser will not directly display this character. What you end up with is this:

```
Die MŸnchner Bibliotek
```

The only way around this from JavaScript's perspective is to either use the codes for characters in HTML or to use the unescape() method to build the character you need. In Chapter 2, we used the unescape function to create the "á" character.

```
my_form.inHello.value = "Buenas d" + unescape( "%92" ) +
                               "as el mundo!"
```

eval()

```
eval( stringToEvaluate )
```

stringToEvaluate is a JavaScript expression.

Numeric Evaluation. The simplest form of the `eval()` statement is to evaluate a string for its numeric value as a numeric expression. For instance, the string "2 + 3" would evaluate to the numeric value 5. Each of the statements below would accomplish the same thing. Each is a string, or a concatenation of strings which, when put together, can be evaluated as a numeric expression. That expression has the numeric value of 5 ,which is assigned to the variable myVar.

```
var myVar = eval( "2 + 3" );
var myVar = eval( "2" + "+ 3" );
var myVar = eval( "2" + "+" + "3" );
```

JavaScript Evaluation. Another use of the `eval()` statement is to build a JavaScript statement which will be executed when eval() is called. Sometimes it is easier to construct a JavaScript statement out of strings than to create the JavaScript you need.

```
var i, char;
for ( i = 0; i<255; i++ )
{
    eval( "document.write( '<P>' + i + '==>' +
          unescape( %" + i + ") );" )
}
```

This seems a long way around, but let's pull it apart.

```
eval( "document.write( '<P>' + i + '==>' +
      unescape( %" + i + ") );" )
```

Let's take the outer-most quotation marks and resolve them. Assume that "i" has the value 25.

```
eval( "document.write( '<P>' + i + '==>' +
      unescape( %25 ) ); " )
```

The first "i" we come across is inside the double quotation marks, so we won't evaluate it yet. The second "i" was outside the double quotation marks and can be evaluated so we replaced the

```
unescape( %" + i + ")
```

with

```
unescape( %25 )
```

Continuing with eval(), a single string is now inside the following method:

```
"document.write( '<P>' + i + '==>' + unescape( %25 ) )"
```

eval() begins by executing the statement as if it were an independent line of code.

```
document.write( '<P>' + i + '==>' + unescape( %25 ) )
```

We have more levels of quotation marks to resolve at this time. Again, "i" has the value 25 and the method unescape() is called to evaluate its argument and return the letter "B".

```
document.write( '<P>25===>B' )
```

Now, we just execute document.write() is if we'd called it in the first place.

    eval() is effective at building statements which seem difficult to program directly. Remember however, that eval puts a lot of overhead in your code and should be avoided if possible.

parsefloat() and parseint()

```
parsefloat(stringToEvaluate)
parseint(stringToEvaluate, radix)
```

stringToEvaluate is a string that represents the value you want to parse.

    Both parsefloat() and parseint() are built into the JavaScript language and are not associated with any object. In both cases, the *stringToEvaluate* is assumed to contain a string which can be evaluated to a numeric value. Both functions begin at the left and look at the characters one-by-one until a character is found which would not allow the string to be evaluated as a number. At that point, the evaluation stops and the number found so far is evaluated and its value returned. Here are some examples:

```
parsefloat( "-13.44" ) == -13.44
parsefloat( "+13.44-23.44" ) == 13.44
parseint( "13.44" ) == 13
parseint( "0xFE" ) == 254
parseint( "0xFExxxx" ) == 254
parseint( "34", 8 ) == 28
```

```
parseint( "JavaScript" ) == "NaN" or 0
```

In each case, the parsing went as far as it could to find a number. Where it stopped depended on where the string stopped, or where the characters which could be evaluated as a number stopped.

If a string cannot be evaluated as a number at all, the behavior of JavaScript varies based on the platform. The method will return the following:

- 0 on Windows platforms,
- "NaN" on all other platforms (Not a Number).

This is another problem with JavaScript. One of the virtues of Java, the namesake of JavaScript, is that it behaves identically on all platforms which support it. To have JavaScript behave differently based on platform is inconsistent with the goals of the Web browser technology, which is to create platform-independent access to information. Hopefully over time, Netscape will remove these incompatibilities.

On those platforms where "NaN" is returned, all arithmetic operations on the NaN value will result in NaN.

isNaN()

```
isNaN( argument )
```

argument is the value you want to evaluate.

On UNIX browsers, isNaN() evaluates whether the argument is a number. This is best used on the results of parseint() and parsefloat() to determine if the results are a number.

This method is currently only available on UNIX browsers. As with parsefloat() and parseint(), the behavior of the JavaScript should not differ by platform. Because Web browser technology is intended to provide platform-independent access to information, having components of the language which either differ by platform, or are unavailable by platform is a big problem. How can you determine whether the incoming client is going to be able to interpret your code?

One possible solution is to use the navigator properties like userAgent to determine which client is going to execute your JavaScript code and route the flow of program control appropriately.

A better solution in our minds is to avoid all of the components of the language which are not consistent across all platforms. Listing 6-7 demonstrates how a browser behaves to isNaN(). Remember that it is the browser which is executing this code. Although the same document is loaded from the server, different client browser platforms may react differently to it.

```
<HTML>
<!-- File: LIST6_07.HTM
     Usage: determine how isNaN() works on a client

     WARNING: IF isNaN() IS NOT IMPLEMENTED ON YOUR
     BROWSER, THIS SCRIPT WILL CAUSE A JAVASCRIPT ERROR.
  -->
<HEAD>
<TITLE>Test isNaN()</TITLE>
</HEAD>

<BODY>
<P>Below this line is an execution of isNaN() in
   JavaScript.  Remember that it is executing on the
   client and different clients will have different
   behavior.  If you get an error, this means that
   your browser has not implmented isNaN().
<SCRIPT>
document.write( "<P>isNAN = ", isNaN( "SSSSSS" ));
</SCRIPT>
</BODY>
</HTML>
```

LISTING 6-7 USE THIS SCRIPT TO TEST HOW YOUR BROWSER PLATFORM REACTS TO ISNAN().

Listing 6-8 demonstrates a possible way to create a new method, called testIntNaN(), which uses some odd behavior of NaN to determine whether a number was found or not. The code attempts to be self-explanatory, so we won't comment on it here.

```
<HTML>

<!-- File: LIST6_08.HTM
     Usage: demonstrate testIntNaN() for testing whether a
            variable contains a number.
  -->

<HEAD>

<TITLE>
Testing for Integers
</TITLE>

<SCRIPT LANG="JavaScript">
```

LISTING 6-8 A PLATFORM-INDEPENDENT WAY TO TEST WHETHER A NUMBER IS NOT A NUMBER ("NaN").

```
function testIntNaN( vTest )
{

// Name: testIntNaN()
// Usage: test a value to see if it is a number
// Parameters: vTest, the value to be tested
// Returns: true or false based on whether vTest is an
//          integer number
// Problems: "-0" (negative zero) evaluates as not a number
//           and returns false mixed text which begins with
//           a number returns true (e.g. "1xyz")

// testIntNaN() is an attempt to get around a glaring hole
// in the JavaScript language.  There is no uniform way at
// this writing to determine if a variable contains a legal
// number.  isNaN() is only defined to work on the UNIX
// Netscape Browser.
//
// On top of that, the behavior of parseInt() varies between
// Macintosh, UNIX, and Windows.  Under Macintosh and UNIX,
// an illegal number will return "NAN".  Under Windows it
// returns the value zero.
//
// This routine takes advantage of some peculiar behavior of
// the current browser.  I believe that this behavior may
// change in the future and that isNaN() may end up working
// across platforms.  Hence the expected (or hoped for)
// useful life of this function is short.
//
// Ways this procedure could break or be obsolete:
// 1) isNaN() becomes supported on all platforms
// 2) "NAN" can be evaluated as a string using indexOf()
// 3) "NAN" stops evaluating as a negative number

// Use parseInt() to test vTest for being a number.  For
// all platforms a valid number in vTest, where a number
// followed by any arbitrary text (e.g. "123xxxxxx"),
// will evaluate to a number (e.g. "123"). On UNIX and
// Macintosh, a non-number (e.g. "xyz" ) will evaluate to
// "NAN" and on Windows it will evaluate to 0.

   var vResult = parseInt( vTest );

   // OK, hang on to your hats.  Here's some very strange
   // behavior we're going to use.  On UNIX and Macintosh,
   // "NAN" evaluates to a number and not a string, so we
   // can't test for the "NAN" characters.  However, "NAN"
```

LISTING 6-8   (CONTINUED) A PLATFORM-INDEPENDENT WAY TO TEST WHETHER A NUMBER IS NOT A NUMBER ("NaN").

```
   // also evaluates to being less than zero.  (I haven't
   // tested to see which negative number it thinks it is.)
   // One of the behaviors of JavaScript is that when you
   // use NAN in a numeric expression, the result of that
   // expression is also NAN.  So, negate NAN and it is
   // still less than zero.

   if ( ( vResult < 0 ) && ( ( -vResult ) < 0 ) )
   {
      // Using the trick, we found that vTest is not a
      // number
      return false;
   }

// For Windows platforms, parseInt() evaluates non-
// numbers to zero. Note also that zero itself would have
// evaluated to zero, so make sure that if we get vResult
// equaling zero, then zero was really what was in vTest.

   if ( vResult == 0 )
   {
      // Look for "0" in vTest
      var vIdx = vTest.indexOf( "0" )

      if ( ( vIdx == -1 ) || ( vIdx > 0 ) )
      {

   // indexOf() returns -1 if it can't find "0" in the
   // value, which means that we're dealing with the
   // Windows version of parseInt() and vTest is not a
   // number.  If zero appears somewhere other than as
   // the first digit, then we're not dealing with a
   // number either.  This is the spot where "-0" is
   // rejected.
         return false;
      }
   }

   // Either vResult is non-zero or it passed the zero
   // tests.  We have a number!

   return true;
}


function testIt( vTest )
{
```

LISTING 6-8   (CONTINUED) A PLATFORM-INDEPENDENT WAY TO TEST WHETHER A NUMBER IS NOT A NUMBER ("NAN").

```
   var vResult = testIntNaN( vTest );
   var vNum = parseInt( vTest );
   if ( vResult )
   {
      this.document.fo_testNaN.in_outputNaN.value =
      "a number";
   }
   else
   {
      this.document.fo_testNaN.in_outputNaN.value =
      "not a number";
   }
   this.document.fo_testNaN.in_number.value = vNum;
}



</script>
</head>

<body>
<H2>Testing for Integers</H2>

<P> Type something in the field below and click outside
    the field to evaluate whether it is a number of not.
    Note that &quot;-0&quot; evaluates to &quot;not a
    number&quot; and that a mixed string which begins with
    one or more numbers such as &quot;123xyz&quot; will
    evaluate to a number.
<H3>A note on parseInt() evaluations.</H3>

<P> In the absence of a specific radix for evaluating the
    string (we're just calling parseInt() with what you type
    in directly) a leading zero will indicate an octal
    number.  Any digit not 0-7 will stop the numeric
    evaluation.  For example, 0097 will evaluate to 0.
    Likewise, beginning the number with 0x will indicate a
    hexadecimal number and anything outside of 0-F will stop
    the numeric evaluation.

<P> Go ahead and experiment to get an idea of how parseInt()
    works!

<HR>

<form name="fo_testNaN">
   Type something here:
```

LISTING 6-8   (CONTINUED) A PLATFORM-INDEPENDENT WAY TO TEST WHETHER A NUMBER IS NOT A NUMBER ("NAN").

```
    <input name="in_testNaN" type="text" >
    <br>
    Then
    <input name="btn_testNaN" type="button"
          value="click here" onClick="testIt(
this.form.in_testNaN.value )">
    to see the result of the evaluation.
    <br>
    Result of the NaN evaluation:
    <input name="in_outputNaN" type="text" >
    <br>
    The evaluated number:
    <input name="in_number" type="text">
</form>

</body>
</html>
```

LISTING 6-8 (CONTINUED) A PLATFORM-INDEPENDENT WAY TO TEST WHETHER A NUMBER IS NOT A NUMBER ("NaN").

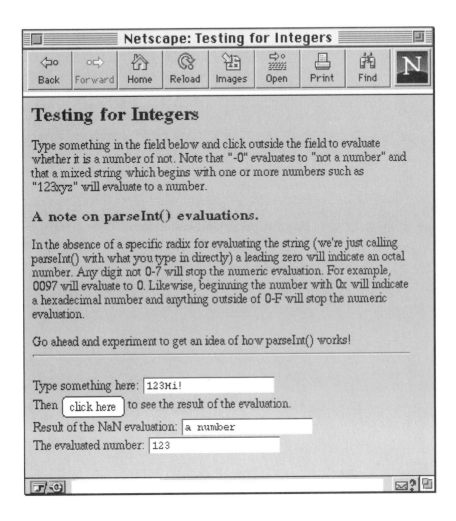

FIGURE 6-31   The page generated by Listing 6-8. Note that the number tested and interpreted by parseInt() stopped at the first character which could not be interpreted as a number.

Scope of Statements

One of the important factors to remember when working with Java-Script is to understand the scope of an object or variable. Because JavaScript will create a variable for you if you haven't declared it explicitly, using an object in a place where it isn't understood will result in a variable being created with that name. When you attempt to use that variable, some property or method of the object you intend will be absent and you'll get the error message:

```
Object has no properties
```

Keeping track of where you are in the hierarchy will help avoid this problem.

with

Client-side: YES   Server-side: YES

```
with (object){statements}
```

If you repeatedly refer to objects, properties, or methods of an object and would like to avoid having to use the object reference repeatedly, the with() statement allows you to declare an object as the default object for all references within a block of code. This means that instead of immediately trying to create a variable of a particular name, JavaScript will first look at the object referenced and determine if the statement's objects can be considered a part of the object referenced in the with() statement.

We saw an example of this in the Math object, where instead of repeatedly using Math.method(), we wrote the following:

```
with (Math)
{
   method();
   method();
   method();
}
```

Any valid object may be used as the referenced object in a with() statement.

this

We've seen earlier that windows and frames have synonyms, and that they can be called using their names. JavaScript has another reserved word in JavaScript for referring to objects.

```
this.objectReference
```

The reserved word "this" provides the complete object reference from within the current object. For instance, Figure 6-32, generated by Listing 6-9, has three forms which have a single text field. In the first two, if a change is made in the field, a function is called. In both cases, the same function is called and a reference to the current form is passed as "this.form". The function then takes the reference and retrieves the name of the form, which is different for each one. Without the "this" synonym, you must pass the name directly. Using "this" helps make functions more flexible since you may want to pass multiple attributes of the form to the function. A single reference to "this.form" is all that is needed.

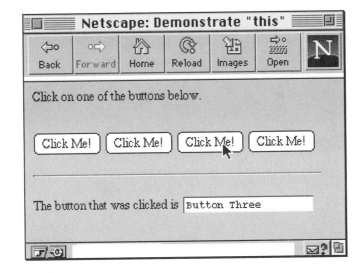

FIGURE 6-32   The page generated by Listing 6-9. The user has clicked on the third button.

```
<HTML>
<!-- File: LIST6_09.HTM
     Usage: show the use of the "this" construct
  -->

<HEAD>
<TITLE>Demonstrate &quot;this&quot;</TITLE>

<SCRIPT lang="JavaScript">

function testIt( aObj )
{
   document.fo_test.in_test.value = aObj.name;
}
</SCRIPT>
</HEAD>

<BODY>
<P>Click on one of the buttons below.
<FORM NAME="fo_test">
   <BR>
   <INPUT NAME="Button One" TYPE="button" VALUE="Click Me!"
          onClick="testIt( this )" >
   <INPUT NAME="Button Two" TYPE="button" VALUE="Click Me!"
          onClick="testIt( this )" >
   <INPUT NAME="Button Three" TYPE="button"
          VALUE="Click Me!"
          onClick="testIt( this )" >
   <INPUT NAME="Button Four" TYPE="button" VALUE="Click Me!"
          onClick="testIt( this )" >
</FORM>
<HR>
<FORM NAME="fo_test">
   <P>The button that was clicked is
   <INPUT NAME="in_test" TYPE="text" >
</FORM>
</BODY>
</HTML>
```

LISTING 6-9 DEMONSTRATE THE USE OF "THIS".

Developing Applications with LiveWire

- **Learn How to Use the LiveWire Compiler to Package JavaScript Applications.**
- **Learn How to Use the LiveWire Application Manager.**

Overview

Developing client/server Internet applications with Java-Script is accomplished through the LiveWire compiler and server extensions. The LiveWire compiler packages HTML files with embedded JavaScript into a LiveWire application. The LiveWire server extensions give a standard Netscape Web server the ability to understand server-side JavaScript and provide a facility to manage LiveWire applications.

This chapter will focus on the steps involved in creating LiveWire applications. Included will be instructions on how to use the LiveWire Application Manager to add and manipulate LiveWire applications. Three major steps are involved in deploying a LiveWire application:

1. Creating the source files.

2. Compiling the source files with the LiveWire command-line compiler.

3. Installing and debugging the application with the LiveWire Application Manager.

Creating the Source Files

As mentioned, the first step in the application development process is to create the source files. You can create the source files using any text editor or, if you prefer, you can use Netscape Navigator Gold. When developing a LiveWire application, two different types of source files can be created:

- HTML files with an `.html` or `.htm` extension.
- JavaScript function files with a `.js` extension.

Creating HTML Files

The LiveWire compiler can package any number of HTML files. These files can be standard HTML files, or they can contain some combination of client-side and server-side JavaScript. As previously stated, client-side Java-Script can be included in an HTML page using the `<SCRIPT>` tag introduced in Chapter 2.

Server-side JavaScript can be included in an HTML page using two different methods:

- `<SERVER>` tag.
- Backquote (`` ` ``) character.

This section focuses on how to include JavaScript in HTML and not on JavaScript itself. For an in-depth presentation of the server-side JavaScript language components see Chapter 8.

The <SERVER> Tag

You were introduced to the `<SERVER>` tag in Chapter 3. As mentioned, the `<SERVER>` tag is used to begin any number of server-side JavaScript statements in an HTML page. It requires a closing `</SERVER>` tag to end the code section.

The `<SERVER>` tag has its limitations—it is *invalid* to use the `<SERVER>` tag within other HTML tags. The following server-side JavaScript statements will *not* be executed:

```
<!-- These are invalid -->
<A HREF=<SERVER>write(request.myurl)</SERVER>>Link</A>
<IMG SRC=<SERVER>write(request.mypic)</SERVER>>
```

The Backquote (`) Character

The second method of including server-side JavaScript in HTML is with the backquote (`) character. The backquote is used to solve the problem illustrated previously so that server-side JavaScript expressions can be included within other HTML tags. A `write()` is not required because using the backquotes will automatically write the content of the enclosed expression.

```
<!-- These are valid -->
<A HREF=`request.myurl`>Link</A>
<IMG SRC=`request.mypic`>
```

Creating JavaScript Function Files

Any functions included in an HTML page can only be called from that page. It is for this reason that LiveWire supports JavaScript function files. These files with a `.js` extension are used to store server-side JavaScript functions so they can be called by multiple HTML files. A `.js` file can contain any number of JavaScript functions. In these files, JavaScript statements not contained in functions are ignored.

JavaScript function files can be very useful for developing libraries of related JavaScript functions. These files allow the included functions to be reused without duplication in each page that needs to access them. When calling one of these functions in a page, it is not necessary to explicitly refer to the appropriate `.js` file. Any function in a `.js` file included in a particular application can be called by any page of that application.

JavaScript function files can also be used to share code with multiple applications. However, every application that wants to use the files explicitly must include them during the compilation process.

 It is important to note that these JavaScript function files only apply to server-side JavaScript code! You may not call these functions in client-side JavaScript sections of an HTML page, but only in server-side JavaScript sections.

You should also avoid having two functions with the same name included in an application. If the following files were compiled into a LiveWire application, which of the duplicate functions gets executed would depend on the order that the files were compiled. The LiveWire compiler would not report an error when building the application and the last definition processed by the compiler would be the one that is used.

Here is the file `a1.js`

```
function a(parm1)
{
        return --parm1;
}
```

The file `a2.js`:

```
function a(parm2)
{
        return ++parm2;
}
```

Here is the file `home.htm` with the ambiguous call to the `function a()`:

```
<SERVER>
write(a(5));
</SERVER>
```

Compiling the Source Files

The second step in the application development process is to package the source HTML and JavaScript function files into a single `.web` file. Netscape servers with LiveWire extensions installed do not automatically process server-side JavaScript in raw HTML files.

In other words, if you were to simply drop an HTML file containing server-side JavaScript into the document root directory, it would not be executed. The client-side JavaScript would be sent to the client and executed as normal. However, the server-side JavaScript would also be sent to the client! It would not be executed, but the source would be displayed as part of the HTML page. The following example illustrates this:

```
<SERVER>x=5;write(x);</SERVER>
<SCRIPT>y=10;document.write(y);</SCRIPT>
<P>This is a test.</P>
```

```
x=5;write(x); 10

This is a test.
```

It is for this reason that HTML files containing server-side JavaScript must be compiled and packaged into a .web file. Only server-side JavaScript contained in a .web file and installed with the LiveWire Application Manager will be executed on the server.

Avoid developing your LiveWire application in the Web server document root or its sub-directories. Server-side JavaScript is intended to be secure and the actual code will never be seen by the client if compiled into a .web file. You may have database connect statements in server-side JavaScript that reveal passwords or have other sensitive information that you do not want the client to have access to. If you develop your LiveWire applications in the Web server document root or its sub-directories you are providing a way for the client to view your server-side JavaScript code as illustrated in the previous example.

The LiveWire Command-line Compiler

The following is the syntax of the command-line compiler:

```
lwcomp [-cdv] -o BinaryFile SourceFile_1 ... SourceFile_n
```

The switches in [ ] are optional. Table 7-1 summarizes the command-line switches and parameters.

TABLE 7-1. Required and optional parameters for the LiveWire command-line compiler.

Parameter	Description	Explanation
-c (optional)	check only	Use this option to verify the syntax of an application without compiling it into a .web file.
-d (optional)	debug output	Use this option to display the generated content of the source files.
-v (optional)	verbose output	Use this option to monitor the compiler's progress in reading and compiling your source files and to report when the .web has been written.
-o *BinaryFile* (required)	output file	Use this option to specify the name of the .web file.
SourceFile (required)	source files	Use this option to specify the source HTML and JavaScript function files.

The LiveWire compiler makes every attempt to catch syntax errors in your source code. Consider the following example where `oops.htm` contains a server-side JavaScript `for` loop with the {...} and (...) switched:

```
<SERVER>
for {x=0; x<10; x++}
(
        write(x);
)
</SERVER>
```

Now, go ahead and check the syntax of the file using the `-c` command-line switch:

```
lwcomp -v -c oops.htm
```

```
Livewire Compiler Version xx
Copyright (C) Netscape Communications Corporation xxxx
All rights reserved
Reading file oops.htm
Compiling file oops.htm
Error: line 5: missing ( after for:
for {x=0; x<10; x++}
....^
```

As expected, the compiler reports an error. Now, let's try the same invalid syntax again, except we will change the code section to client-side JavaScript:

```
<SCRIPT>
for {x=0; x<10; x++}
(
        document.write(x);
)
</SCRIPT>
```

If you were to compile the above code, no error would be reported. **The LiveWire compiler only checks the syntax of server-side JavaScript code!** So, client-side JavaScript code must be verified separately using Netscape Navigator.

Using the LiveWire Application Manager to Install and Debug your Applications

The third step in the application development process is to install the .web file as an application and verify its correct operation using the LiveWire Application Manager. The Application Manager allows you to perform the following functions:

- Add a new application and modify an existing application.
- Delete an existing application.
- Start, Stop, or Restart an application.
- Run or Debug an application.

If you have the LiveWire server extensions installed and enabled on your Netscape server, you can access the Application Manager using the following URL: "http://hostname/appmgr/", where you replace hostname with the actually hostname of your Netscape Web server.

Make sure that you restrict access to the Application Manager URL. To do this, you must go to the Programs\LiveWire area in the Netscape Administration Server which has an option to require the administration server password for the LiveWire Application Manager. If you don't enable this option, anyone could delete an application off your server!

You must connect to the Application Manager using Netscape Navigator 2.x or higher because it makes use of frames and, of course, client-side JavaScript. When you connect, you should see something similar to Figure 7-1.

Adding and Modifying an Application

To add an application, click on the Add link in the Applications frame of the Application Manager. A form is then displayed in the Information frame as in Figure 7-2.

Table 7-2 explains the purpose of each of the form elements in the Add Application page.

Once you enter this information, click the Enter button to add the application and automatically start it. If for some reason you need to change one of the values for a given application, click on that application in the list and select the Modify link. A form is displayed similar to Add Application that allows you to change every element except the name of the application.

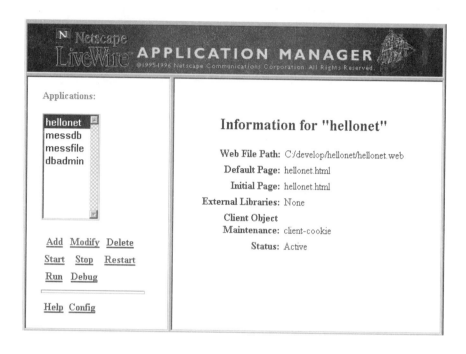

FIGURE 7-1   The LiveWire Application Manager.

Deleting an Existing Application

If you want to remove an application, simply click on the application in the LiveWire Application Manager list and select the Delete link. You will be prompted to confirm that you want to delete the application in question. The application manager stops the application and removes its entry in the LiveWire configuration file. However, it does not physically delete the .web file or the source. If you want to do this, you must do it manually.

Starting, Stopping, or Restarting an Application

A LiveWire application can be in two possible states:

- Stopped
- Active

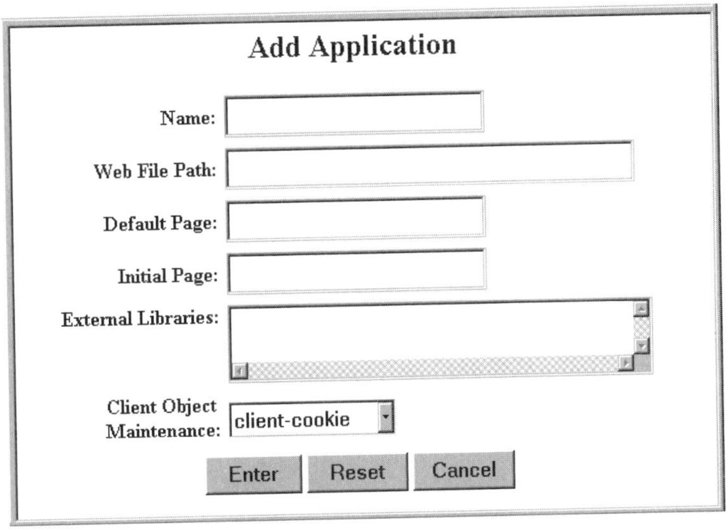

Add Application

Name:	
Web File Path:	
Default Page:	
Initial Page:	
External Libraries:	
Client Object Maintenance:	client-cookie

Enter   Reset   Cancel

FIGURE 7-2   The form presented when adding an application to LiveWire.

TABLE 7-2. Form elements of the Add Application Frame.

Element	Description
Name (required)	This is the name of the application. This name is used as the base URL for accessing the application. For example, if you named an application "order", the base URL for the application would be "http://hostname/order/". If an order sub-directory existed in the Web server document root, the HTML files in that directory would not be accessible via the Web when the LiveWire application was installed using the same name.
Web File Path (required)	This is the full operating system path to .web file created with the LiveWire compiler.
Client Object Maintenance (required)	The server-side JavaScript client object with its associated properties can be maintained using several different techniques. Not all techniques work in every environment, so you must choose the technique required for your application environment. See the section on the client object in Chapter 8 for more details.

TABLE 7-2. (Continued) Form elements of the Add Application Frame.

Default Page (optional)	This is the page that gets displayed when only the base URL for the application is specified.
Initial Page (optional)	This page gets executed the first time a user connects to an application. After the initial access to the application, the default page will be displayed instead.
External Libraries (optional)	Server-side JavaScript has the ability to call operating system shared libraries (.dll for Windows or .so for UNIX). This is where you specify those libraries.

If a particular application is stopped, it will be unavailable to users. You can tell what the current status of an application is by clicking on its name in the list in the Application Manager. The Information frame gives all of the details about the application, including its current status, stopped or active.

Table 7-3 suggests when and for what reasons you would want to start, stop, or restart an application.

TABLE 7-3. Reasons for changing the state of a LiveWire application.

Operation	Use
Start	Use this option to start a stopped application.
Stop	Use this option to stop an active application. You may want to temporarily stop an application and make it unavailable to your users. For example, if you were doing database maintenance on the database that the application connects to, you would probably want to stop the application until the maintenance is complete.
Restart	Use this option to restart an active application. This option is valuable when you have made changes to an application and have recompiled it and you want those changes to take effect without stopping the application.

Running or Debugging an Application

Once a LiveWire application has been successfully compiled and installed, you may access the application using the following URL:

```
http://hostname/applname/pagename.html
```

As previously explained, `hostname` refers to the name of the Web server with LiveWire installed, `applname` refers to the name of the application as specified when the application was added in the Application Manager, and `pagename` refers to any of the HTML documents that were compiled as part of the `applname` project. If `pagename` is not specified, you are connected to the default page for this project as reported to the LiveWire Application Manager when the application was added.

Because JavaScript is a run-time language, only certain syntax errors can be caught by the compiler. If you try to perform an operation on a variable that is not yet defined, the compiler will not complain about it. Most of the debugging of server-side JavaScript code will need to be done while the application is active. It is for this reason that the Application Manager has a debugging facility.

To access the debugging facility, choose the application you want to debug from the list in the LiveWire Application Manager and click on the <u>Debug</u> link or use the following URL where `applname` is the name of the application:

```
http://hostname/appmgr/debug.html?name=applname
```

Either way, something similar to Figure 7-3 will be displayed. The trace screen shot is for the "Hello Net" application created in Chapter 3.

The left frame is the debugger's trace window. The right frame actually contains the running program. In the trace window, the debugger reports when the following events occur:

- When an object is created.
- When a value is assigned to a property.
- When a particular page is requested.
- When a database operation has occurred, if any.
- When a run-time error occurs.

In addition to the standard information that is reported in the trace window, you can report additional information using the top-level server-side JavaScript function `debug()`. As with the `write()` function, the `debug()` function accepts any valid server-side JavaScript expression. The difference is that with the `debug()` function, the result appears in the trace window instead of the application window.

Some restrictions apply when debugging LiveWire applications:

- The debugger's trace facility should only be running once per application at the same time. The Navigator meteor shower will never stop while trace is running.

```
Creating request object:          Hello Net!
yourname = "Brian"
ip = "1.2.3.4"
protocol = "HTTP/1.0"             I know the following things about you:
method = "POST"
agent = "Mozilla/2.01Gold           • Your IP address is 1.2.3.4.
(Win95; I)"                         • Your Browser is Mozilla/2.01Gold (Win95; I).
                                    • Using the HTTP/1.0 protocol, you used the POST method
Creating client object:               to retrieve this document.
counter = "0"                       • You have previously accessed this application 1 times.
                                    • You reported your name to be Brian.
Creating server object:
hostname = "hostname"            Let me tell you a little about myself:
host = "hostname"
protocol = "http:"                  • My hostname is hostname.
port = "80"                         • This application has been accessed 2 times.
counter = "3"                       • This server has been accessed 4 times.

Serving page...
Property assignment:
client.counter = "1"
Property assignment:
project.counter = "2"
Property assignment:
server.counter = "4"

Final client object:
counter = "1"
```

FIGURE 7-3   Tracing the "Hello Net" application.

- Only one client should connect to the application while the trace facility is operating.

Controlling Access to your LiveWire Applications

As with the LiveWire Application Manager, by default, anyone can access a LiveWire Application once it is installed. When developing intranet and some Internet applications, it may be necessary to restrict access to certain users or domains. You can do this by applying a configuration style to the URL for the secure application. See your Web server documentation for details.

Creating a LiveWire Application for your Web Server's Root

In addition to being able to add LiveWire applications that map to URL paths below the server's root, i.e., `http://hostname/applname/page-name.html`, you can also map a single LiveWire application to replace the server's standard document root:

```
http://hostname/pagename.html
```

You do this by selecting the Config link in the LiveWire Application Manager. After selecting the Config link, the window in Figure 7-4 appears in the "Information" frame of the Application Manager.

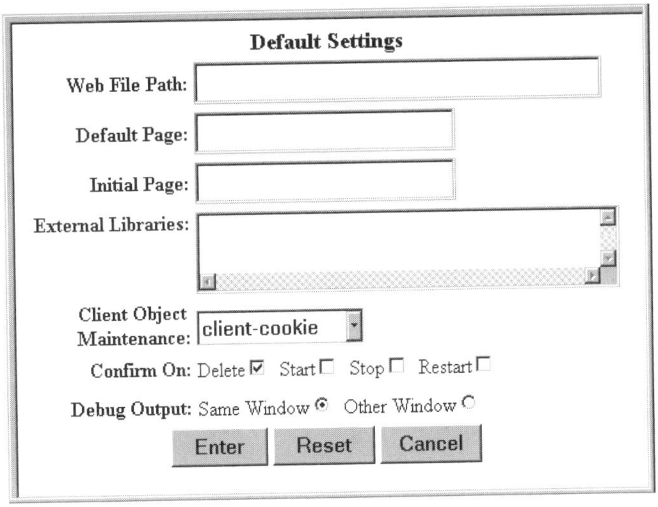

Default Settings

Web File Path:

Default Page:

Initial Page:

External Libraries:

Client Object Maintenance: client-cookie

Confirm On: Delete ☑ Start ☐ Stop ☐ Restart ☐

Debug Output: Same Window ⦿ Other Window ○

Enter   Reset   Cancel

FIGURE 7-4   The LiveWire Application Manager Default Settings.

As with other LiveWire applications, you must enter the Web file path, the default page, and so forth. Once you click the Enter button, your server root will be mapped to this LiveWire application and the standard document root will be inaccessible as long as the application is installed.

Changing Application Manager Settings

In this same <u>Settings</u> window, you can also configure the behavior of certain features of the Application Manager. Specifically, you can choose which Application Manager operations will require confirmation before they are performed. If you have a critical application that needs high availability, you may want to check the "confirm on stop" check-box to insure that you don't inadvertently stop the application.

If you would prefer not to have the debugger's trace page and the running program in the same window, you can change Debug Output to Other Window. If you do this, selecting Debug in the Application Manager will bring up the trace window and the application window in separate Navigator windows rather than as two frames of the same Navigator window.

Summary

In this chapter, you learned the steps involved in creating a LiveWire application. You also learned in detail how to accomplish this by using the LiveWire command-line compiler and LiveWire Application Manager. Now you must learn how to create server-side JavaScript to include in the HTML files as part of your applications. This is the subject of Chapter 8.

Server-side JavaScript Language

- Objects and functions shared with client-side JavaScript.
- Top-level functions.
- Pre-defined objects, their properties, and methods.
- Object-types, their properties, and methods.

Overview

The JavaScript language, in itself, is the same in both client-side and server-side JavaScript. This means that you can use the same statements (i.e., `for`, `if`, `while`, `function`, `return`) and the same operators (i.e., `+`, `=`, `<`, `&&`) in server-side JavaScript as you learned to use with client-side JavaScript in Chapter 5. However, some differences exist in the objects, object-types, and functions offered on the client versus what is offered on the server.

This chapter will focus on server-side JavaScript language components. Specifically, these major areas will be addressed:

- Objects and functions shared with client-side JavaScript.
- Top-level functions.
- Pre-defined objects, their properties, and methods.
- Object-types, their properties, and methods.

To clarify, <u>top-level functions</u> are functions that are not associated with any particular object and can be called without any object qualifier. A <u>pre-defined object</u> is unique—only one object of this type can exist in the current scope. The system automatically handles the creation of these objects. An <u>object-type</u> is a functional attribute where many objects can have the same object-type and their creation is determined by the programmer.

Objects and Functions Shared with client-side JavaScript

Figure 8-1 illustrates the functions, pre-defined objects, and object-types that are shared with client-side JavaScript. Refer to Chapter 6 for more information on these items since the syntax and semantics are exactly the same for server-side JavaScript as in client-side JavaScript.

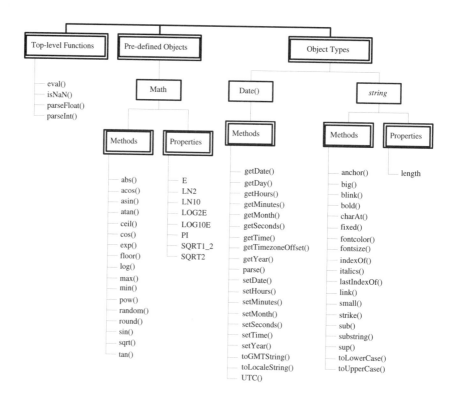

FIGURE 8-1   The components of JavaScript common to both the client and the server.

Top-level Functions

The diagram in Figure 8-2 shows all of the current server-side Java-Script top-level functions.

These functions are used for the following general activities:

- Generating output.
- Redirecting a page to a new URL.

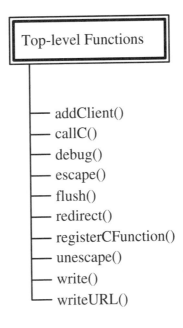

FIGURE 8-2   Server-side JavaScript top-level functions.

- Maintaining the client object.
- Adding values to URL query strings.
- Calling external libraries.

Generating Output

The following functions are used in generating output where *expression* is any valid server-side JavaScript expression:

- `debug(expression)` is used to display the value of an expression in the debugger's trace facility.

See the section on debugging in Chapter 7 for more information on the trace facility. You can use this function to extend the trace facility so that it will report information that will assist in debugging your specific application. For example, you may want to report the value returned from one of your user-defined functions to ensure that a particular value is being calculated correctly. The end user never sees the results of using the debug function; the results are meant only for the programmer using the trace facility. Below is a common example of the use of the debug() function:

```
debug("Invoice Discount = "+discount(request.totalamt))
```

- write(*expression*) is used to output the value of a server-side JavaScript expression to the client browser.

 tip It is the responsibility of the programmer to make sure that the expression and associated HTML tags make sense at the current position in the HTML page. Often, the expression will need to include HTML tags along with data values so the output isn't just one continuous stream of unformatted text.

Using the write() function in conjunction with conditional expressions such as while or if allow the server-side JavaScript programmer the ability to generate dynamic output based on user input or other run-time information.

The following example demonstrates the use of a conditional expression to generate dynamic output. Notice that the opening and closing <P> paragraph tags and the opening and closing <B> bold tags are included within the write expression—this is done to ensure the proper formatting of the data on the client:

```
if (request.method == "POST")
{
    write("<P>The total amount of the invoice is <B>"
        +request.totalamt+"</B></P>.")
}
```

- flush() is used to send the data from previous write statements to the client browser. It requires no parameters. It returns true if successful and false if unsuccessful.

To ensure good performance, data are not sent to the client after each write statement but are buffered and sent over in large blocks. The flush() statement forces LiveWire to send the current buffered data to the client.

Redirecting a page to a new URL

The redirect(*URL*) function is used to immediately redirect the current page to the page specified by the *URL* parameter. The URL may be either relative or absolute, i.e., it doesn't necessarily need to be a page contained within the current LiveWire application, but it could be.

For example, you may create a LiveWire application that makes use of both server-side and client-side JavaScript. You can create a server-side Java-Script function to check the version number of the browser to determine if it supports client-side JavaScript. If the browser is not valid, you can redirect to a page explaining this. Without the use of redirection, the default page for the application would be sent to the client browser. The browser would not display the page correctly without client-side JavaScript support.

```
<SERVER>
// Check user agent
if (!ValidAgent())
        redirect("invalid.htm");
</SERVER>
```

Maintaining the Client Object

The `addClient()` and `writeURL()` functions are associated with maintaining the state of the `client` object when using the `client` URL and `server` URL methods. A brief description follows, but you should see the `client` object section of this chapter for more detailed information:

- `addClient()` is used to add the client object properties to a URL.
- `writeURL()` is used to generate a URL that preserves the URL encoding scheme.

Adding Values to URL Query Strings

The `escape()` and `unescape()` functions are used to encode and decode character strings with non-alphanumeric values. The `escape()` function can be used to manually add property values to a URL query string. Table 8-1 represents the translation that takes place when a string is encoded using the `escape()` function.

TABLE 8-1. The character encoding scheme used by `escape()` *and* `unescape()`*.*

Character	Encoded Character
A-Z, a-z, 0-9	same
space	+
all other characters	%*xx*, where *xx* is the hexadecimal ASCII value of the character.

Calling External Libraries

The following functions are associated with calling external operating system libraries. Please refer to your LiveWire documentation for more details on the use of these functions.

- `callC()` is used to call an external function in server-side JavaScript that is contained in an operating system shared library.
- `registerCFunction()` is used to register an external function which will be used in server-side JavaScript.

Re-mapping Top-level Functions

 warning   Do not create user-defined functions with the same name as built-in top-level functions.

The compiler or run-time environment does not check to see if you have created user-defined functions with the same name as a built-in top-level function. If you create such a function, you will not have access to the system function of the same name. Consider the following example:

```
<SERVER>
function redirect(url)
{
    write("<P>This top-level function has been re-
mapped.");
    write("You would have been redirected to the
URL:</P>");
    write("<P ALIGN=CENTER>"+url+"</P>");
}
redirect("http://www.foo.bar/");
</SERVER>
```

```
This top-level function has been re-mapped. You would have
been redirected to the URL:

http://www.foo.bar/
```

Pre-defined Objects, their Properties, and Methods

As previously stated, pre-defined objects are a class of objects that have only one object of each type. The system automatically handles the creation of these objects. The following pre-defined objects are more or less just containers for programmer-defined properties—which object is chosen generally depends on the lifetime requirements of the property. Each of these objects has a slightly different purpose and lifetime.

request. This object contains data from the current request for this page. The `request` object contains properties for each of the HTML form elements and/or URL query string values submitted to the current page. It also contains some pre-defined properties associated with the request, such as the IP address of the client that issued the request. The `request` object is initialized each time the Web server responds to a request from a browser.

client. The `client` object stores data for an individual Web browser. This is the object used to keep state between each client and the server so the server knows what the client has done previously. A `client` object exists for each Web browser that accesses the server.

project. The `project` object contains data common to the entire application. This object can be used to share data between multiple clients using the same application. The properties of this object remain until the current application is restarted.

server. The `server` object contains data common to all applications on the server. The properties of this object remain until the Web server is restarted.

tip   Server-side object properties are always stored as strings. The properties of request, client, project, and server are stored as strings even if the actual value stored is numeric. You must use the standard parseInt and parseFloat to extract numeric values.

Since numeric server-side object properties are stored as strings, you must use `parseInt` or `parseFloat` before performing any operations on those properties. For example, when incrementing an integer stored in the `client` object, you must first convert it back to a number from a string:

```
client.value1=25
client.value1=1+parseInt(client.value1,10)
```

In addition to the four standard server-side objects, the `database` object and its associated methods are used to connect to and query SQL databases.

Figure 8-3 summarizes all pre-defined server-side JavaScript objects with their methods and properties.

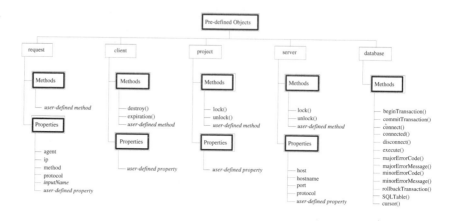

FIGURE 8-3   Server-side JavaScript's pre-defined objects.

The `request` Object

The `request` object for the current page is initialized whenever the client browser requests a copy of that page from the Web server. The client browser may request the page using one of these HTTP retrieval methods:

- GET - This method retrieves the entire content of the requested page in the response, including both the header and body. The GET method is used when you click on an HTML hot-link, or when you manually select a URL in your browser.
- HEAD - This method is identical to GET except the server does not return the body of the page in the response.
- POST - This method is used to request that the Web server accept information from the client browser. One common use of the POST method is to provide a block of data to the server as the result of submitting an HTML form.

Table 8-2 lists the pre-defined properties of the `request` object.

Using the `request.agent` Property to Verify a Browser

The function in Listing 8-1 uses the `request.agent` property to see if the current client browser is Netscape Navigator 2.0 or higher. Based on what is returned from `ValidAgent()`, the program can adapt to use only

TABLE 8-2. The properties of the `request` ***object.***

Property	Description
agent	This property reports the name and version number of the client browser issuing the request. For Netscape Navigator 3.0 Gold running in Windows 95, the following `agent` would be reported: `Mozilla/3.0Gold (Win95; I)`. This can be used to display a dynamic page based on the level of HTML and JavaScript supported by the browser.
ip	This property reports the IP address of the client browser issuing the request. This can be used to display a dynamic page based on the user's location. This is reported as a standard dot-notation address of the form *nnn.nnn.nnn.nnn*, where *nnn* is the decimal representation of a single byte quantity.
method	This property reports the HTTP method used to request the page, i.e., GET, HEAD, or POST.
protocol	This property reports the level of HTTP supported by the browser. This is reported as `HTTP/Version`, such as `HTTP/1.0`.

those techniques supported by the browser, or it can simply require a certain version number to access the application.

Automatically Setting Properties of the `request` Object

In addition to the pre-defined properties, other properties of the `request` object are automatically set using the following techniques:

- Submitting a form.
- Adding a query component to a URL.

Submitting a Form

Submitting a form to a page populates the `request` object with properties and values for each form element on the page. Consider the following code from `hellonet.htm` in Chapter 3:

```
...
<SERVER>
// Only report name if value posted from form
if (request.method == "POST")
{
    write("<LI>You reported your name to be <B>"
        +request.yourname+"</B>.")
}
```

```
function ValidAgent()
{
   agent_name = request.agent.substring(0,
               request.agent.indexOf("/")).toUpperCase();
   agent_version = parseFloat(request.agent.substring(
               request.agent.indexOf("/") + 1,
               request.agent.length));
   if (agent_name == "MOZILLA")
   {
      if (agent_version < 2.0)
      {
         // Using an Older Version of Netscape Navigator
         valid = false;
      }
      else
      {
         // Using a Correct Version of Netscape Navigator
         valid = true;
      }
   }
   else
   {
      // Not Using Netscape Navigator
      valid = false;
   }
   return valid;
}
```

LISTING 8-1   VERIFY THAT THE CURRENT BROWSER IS NETSCAPE NAVIGATOR 2.0 OR HIGHER.

```
</SERVER>
...
<SERVER>
if (request.method == "GET")
{
    write("<P>Tell me more about yourself:</P>")
    write("<FORM METHOD=\"POST\"
ACTION=\"hellonet.htm\">")
    write("<UL>")
    write("<LI>Enter your name: ")
    write("<INPUT TYPE=\"TEXT\" NAME=\"yourname\"
size=20>")
    write("</UL>")
```

```
write("<INPUT TYPE=\"SUBMIT\" VALUE=\"Submit\">")
write("<INPUT TYPE=\"RESET\" VALUE=\"Reset\">")
write("</FORM>")
}
...
```

The form contains a TEXT box input type with the name `yourname`. When this form is submitted, the `request` object automatically contains the `request.yourname` property with the value entered in the form.

In this example, the same page is used to both display and process the form depending on the value of `request.method`. However, we could have just as easily had separate pages for displaying the form and processing it. In this case, we would not have needed to check for the `request.method`.

If you want to retain form values set in the `request` **object, you must assign them to an object with a longer lifetime, such as the** `client` **object**; otherwise, the values will be lost on the next request for the page as the object will be reinitialized. Something similar to the following code would work to retain the `yourname` value beyond the next request for `hellonet.htm` from the current browser:

```
client.yourname = request.yourname
```

Adding a Query Component to a URL

Those name/value pairs included with a base URL are automatically assigned to the `request` object as properties. The syntax for including name/value pairs with a URL is

```
baseURL?name1=value1&name2=value2&name3=value3
```

The name/value pairs begin with a question mark (?) after the base URL and are separated by the ampersand (&). If you only want to include one name/value pair, you do not need to use the ampersand. The link below illustrates the use of a query component to a URL:

```
<A HREF= "hellonet.htm?city=New+York&age=25">Hello
Net!</A>
```

If `hellonet.htm` is accessed using this link, the `request` object will contain a `request.city` property with a value of `"New York"` and a `request.age` property with a value of `"25"`. The values specified in the URL must have non-alphanumeric values encoded and the spaces replaced with the plus (+) character. The top-level server-side function `escape()` will encode a string according to this criteria. These values will be retained as properties of the `request` object for this page as long as they remain included with the base URL.

The `client` **Object**

The `client` object is used to store data for each Web browser that connects to an application. This is very important because it provides a way for the Web server to retain information about the client across multiple requests.

A `client` object is associated with each browser that accesses the Web server. However, a browser can only have access to its own `client` object. By default, if a browser does not access the Web server for ten minutes, the `client` object for this browser is destroyed and will be reinitialized the next time this browser accesses the server. This is done because there is no guarantee in the connection-less environment of HTTP that the browser will ever return and the server must free up valuable system resources.

The following two methods can be used to affect the lifetime of the `client` object:

- `client.expiration(`*seconds*`)` is used to alter the standard expiration time for the client object. If the browser does not access the server within the seconds specified, the client object will be expired.
- `client.destroy()` is used to force the current client object to expire now and be reinitialized.

Unlike the `request` object, the `client` object has no pre-defined values. The programmer can use the `client` object to store application data related to a specific browser. In the "Hello Net" application of Chapter 3, the `client.counter` property was created to keep track of how many times each browser accessed the application.

```
if (client.counter == null)
    client.counter = 0;
else
    client.counter = parseInt(client.counter,10) + 1;
```

As mentioned previously, the client object can be used to retain information across multiple requests. Let's say you have an application that requires the customer to enter an ID number in a form. Rather than requiring the customer to re-enter the ID after every submission, you could store the ID in the `client` object.

```
...
<SERVER>
if (request.method == "POST")
```

```
{
    client.custid = request.custid;
}
</SERVER>
...
<INPUT TYPE="TEXT" NAME="custid" SIZE="15" MAXLENGTH="30"
`(client.custid != null) ? "VALUE='" + client.custid +"'"
: " "`>
...
```

The above example uses server-side backquotes and a conditional expression to set the VALUE parameter of the `custid` input text box. If a value exists for `client.custid`, it will be the default value for the input box. In this way, the customer is not required to re-enter the ID in the input box after the first time until the `client` object expires.

Maintenance Techniques for the `client` Object

The `client` object with its associated properties can be maintained using several different techniques. You choose the technique when you add the application in the LiveWire Application Manager. Not all techniques work in every environment and, depending on your needs, one technique may be more suited to your application than another. You must choose the best technique for your application environment.

- `client-cookie` stores the client object properties on the browser using the Netscape Cookie Protocol.
- `client-url` encodes the client object properties as name/value pairs as part of the URL.
- `server-ip` stores the client object properties on the server based on the IP address of the browser.
- `server-cookie` stores a generated key on the browser using the Netscape cookie protocol. It stores the client object properties on the server based on the key stored in the browser.
- `server-url` encodes a generated key as part of the URL and it stores the client object properties on the server based on the key encoded in the URL.

When using either the client-cookie or client-url technique, you must ensure that any changes to the client object are made before executing the top-level flush() function. You must also make sure that those changes are made before 64K bytes of data are sent to the browser because an automatic flush() is performed at that point.

Using `client-cookie` to Maintain the client object

By choosing `client-cookie`, LiveWire uses the Netscape Cookie Protocol to send name/value pairs to the browser from the Web server. These name/value pairs are stored in a cookie file on the browser.

The `client-cookie` technique has the following restrictions on the amount and size of the client object properties:

- A maximum of twenty properties can be stored per application.
- Each property can have a maximum size of 4096 characters, including both the name and the value.
- **And most importantly, your browser must support the Netscape Cookie Protocol.** Netscape Navigator 1.1 or higher supports the Cookie Protocol, as does Microsoft Internet Explorer 2.0 or higher.

If these restrictions are unacceptable, you will need to choose another technique.

Using the `client-cookie` Technique to Communicate between Client-side and Server-side JavaScript

Client-side and server-side JavaScript are not dependent on each other in any way. They operate independent of each other and they share only one common data-structure between them—the client object and its properties when the `client-cookie` technique is chosen.

Server-side JavaScript can set cookie values by creating or modifying properties of the `client` object if the `client-cookie` state maintenance technique is used. Server-side JavaScript encodes the `client` object properties in the browser cookie associated with the application's base URL. The properties are encoded as follows:

```
NETSCAPE_LIVEWIRE.client_propname=client_propvalue;
```

Client-side JavaScript can retrieve the entire cookie by using the `document.cookie` property. Consider the following example:

```
<HTML>
<BODY>
<SERVER>
client.name = "John Doe";
client.address = "1234 Elm Street";
client.city = "Anytown, USA";
</SERVER>
<SCRIPT>
```

```
document.write(document.cookie);
</SCRIPT>
</BODY>
</HTML>
```

```
NETSCAPE_LIVEWIRE.city=Anytown,+USA;
NETSCAPE_LIVEWIRE.address=1234+Elm+Street;
NETSCAPE_LIVEWIRE.name=John+Doe
```

Having a way to share data between client-side and server-side Java-Script can be very useful. There are certain operations that only client-side JavaScript can perform, such as popping up an alert box. There are also certain operations that only server-side JavaScript can perform, such as accessing a database. A convenient way to pass information between the two is a must for any developer who wants to exploit the strengths of both.

Client-side JavaScript does not have a built-in way to extract the individual elements of the cookie, but we can create some functions that retrieve and decode the properties of the server-side `client` object when they are stored in a cookie. We can also use client-side JavaScript to *set* properties of the server-side `client` object.

Listing 8-2 gives the code for our cookie manipulation functions. The `plus()` and `unplus()` functions are used to encode and decode spaces to pluses (+). The cookie protocol needs spaces converted to pluses for the storage of name/value pairs. The `getclientprop()` function accepts the name of a server-side `client` object property as a parameter and returns its value. The `setclientprop()` function accepts the name and value of a server-side `client` object property and stores it in a cookie according to the `client` object cookie naming conventions.

```
<SCRIPT>
// Replaces the plus (+) encoding with a space and returns
// the new string
function unplus(old_str)
{
    new_str = "";
    for (index = 0; index < old_str.length; index++)
    {
        if (old_str.charAt(index) == "+")
            new_str+=" ";
        else
```

LISTING 8-2   CLIENT-SIDE JAVASCRIPT ROUTINES TO SET AND EXTRACT PROPERTIES OF THE SERVER-SIDE CLIENT OBJECT.

```
            new_str+= old_str.charAt(index);
        }
    return new_str;
}

// Replaces a space with the plus (+) encoding and returns
the new string
function plus(old_str)
{
    new_str = "";
    for (index = 0; index < old_str.length; index++)
    {
        if (old_str.charAt(index) == " ")
            new_str+="+";
        else
            new_str+= old_str.charAt(index);
    }
    return new_str;
}

// Retrieves server-side JavaScript client object proper-
ties from cookie
function getclientprop(field)
{
    if (document.cookie.length > 0)
    {
        var search_in = document.cookie;
        var search_for = "NETSCAPE_LIVEWIRE." + field + "=";
        start = search_in.indexOf(search_for);
        if (start != -1)
        {
            start+=search_for.length;
            end = search_in.indexOf(";", start);
            if (end == -1) end = search_in.length;
            value = unescape(unplus(
                            search_in.substring(start, end)));
        }
        else
            value = null;
    }
    else
        value = null;

    return value;
}
```

LISTING 8-2   (CONTINUED) CLIENT-SIDE JAVASCRIPT ROUTINES TO SET AND EXTRACT PROPERTIES OF THE SERVER-SIDE CLIENT OBJECT.

```
// Sets server-side JavaScript client object properties in
cookie
function setclientprop(field, value)
{
   document.cookie = "NETSCAPE_LIVEWIRE." + field + "=" +
 escape(plus(value));
}
</SCRIPT>
```

LISTING 8-2   (CONTINUED) CLIENT-SIDE JAVASCRIPT ROUTINES TO SET AND EXTRACT PROPERTIES OF
THE SERVER-SIDE CLIENT OBJECT.

The following example illustrates the use of the functions in Listing 8-2
to retrieve and set `client` object properties stored in cookies:

```
<SERVER>
if (client.a == null)
      client.a = "Original 'a' value";
if (client.b == null)
      client.b = "Original 'b' value";
if (client.c == null)
      client.c = "Original 'c' value";
</SERVER>

<SCRIPT>
document.write("<B>Cookie: </B>" + document.cookie +
"<P>");
document.write("<B>'a' displayed in CS JS</B>: " +
getclientprop("a") + "<BR>");
document.write("<B>'b' displayed in CS JS</B>: " +
getclientprop("b") + "<BR>");
document.write("<B>'c' displayed in CS JS</B>: " +
getclientprop("c") + "<BR>");
setclientprop("a","Changed 'a' value");
setclientprop("b","Changed 'b' value");
setclientprop("c","Changed 'c' value");
document.write("<P><B>Cookie: </B>" + document.cookie +
"<P>");
</SCRIPT>

<SERVER>
write("<B>'a' displayed in SS JS</B>: " + client.a +
"<BR>");
write("<B>'b' displayed in SS JS</B>: " + client.b +
"<BR>");
```

```
write("<B>'c' displayed in SS JS</B>: " + client.c +
"<BR>");
</SERVER>
```

The following steps are performed in the previous section of code:

1. The a, b, and c properties of the `client` object are set in server-side JavaScript if they don't currently have a value.

2. The values of these properties are displayed in client-side JavaScript using our `getclientprop()` function to retrieve the values from the cookie.

3. The values of a, b, and c are changed in the cookie using our client-side `setclientprop()` function.

4. The values of these properties are displayed in server-side JavaScript.

As shown below, when the values are changed on the client, the cookie is updated, but server-side JavaScript still uses the old values. This is because the server and the client only let each other know about changes made to cookies at the next HTTP request/response sequence. What this means is that the server will not know about the changes made to the cookie until the next time the client issues a request for a page.

```
Cookie: NETSCAPE_LIVEWIRE.c=Original+'c'+value;
NETSCAPE_LIVEWIRE.b=Original+'b'+value;
NETSCAPE_LIVEWIRE.a=Original+'a'+value

'a' displayed in CS JS: Original 'a' value
'b' displayed in CS JS: Original 'b' value
'c' displayed in CS JS: Original 'c' value

Cookie: NETSCAPE_LIVEWIRE.c=Changed+%27c%27+value;
NETSCAPE_LIVEWIRE.b=Changed+%27b%27+value;
NETSCAPE_LIVEWIRE.a=Changed+%27a%27+value

'a' displayed in SS JS: Original 'a' value
'b' displayed in SS JS: Original 'b' value
'c' displayed in SS JS: Original 'c' value
```

We can initiate a new request by hitting the Reload button in the browser. This causes the same page to be displayed, but now the new value is known both to the client and the server. As part of the client's request, the browser shipped a copy of the cookie to the server.

```
Cookie: NETSCAPE_LIVEWIRE.c=Changed+'c'+value;
NETSCAPE_LIVEWIRE.b=Changed+'b'+value;
NETSCAPE_LIVEWIRE.a=Changed+'a'+value

'a' displayed in CS JS: Changed 'a' value
'b' displayed in CS JS: Changed 'b' value
'c' displayed in CS JS: Changed 'c' value

Cookie: NETSCAPE_LIVEWIRE.c=Changed+%27c%27+value;
NETSCAPE_LIVEWIRE.b=Changed+%27b%27+value;
NETSCAPE_LIVEWIRE.a=Changed+%27a%27+value

'a' displayed in SS JS: Changed 'a' value
'b' displayed in SS JS: Changed 'b' value
'c' displayed in SS JS: Changed 'c' value
```

Using `client-url` to Maintain the `client` Object

By choosing `client-url`, LiveWire encodes the full properties of the `client` object as dynamic URLs. The name/value pairs are appended to URLs that reference other portions of the application. The main advantage of this approach is that all Web browsers can support it so you are not locked into just using browsers that support cookies. However, it requires the largest amount of network resources of any of the techniques.

The following two HTML files illustrate the use of `client-url` encoding. You should compile the two files into a LiveWire application and install the application with the following parameters:

- `client-url` technique of client object maintenance.
- The default and initial pages as `setclient.htm`.

Here is `setclient.htm`:

```
<HTML>
<BODY>
<SERVER>
client.name = "Brian Holman";
client.rank = "Major";
client.serialno = 1234;
```

```
</SERVER>
<A HREF=`writeURL('getclient.htm')`>Click to display
client object</A>
</BODY>
</HTML>
```

Here is `getclient.htm`:

```
<HTML>
<BODY>
<SERVER>
write("<B>Name:</B> " + client.name + "<BR>");
write("<B>Rank:</B> " + client.rank + "<BR>");
write("<B>Serial #:</B> " + client.serialno + "<BR>");
</SERVER>
</BODY>
</HTML>
```

Now when we connect to `setclient.htm`, the following HTML is actually sent to the browser from the server:

```
<HTML>
<BODY>
<A HREF=
getclient.htm?NETSCAPE_LIVEWIRE.name=Brian+Holman&NETSCA
PE_LIVEWIRE.rank=Major&NETSCAPE_LIVEWIRE.serialno=1234>C
lick to display client object</A>
</BODY>
</HTML>
```

Notice that in addition to the document name portion of the `A HREF`, the `writeURL()` function appended all of the name/value pairs of the `client` object to the base URL. So, when you select the link to go to `getclient.htm` from `setclient.htm`, all of the name/value pairs will be transferred as part of the URL (illustrated in Figure 8-4).

So, when writing code to support the `client-url` technique, any references to other pages within an application must use the `writeURL()` function, otherwise the client object properties will not be retained.

Using `server-ip` to Maintain the `client` Object

The `server-ip` maintenance technique stores the properties of the `client` object associated with each browser in a data structure on the server. It identifies each individual `client` object by the IP address of the browser. The problem with this technique is that it will not work for multi-user sys-

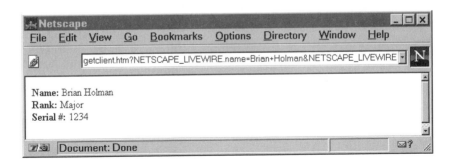

FIGURE 8-4   Encoding the client object properties as part of the URL.

tems that share the same IP address for multiple users or for users that access the Web server through a proxy. If neither of these two problems are important for your application, this may be a very useful technique where you don't have to hassle with generating dynamic URLs if your browsers don't have cookie support.

Using `server-cookie` to Maintain the `client` Object

The `server-cookie` maintenance technique stores the properties of the `client` object associated with each browser in a data structure on the server. It identifies each individual `client` object by the ID number stored in a cookie on the client browser. All browsers that use your application must support the Netscape cookie protocol.

The advantage this technique has over `client-cookie` is that only an ID number is stored in the cookie on the browser. The actual properties are stored on the server, so the normal cookie restrictions don't apply. In other words, you are no longer limited to a maximum of twenty cookies (client properties) because the ID number only counts as one cookie and the real properties are stored on the server.

Using `server-url` to Maintain the `client` Object

By choosing `server-url` to maintain the `client` object, LiveWire encodes the properties of the `client` object in a data structure on the server and then stores an ID number for that data structure as part of the URL. This ID number is appended to URLs that reference other portions of the application. The main advantage of this approach is that all Web browsers can support it and, unlike the `client-url` technique, it doesn't lead to enormously long generated URLs because only a reference to the properties is appended in the URL not the properties themselves.

To demonstrate the difference between `server-url` and `client-url`, modify the application created in the `client-url` section in the LiveWire Application Manager and change it to `server-url` maintenance technique. Now, when you connect to `setclient.htm`, the following HTML is sent to the browser from the server:

```
<HTML>
<BODY>
<A
HREF=getclient.htm?NETSCAPE_LIVEWIRE_ID=002548861853>Cli
ck to display client object</A>
</BODY>
</HTML>
```

So, when you select the link to go to `getclient.htm` from `setclient.htm`, the server ID associated with the client properties will be transferred as part of the URL (illustrated in Figure 8-5).

FIGURE 8-5 Encoding a server reference to the client object properties as part of the URL.

As with the `client-url` technique, any references to other pages within an application must use the `writeURL()` function, otherwise the client object properties will not be retained.

The `project` Object

As previously mentioned, the `project` object contains data common to an entire application. Every client browser that accesses a particular LiveWire application has access to the same `project` object. This object can be used to share data between multiple clients using the same application. The properties of this object remain until the current application is restarted.

As with the `client` object, the `project` object contains no pre-defined properties. The programmer can use the `project` object to store application data common to all clients. In the "Hello Net" application of Chapter 3, the `project.counter` property was created to keep track of how many times any browser accessed the application.

```
project.lock();
if (project.counter == null)
    project.counter = 0;
else
    project.counter = 1 + parseInt(project.counter,10);
project.unlock();
```

Locking the `project` Object

Because there is the potential for multiple clients to try to update the same property of the `project` object at the same time, a locking mechanism is used to ensure that only one client can update the `project` object at a time. This is accomplished through the `project.lock()` and `project.unlock()` methods illustrated above. When one client has a lock on the `project` object, all other clients trying to establish a lock must wait until the first client releases the lock.

If the client holding the lock takes too long, the other client will time-out. The section of code between the `lock()` and `unlock()` functions is known as a critical section. **It is important that you keep your critical sections small to allow other clients a chance to update the `project` object.** It is bad practice to include any loops in a critical section. You just want to lock the object, make the change, and unlock the object as quickly as possible.

The `server` Object

The `server` object contains data common to all LiveWire applications on the same server. Every client browser that accesses any application on this server has access to the same `server` object. This object can be used to share data between multiple applications on the same server. The user-defined properties of this object remain until the Web server on the assigned port is restarted. The `server` object has some pre-defined properties. Table 8-3 summarizes those properties.

The programmer can use the `server` object to store user-defined properties common to all applications on the server. In the "Hello Net" application of Chapter 3, the `server.counter` property was created to keep a total

TABLE 8-3. Server Object Properties

Property	Description
host	This property reports the full hostname of the Web server. For example, `www.foo.bar`.
hostname	This property reports the full hostname of the Web server, including the number of the port that the Web server is running on. For example, `www.foo.bar:80`.
port	This property reports the number of the port that the Web server is running on.
protocol	This property reports the communications protocol being used by the server. This will be `http:` on a standard server or `https:` on a secure server with encrypted communication.

access count of any page of any application on the server. As illustrated, the same locking mechanism used with the `project` object applies to the `server` object to ensure that only one client at a time updates a property of the `server` object.

```
server.lock();
if (server.counter == null)
    server.counter = 0;
else
    server.counter = 1 + parseInt(server.counter,10);
server.unlock();
```

It is important to note that when we refer to a Web server, we are referring to a server listening on a particular port, such as port 80. You may have another Web server running on another port. *Each server running on a separate port has its own* `server` *object and* `project` *objects, and the servers do not share any data.*

The `database` Object

Most of the information about databases beyond this point requires a basic knowledge of the industry-standard database Structured Query Language (SQL).

The `database` object has no pre-defined properties and the programmer is not allowed to add any user-defined properties. It has the same lifetime as the `project` object. Every client browser that accesses a particular LiveWire application has access to the same `database` object.

The `database` object consists entirely of methods used for SQL database access. These methods are grouped into the following areas for discussion:

- Establishing Database Connections.
- Sending SQL Statements to the Database.
- Creating Database Transactions.
- Detecting Database Error Conditions.

Establishing Database Connections

The `connect()`, `connected()`, and `disconnect()` methods of the `database` object are used respectively to establish, verify, and terminate a connection to a particular database on a database server. The following code illustrates their use:

```
// if not yet connected to a database then connect
if(!database.connected())
{
        database.connect("INFORMIX", "myhost", "me",
"mypassword", "mydatabase");
}

// if still not connected then something must be wrong
if (!database.connected())
{
        write("Error: Unable to connect to database.");
}
...
Perform database query operations
...
// Now that we're done, disconnect from database
database.disconnect();
```

The syntax for each of these functions is specified in Tables 8-4, 8-5, and 8-6.

Database connections can be made using one of two different methods—locking or non-locking. Each have their respective advantages and disadvantages and deciding which one to use is application- and environment-specific.

Non-locking Database Connection

Once a database connection is initially established by a single client, it can be used by all clients accessing the database in the same application. With this approach, an implicit disconnect will happen if the application is

TABLE 8-4. Establish a connection to a database.

database.connect("*dbtype*", "*dbhost*", "*user*", "*pass*", "*database*");	
Parameter	**Description**
dbtype	This is the database type for the database server you are connecting to. The currently supported databases are: • INFORMIX • ORACLE • SYBASE • ILLUSTRA In addition to the above databases, you may also be able to use the ODBC type to access additional databases if the ODBC protocol is supported on your platform. You must also have the ODBC driver for the necessary database server installed and configured properly.
dbhost	The name of the database server of the type specified in *dbtype*.
user	The name of the database user that has the necessary rights to access *database*.
pass	The password for the user specified by *user*.
database	The name of the database to connect to on the *dbhost* server.

TABLE 8-5. Terminate the current connection to a database.

database.disconnect();	
Parameter	**Description**
none	N/A

TABLE 8-6. Verify a connection to a database.

database.connected();	
Parameter	**Description**
none	N/A

TABLE 8-6. (Continued) Verify a connection to a database.

Return Value	Condition
true	Returns true if the database object is currently connected to a database.
false	Returns false if the database object is not connected to a database.

stopped. When the application is restarted, the first client to connect to the application will cause the database connection to be re-established. The main advantage to this type of database connection is that clients can issue database operations concurrently and will not have to wait for each other's operations to complete.

However, this approach has the following disadvantages:

- Every client using the database will be using it with the privileges of the *user* specified in the `connect()` statement. Therefore, the burden of database security rests on the server-side JavaScript programmer. If the database *user* you are using allows more privileges than you want the LiveWire application to have, you must enforce the appropriate database access when you write the application. You may want to use the IP address of the client browser as a means of recognizing the source of a query since the same database user is being used for all clients.
- The application can only access tables in a single database—the one specified in the `connect()` statement.

Keep in mind the following when coding an application to support this type of connection:

- Before issuing any database statements, you should check and see if the database is open using `connected()` and if not, you should open it using `connect()`.
- You should never use the `disconnect()` statement anywhere in your application.
- To ensure concurrent access to the database, no database statements should be contained within `project` or `server` critical sections (the code between the `lock()` and `unlock()` methods).

Locking Database Connection

When using the locking approach, all database operations are included within a critical section of the `project` object, which forces database operations to be handled serially. This means that only one client at a time will be allowed to use the database object and all others must wait for it to complete its operations.

Here is the way you should code this approach:

1.Lock the project with the `project.lock()` method.

2.Connect to a database using the `database.connect()` method.

3.Perform the necessary database operations.

4.Disconnect from the database using the `database.disconnect()` method.

5.Unlock the project object with the `project.unlock()` method.

Since only one client at a time will be allowed to perform database operations, you can now have each individual client authenticate itself with the database. You can do this by prompting the client for its database user ID and password as part of the page that connects the client to the database. You could also connect to a different database depending on some condition determined at run-time for an individual client browser. Neither of these are possible using the non-locking approach.

 When using the locking approach, it is not a good idea to issue queries that take a long time to process because this will effectively lock out all other users from the database until the query is complete.

Sending SQL Statements to the Database

The `database` object has two methods for issuing SQL statements—`execute()` and `SQLTable()`. If you want your application to remain portable across different vendors' database management systems, you should restrict yourself to ANSI-standard SQL without vendor-specific SQL extensions. However, vendor-specific extensions are supported with these two methods.

The `execute()` method is used when you want to send SQL statements to the database from which it is not possible for rows to be returned. For example, you would probably want to use `execute()` when creating a new table in a database or when dropping a table from a database. You would also want to use `execute()` when you are inserting or updating values in a table. Consider this example from which no rows are returned:

```
// SQL statements that return no data
database.execute("DROP TABLE Stuff");
```

```
database.execute("CREATE TABLE Stuff (Number INTEGER,
Name CHAR(30))");
database.execute("INSERT INTO Stuff VALUES (5,
'Seven')");
database.execute("INSERT INTO Stuff VALUES (3,
'Three')");
database.execute("UPDATE Stuff SET Name = 'Five' WHERE
Number = 5");
```

The syntax of the `database.execute()` command is specified in Table 8-7.

TABLE 8-7. Send an SQL statement to a database.

database.execute(*sqlString*);	
Parameter	**Description**
sqlString	This is any valid SQL query that does not return rows as a result.
Return Value	**Condition**
0	Returns 0 if the operation was completed successfully.
>0	Returns greater than 0 if the operation failed for some reason. See "Detecting Database Error Conditions" in the next section for more information.

You may also make changes to a database using methods of the `database.cursor()` object-type that will be discussed later in this chapter.

The `SQLTable(`*sqlQueryString*`)` method is used to issue SQL queries to the database and to place the results, if any, automatically in an HTML table. The *sqlQueryString* parameter is any valid SQL statement from which you expect rows to be returned. When you are querying the database for rows that meet a certain criteria, it may or may not return any rows. There is always the possibility, however, of the query returning rows when using the SELECT statement. Consider this example, which is a follow-on to the previous code section with the results of the example shown in Figure 8-6.

```
database.SQLTable("SELECT * FROM Stuff");
```

number	name
5	Five
3	Three

FIGURE 8-6 The result of using the `database.SQLTable()` method.

The `SQLTable()` method is an easy way to return the results of a query to an HTML page. However, you have no control over the formatting of the table. If you don't want to display the results in table form, or you want to display a more informative header than the field name, you will need to use the `database.cursor()` object-type discussed later in this chapter in the section titled "Object-Types, their Properties, and Methods".

Creating Database Transactions

When working with databases, sometimes an unforeseen situation can halt a program while it is in the middle of a database operation. This can compromise the integrity of the database because the entire operation will not have completed successfully. It is for this reason that we have database transactions. A database transaction is a sequence of changes to a database that either must be accomplished completely or not at all. The database server ensures that the operation is either committed to disk or the database is restored to its previous state.

The following functions are used to explicitly control database transactions:

- `database.beginTransaction()` starts a new database transaction.
- `database.commitTransaction()` commits to the database all of the database operations since the last `beginTransaction()`.
- `database.rollbackTransaction()` returns the database to the state it was in before the last `beginTransaction()`.

None of the above methods require any parameters. Each of these methods return zero (0) if successful or a number greater than zero if not successful. The procedure listed below shows how to use these functions for the creation and control of database transactions:

1. Start a transaction using the `database.beginTransaction()` method.

2. Make changes to the database using either the `database.execute()` method or a modifiable cursor.

3. If the changes are acceptable, use `database.commitTransaction()` to commit the changes; otherwise, use `database.rollbackTransaction()` to abort the changes.

With most SQL database management systems, transaction logging must be enabled to have the ability to rollback a transaction. This is often done on the database level. You should refer to your database administrator's guide for more information.

Detecting Database Error Conditions

Many of the database methods return a status code depending on whether an operation is completed successfully or not. The transaction-related methods just mentioned and the `execute()` method all return this status code. In addition, some of the methods of the `database.cursor()` object-type also return this status code.

Table 8-8 explains the meaning of each of the possible database status codes returned by the methods mentioned.

TABLE 8-8. Status codes returned by certain database methods.

Status	Description	Status	Description
0	No error	13	Unsupported feature
1	Out of memory	14	Null reference parameter
2	Object never initialized	15	Database object not found
3	Type conversion error	16	Required information is missing
4	Database not registered	17	This object cannot support multiple readers
5	Error reported by server	18	Object cannot support deletions
6	Message from server	19	Object cannot support insertions
7	Error from vendor's library	20, 21	Object cannot support updates

TABLE 8-8. (Continued) Status codes returned by certain database methods.

Status	Description	Status	Description
8	Lost connection	22	Object cannot support indices
9	End of fetch	23	Object cannot be dropped
10	Invalid use of object	24	Incorrect connection supplied
11	Column does not exist	25	Object cannot support privileges
12	Invalid positioning within object (bounds error)	26	Object cannot support cursors
		27	Unable to open

For status codes 5 and 7, additional methods are given to return the specific server or library error code and description:

- database.majorErrorCode() returns a number corresponding to the database server error code.
- database.majorErrorMessage() returns the error message string corresponding to the major error code reported.
- database.minorErrorCode() returns a number corresponding to the database library error code.
- database.minorErrorMessage() returns the error message string corresponding to the minor error code reported.

The following code gives an example of the use of these error reporting functions. The error message reported is for Informix, but something similar would be displayed for the other database vendors.

```
// Try to create a table that already exists
var errno = database.execute("CREATE TABLE Stuff (Number
INTEGER, Name CHAR(30))");

if (errno > 0)
{
    write("<B>Status Code:</B> " + errno + "<P>");
    if (errno == 5 || errno == 7)
    {
        write("<B>Major Error:</B> " +
        database.majorErrorCode() + ":" +
        database.majorErrorMessage() + "<P>");
        write("<B>Minor Error:</B> " +
        database.minorErrorCode() + ":" +
```

```
        database.minorErrorMessage() + "<P>");
    }
}
```

```
Status Code: 7

Major Error: -310:[VENDORLIB] Vendor Library Error: Table
(stuff) already exists in database.

Minor Error: 0:
```

Object-Types, their Properties, and Methods

An object-type can have many objects of the same type, whereas a pre-defined object can have only one of any given type. The programmer handles the creation of new objects of a given object-type. Only two object-types are specifically related to server-side JavaScript—the `database.cursor` and `File` object-types. Declare a new object of an object-type as follows:

var *varname* = **new** *objtype* (*parameters*) ;

where *varname* is any valid JavaScript variable name and *objtype* is the desired object-type with any required or optional *parameters* specified. For example,

var myfile = **new File**("stuff.txt");

Once an object of a particular object-type has been created in this way, you are allowed to use its methods and access and manipulate its properties.

The `database.cursor` Object-type

Objects of the `database.cursor` object-type can be used to issue a database query and access the results of that query on the currently open database. When a query has the potential of returning more than one row as a result, you can use a *cursor* to process each row individually. When on a particular row, you can display or update the elements in that row, delete the row, or insert a new row. The methods and properties of the cursor object-type allow you to perform these operations:

- Open and close a cursor.
- Retrieve the results of the query associated with a cursor.
- Update, delete, and insert rows in a cursor.

In addition to these functional areas, we will also discuss how SQL data-types get converted to JavaScript data-types, and vice versa.

Opening and Closing a Cursor

A new object of the `database.cursor` object-type is created using the convention specified in Table 8-9. For example,

```
var mycursor = database.cursor("SELECT * FROM Stuff ");
```

Once the object is created, the cursor is automatically opened and the query is sent to the database for processing. When you have finished with a cursor, you should close it to free database resources. This is accomplished by using the `close()` method, as explained in Table 8-10.

If you don't explicitly close a cursor, it will be automatically closed at the end of the current HTTP request. In other words, cursors have the same lifetime as the server-side `request` object. So, if you want to retain information from a cursor for longer that this, you will need to store the desired information as properties of either the `client`, `project`, or `server` object depending on your need.

TABLE 8-9. Create a new database cursor.

`cursorname = new database.cursor(sqlQueryString, update);`	
Parameter	**Description**
sqlQueryString	This parameter is any valid SQL statement from which you expect rows to be returned.
update	This parameter can be either `true` or `false`. If it is true, you will have the ability to update the database corresponding to the cursor. If it is not specified, the default is `false`.
Return Value	**Condition**
cursorname	Returns a new `database.cursor` object.

TABLE 8-10. Close an existing database cursor.

cursorname.**close**();	
Parameter	**Description**
cursorname	This is the name of the database cursor that you would like to close. When the close() method is executed, the database frees the resources allocated to this cursor.

Retrieving the Results of the Query Associated with a Cursor

One of the most useful features of a cursor is the ability to access the individual elements of a multi-row result set and format the results in an application-specific way. The generic features of the database.SQLTable() method are, in many cases, simply not adequate. The following methods of the cursor object-type allow you much more control over how the results of a particular query get displayed:

- *cursorname*.columns() returns an integer corresponding to the number of columns in a particular result set.
- *cursorname*.columnName(*index*) returns a string corresponding to the name of a particular column in the result set. The *index* value can be from 0 to n-1, where n is the number of columns.
- *cursorname*[*index*] returns the value corresponding to a particular column in the current row of the result set. Again, the *index* value can be from 0 to n-1, where n is the number of columns.
- *cursorname*.next() advances the row pointer to the next row of the result set. If the row pointer has reached the end of the result set, it returns false; otherwise, it returns true.

You can use these methods to customize the results of database queries for your applications. The example of Listing 8-3 illustrates the use of all these methods to create an enhanced version of the database.SQLTable() method. The prettyresults function displays the results of a query in the same way as SQLTable(), with the following enhancements as shown in Figure 8-7:

- A table caption is supported.
- Column names are capitalized.
- The table header and row elements have a background color.

The example in Listing 8-3 and Figure 8-7 works with any query because it determines the characteristics of the result set at run-time. However, there are times when we would like to refer to a column by its name rather than its column number. To do this, we must know the characteristic of

```
function prettyresults(query, caption)
{
    cursor = database.cursor(query, false);
    write("<TABLE>");
    write("<CAPTION>"+caption+"</CAPTION>");
    write("<TR>");
    for (col=0; col < cursor.columns(); col++)
    {
        write("<TH BGCOLOR='white'>" +
            cursor.columnName(col).toUpperCase() + "</TH>");
    }
    write("</TR>");

    while (cursor.next())
    {
        write("<TR>");
        for (col=0; col < cursor.columns(); col++)
        {
            write("<TD BGCOLOR='lightblue'>" + cursor[col] +
                "</TD>");
        }
        write("</TR>");
    }
    write ("</TABLE>");
    cursor.close();
}

prettyresults("SELECT * FROM Stuff", "The Stuff Table");
```

LISTING 8-3   USING A DATABASE CURSOR TO DISPLAY THE RESULT OF A QUERY.

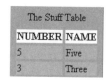

FIGURE 8-7   Using prettyresults() to display the results of a query.

the result set at the time of coding. So, for the query that retrieves the results of the `Stuff` table, we could refer to the elements of a particular row in one of two ways:

- `cursor[0]` and `cursor[1]`, or
- `cursor.Name` and `cursor.Number`.

In general, *cursorname.columnname* returns the value corresponding to a particular column in the current row of the result set.

Linking to and Displaying Database BLOB Fields

Most SQL Databases support a special data-type for the storage of complex multimedia data such as images, sounds, animation, etc. These types of data are stored in a general-purpose "binary large object" data-type. The actual name of the SQL data-type for binary large objects is database-server specific. Table 8-11 shows the binary large object data-types for the most popular databases supported by LiveWire.

TABLE 8-11. The BLOB data-types available for the most popular database systems.

SQL Database	BLOB Data-types
Informix	byte
Oracle	raw, long raw
Sybase	binary, varbinary, image

When traversing a cursor, you can access a BLOB column using these methods:

- *cursorname.columnname*`.blobImage()` to display the content of the BLOB on the current page, if it is an image type supported by Netscape.
- *cursorname.columnname*`.blobLink()` to create a hyperlink to a BLOB that can be of any MIME type.

Below is a portion of Listing 8-4 (see CD-ROM for full source). It illustrates the use of `blobImage()` and `blobLink()` in displaying and linking to BLOB columns in a database. The results of this code are shown in Figure 8-8.

The following HTML is produced from the JavaScript code of Listing 8-4. It shows how the `IMG` and `A HREF` tags are generated from calls to `blobImage()` and `blobLink()`:

```
// Open the Cursor
cursor = database.cursor("SELECT * FROM Army", false);

// Display the First Record with BLOB as IMG
cursor.next();
write("<B>Name</B>: " + cursor.Name + "<BR>");
write("<B>Rank</B>: " + cursor.Rank + "<BR>");
write("<B>Serial #</B>: " + cursor.SerialNum + "<BR>");
write("<B>Picture</B>: " + cursor.Picture.blobImage("gif",
"Photo","top") + "<P>");

// Display the Second Record with BLOB as Link
cursor.next();
write("<B>Name</B>: " + cursor.Name + "<BR>");
write("<B>Rank</B>: " + cursor.Rank + "<BR>");
write("<B>Serial #</B>: " + cursor.SerialNum + "<BR>");
write("<B>Picture</B>: " +
cursor.Picture.blobLink("image/gif", "Photo") + "<P>");
cursor.close();
```

LISTING 8-4   PARTIAL LISTING.

Name: Brian Holman
Rank: Major
Serial #: 1234
Picture:

Name: Bill Lund
Rank: General
Serial #: 4321
Picture: Photo

FIGURE 8-8   Using blobImage() and blobLink() to display database BLOB fields.

```
<HTML>
```

```
<BODY>
<B>Name</B>: Brian Holman<BR>
<B>Rank</B>: Major<BR>
<B>Serial #</B>: 1234<BR>
<B>Picture</B>: <IMG SRC="LIVEWIRE_TEMP1" ALT="Photo"
ALIGN=top><P>

<B>Name</B>: Bill Lund<BR>
<B>Rank</B>: General<BR>
<B>Serial #</B>: 4321<BR>
<B>Picture</B>: <A HREF="LIVEWIRE_TEMP2">Photo</A><P>
</BODY>
</HTML>
```

You should always enclose the results of both the `blobImage()` and `blobLink()` methods within the `write()` function, otherwise the generated HTML will not be sent to the client.

Since the actual content of the BLOB is stored in the database server and not on the Web server, LiveWire creates a temporary file in memory on the Web server for the BLOB. This is why, in the above HTML source, the file names were called `LIVEWIRE_TEMP1` and `LIVEWIRE_TEMP2`. These memory files have a limited lifetime and the memory will be released when one of the following two events occur:

- The temporary file is transferred from the Web server to the client browser.
- 60 seconds have elapsed since the request was processed.

So, when the `blobImage()` method is used, the image is transferred as part of the page and the memory is subsequently freed. If the user waits longer than 60 seconds to click on a `blobLink()` or to load images from a `blobImage()`, the BLOB would no longer be available.

The full syntax for `blobImage()` and `blobLink()` are explained in Tables 8-12 and 8-13, respectively.

TABLE 8-12. *Display a database BLOB field as an image with the IMG tag.*

cursorname.columnname.blobImage(format [, text][,align] [,width][,height][,border][,ismap])	
Parameter	**Description**
cursorname	The name of the current database cursor object.

TABLE 8-12. (Continued) Display a database BLOB field as an image with the IMG tag.

columnname	The name of the BLOB column of the cursor result set.
format	A string specifying the format of the image. This could be "gif", "jpeg", or any other MIME image-type.
text	A string specifying the text to display when the image is not loaded. This is the same as the ALT attribute of the IMG tag and is optional.
align	A string specifying the alignment of the image, such as "left", "right", "top", "bottom", etc. This is the same as the ALIGN attribute of the IMG tag and is optional.
width	A number specifying the width of the image in pixels. It is the same as the WIDTH attribute of the IMG tag and is optional.
height	A number specifying the height of the image in pixels. It is the same as the HEIGHT attribute of the IMG tag and is optional.
border	A number specifying the border of the image in pixels. It is the same as the BORDER attribute of the IMG tag and is optional.
ismap	A boolean value (either `true` or `false`) specifying whether or not the image is an image map.
Return Value	**Condition**
string	Returns a string corresponding to the <IMG> HTML tag with its optional attributes specified in the parameters for the associated BLOB field.

TABLE 8-13. Create a hyperlink to a database BLOB field.

`cursorname.columnname.blobLink(`*mimetype, linktext*`)`	
Parameter	**Description**
cursorname	The name of the current database cursor object.
columnname	The name of the BLOB column of the cursor result set.
mimetype	A string specifying the MIME type of the BLOB field. For example, `image/gif` or `audio/wav`.

TABLE 8-13. (Continued) Create a hyperlink to a database BLOB field.

linktext	A string specifying the text to be displayed for this link.
Return Value	**Condition**
string	Returns a string corresponding to the A HREF HTML tag for the associated BLOB field.

Updating, Deleting, and Inserting Rows in a Cursor

The most common way of updating, deleting, or inserting rows in a database table is to simply issue the appropriate SQL statements using the database.execute() method explained previously. However, the updateRow(), insertRow(), and deleteRow() methods of the cursor object-type can also be used to make changes to a particular database table. These changes are made without requiring the programmer to write SQL statements. This is a very elegant way of doing things and you are less likely to write SQL statements that are not portable across database environments.

Listing 8-5 illustrates the use of the insertRow() and updateRow() methods in place of standard SQL.

number	name
5	Five
3	Three

FIGURE 8-9   The result of executing Listing 8-5.

As with the example used for database.execute(), the resulting Stuff table would contain the information in Figure 8-9.

To be able to use the updateRow(), insertRow(), and deleteRow() methods, the cursor must be created with the *update* parameter set to true. The SELECT statement issued as part of the cursor's SQL query parameter must be a single SELECT for only one table, i.e., "SELECT * FROM *tablename*".

Use the convention *cursorname.columnname=newvalue* to make changes to any non-BLOB column before calling either updateRow() or insertRow(). You must use the blob() function to update a BLOB column. Specifically, *cursorname.columnname=blob (file)*, where *file* is the path of a valid operating system file on the server. Below is a portion of Listing 8-4 that illustrates how to update both standard columns and BLOB columns:

```
// Open Updateable Cursor
cursor = database.cursor("SELECT * FROM Stuff", true);
// Equivalent to SQL: INSERT INTO Stuff VALUES (5, 'Seven')
cursor.Name = "Seven";
cursor.Number = 5;
cursor.insertRow("Stuff");
// Equivalent to SQL: INSERT INTO Stuff VALUES (3, 'Three')
cursor.Name = "Three";
cursor.Number = 3;
cursor.insertRow("Stuff");
// Close Cursor
cursor.close();

// Equivalent to SQL: UPDATE Stuff SET Name = 'Five' WHERE
Number = 5
cursor = database.cursor("SELECT * FROM Stuff WHERE Number
= 5", true);
while (cursor.next())
{
    cursor.Name = "Five";
    cursor.updateRow("Stuff");
}
cursor.close();
```

LISTING 8-5   USING UPDATEABLE CURSORS INSTEAD OF SQL STATEMENTS TO ALTER A DATABASE RECORD.

```
cursor = database.cursor("SELECT * FROM Army", true);
cursor.Name = "Brian Holman";
cursor.Rank = "Major";
cursor.SerialNum = 1234;
cursor.Picture = blob("brian.gif");
cursor.insertRow("Army");
cursor.Name = "Bill Lund";
cursor.Rank = "General";
cursor.SerialNum = 4321;
cursor.Picture = blob("bill.gif");
cursor.insertRow("Army");
cursor.close();
```

You should use these procedures when calling one of the database-altering methods.

Updates:

1. Open the cursor for update.

2. Find the appropriate record in the cursor and make it the current row.

3. Make the desired changes to the columns of the current row.

4. Call the `updateRow()` method.

5. Close the cursor.

Insertions:

1. Open the cursor for update.

2. Populate the columns of the cursor with the desired information. (The current row position is not important for insertions since the current row is just used as a holder for the insertion data and is never actually updated.)

3. Call the `insertRow()` method.

4. Close the cursor.

Deletions:

1. Open the cursor for update.

2. Find the appropriate record in the cursor and make it the current row.

3. Call the `deleteRow()` method.

4. Close the cursor.

Tables 8-14, 8-15, and 8-16 explain the syntax of the `updateRow()`, `insertRow()`, and `deleteRow()` methods.

Data-type Conversion between the DBMS and JavaScript

Most database management environments, including those supported by LiveWire, provide a rich set of data-types. These include data-types for

TABLE 8-14. Update the record corresponding to the current row of a cursor.

cursorname.updateRow(*tablename*)	
Parameter	**Description**
cursorname	The name of the current database cursor object.
tablename	The name of the database table you would like to update.
Return Value	**Condition**
0	Returns 0 if the operation was completed successfully.
>0	Returns greater than 0 if the operation failed for some reason. See "Detecting Database Error Conditions" in this chapter for more information.

TABLE 8-15. Insert a new row into a database table.

cursorname.insertRow(*tablename*)	
Parameter	**Description**
cursorname	The name of the current database cursor object.
tablename	The name of the database table into which you would like to insert the row.
Return Value	**Condition**
0	Returns 0 if the operation was completed successfully.
>0	Returns greater than 0 if the operation failed for some reason.

TABLE 8-16. Delete the record corresponding to the current row of a cursor.

cursorname.deleteRow(*tablename*)	
Parameter	**Description**
cursorname	The name of the current database cursor object.
tablename	The name of the database table from which you would like to delete the row.

***TABLE 8-16. (Continued) Delete the record corresponding to the current row of a
cursor.***

Return Value	Condition
0	Returns 0 if the operation was completed successfully.
>0	Returns greater than 0 if the operation failed for some reason.

fixed-length character strings, variable-length character strings, dates and
times, money, floating point numbers, fixed precision numbers, integers, and
binary data.

However, JavaScript supports a much more limited set of data-types.
Specifically, JavaScript supports only strings, numbers, dates, and BLOB
data-types. Obviously, some type of translation from DBMS data-types to
JavaScript data-types must occur when accessing and setting database fields
in JavaScript. Table 8-17 shows the JavaScript data-types that correspond to
DBMS data-types.

TABLE 8-17. DBMS-to-JavaScript Data-type Conversion.

DBMS Data-types	JavaScript Data-types
fixed-length character strings, variable-length character strings	strings
money, floating point numbers, fixed precision numbers, integers	numbers
dates and times	dates
binary data	BLOBs

It is important that when you are assigning data to a column of a database type that you use the correct JavaScript data-type. For example, if you
are assigning a date to the Informix `datetime` data-type, you would need to
assign it from a JavaScript date data-type.

The `File` Object-type

Objects of the `File` object-type can be used to create and access disk
files on the Web server. Objects of this type have no properties, but they do
have a group of associated file access methods. These methods can be grouped
into eight areas:

- Opening and closing a file.

- Getting information about a file.
- Reading from a file.
- Writing to a file.
- Converting bytes to strings as vice versa.
- Detecting errors.

Ensuring File Integrity

When an object of the File object-type is created and opened, all clients using an application have access to it. Under most circumstances, you should not allow more than one client to access a file at a time because one client could change the current file position from that expected by another client. This can lead to data corruption when the clients are trying to write to the same file at the same time. It can also lead to unexpected results when clients are trying to read from the same file.

The way to prevent multiple clients from writing to a file at the same time is to use the project.lock() and project.unlock() methods explained previously in this chapter to enclose any File methods used in a critical section. This will prevent multiple clients in the same application from accessing a file at the same time. If two different applications on the server have the potential to write to the same file at the same time, you should use the server.lock() and server.unlock() methods.

Opening and Closing a File

Once a new object of the File object-type is created, you can open and close a file by using its open() and close() methods as shown below:

```
// Create an empty file
myfile = new File("myfile.txt");
myfile.open("w");
myfile.close();
```

 Files are stored relative to the Web server's config sub-directory if the full operating system path is not given.

The file access rights for server-side JavaScript are dependent upon those rights granted to the user account that the Web server is running under. You should be careful in how you provide file access to the client browser using server-side JavaScript. In general, you should probably hard-code the *file-name* used and not allow the client user to input one.

The syntax for the methods related to opening and closing files are in Tables 8-18, 8-19, and 8-20.

TABLE 8-18. Create a new object of the `File` ***type.***

`fileobj` = **new File**(`filename`)	
Parameter	**Description**
filename	This is any valid operating system filename for the system the Web server is running on. If a relative filename is given, its base path will be the configuration subdirectory for the running Web server. So, if you were just to specify a filename without a path, it would be stored in the `config` subdirectory of your Web server.
Return Value	**Condition**
fileobj	Returns a new `File` object.

Getting and Changing the Current Position in a File

When opening a file, the current position in the file is either set to the beginning or end of the file depending on the *mode* used. Reading from and writing to a file are done relative to the current position. Once an operation is complete, the current position will change to reflect the result of the operation, i.e., if you write ten bytes, the current position will be incremented by ten bytes.

The `getPosition()` and `setPosition()` methods allow you to determine and set the current file position, respectively. Tables 8-21 and 8-22 show the syntax for these two methods.

The example of Listing 8-6 illustrates the use of the `setPosition()` function using the different *position* parameters.

Getting Information about a File

Some methods of the `File` object-type are related to getting information about the current state of the file:

- `getLength()` returns the number of bytes in the file.
- `eof()` returns true if the file pointer is beyond the end of the file; otherwise, it returns false.
- `exists()` returns true if the file exists; otherwise, it returns false.

TABLE 8-19. Open a file.

fileobj.open(mode)	
Parameter	**Description**
mode	A string containing the mode with which you would like to open the file. The following modes are supported and are equivalent to those used with the standard C library call `fopen()`: "r" - open a existing text file for reading. "w" - create a new text file for writing and discard the previous contents, if any. "a" - open or create a text file for writing at the end of the file. "r+" - open an existing text file for reading or writing starting at the beginning of the file. "w+" - create a text file for reading and writing and discard the previous contents, if any. "a+" - open or create a text file for reading and writing starting at the end of the file. If the mode includes a `"b"` after the initial mode, such as `"rb"`, the file will be opened as a binary file rather than a text file.
Return Value	**Condition**
true	Returns true if the file was able to be opened according to the mode specified.
false	Returns false otherwise.

TABLE 8-20. Close a file.

fileobj.close()	
Return Value	**Condition**
true	Returns true if the file could be closed.
false	Returns false if the file is not currently open.

None of the above methods have any required or optional parameters. Listing 8-7 illustrates the use of these methods.

TABLE 8-21. Get the current position in a file.

fileobj.getPosition()	
Return Value	**Condition**
-1	Returns -1 if an error was encountered in determining the current position in the file.
0 or greater	Returns the current position in the file in bytes with the first byte of the file being 0.

TABLE 8-22. Set the current position in a file.

fileobj.setPosition(*position* [,*reference*])	
Parameter	**Description**
position	An integer containing the new position for the file pointer.
reference	An integer explaining where to reference the *position* from: 0 - *position* is relative to the beginning of the file. 1 - *position* is relative to the current position. 2 - *position* is relative to the end of the file. If no *reference* is specified, the *position* will be relative to the beginning of the file.

Reading from a File

Three different methods of the `File` object-type read data from a file:

- `read(count)` - reads the next count bytes from a file and returns a string.
- `readln()` - reads a line of text from a file and returns it as a string.
- `readByte()` - reads a single byte from a file and returns it as an integer.

Please refer to the previous two code examples to see cases of using the `read()` and `readln()` methods. Tables 8-23, 8-24, and 8-25 give the syntax of the methods associated with reading from a file.

Writing to a File

The parallel functions for writing that correspond to those functions for reading from a file are:

```
<SERVER>
// Create a new file object
myfile = new File("mime.types");

// Open the file for reading from the beginning of the file
myfile.open("r");

// The first 10 bytes of the file
myfile.setPosition(0)
write("1: " + myfile.read(10) + "<BR>");

// 10 bytes of the file, starting at position 50
myfile.setPosition(50);
write("2 : " + myfile.read(10) + "<BR>");

// 10 bytes of the file, going 15 ahead of the current
position
myfile.setPosition(15,1);
write("3: " + myfile.read(10) + "<BR>");

// 10 bytes of the file relative to the end of the file
myfile.setPosition(-10,2);
write("4: " + myfile.read(10) + "<BR>");

// Close the file
myfile.close();
</SERVER>
```

```
1: #--Netscap
2: ation # Do
3: above line
4: i,exe,bat
```

LISTING 8-6   CHANGING POSITION WITHIN A FILE.

- write(*string*) - writes a string to a file starting at the current file position.
- writeln(*string*) - writes a string to a file starting at the current file position followed by a newline.
- writeByte(*integer*) - writes a single byte to a file starting at the current file position whose value is specified by integer.

```
<SERVER>
// Create a new file object
myfile = new File("mime.types");

// Open the file for reading if file exists
if (myfile.exists())
{
    myfile.open("r");

    // Display the file length in bytes
    write("<B>File length</B>: " + myfile.getLength()
    + "<P>");

    // Display each line of the file until end-of-file
    // reached then report the number of lines read
    var linect = 0;
    while (!myfile.eof())
    {
        write(myfile.readln() + "<BR>");
        linect++;
    }
    write("<B>Line Count</B>: " + linect + "<P>");
}

// Close the file
myfile.close();
</SERVER>
```

File length: 2402

```
#--Netscape Communications Corporation MIME Information
# Do not delete the above line. It is used to identify the
file type.

type=application/octet-stream exts=bin,exe
type=application/oda exts=oda
type=application/pdf exts=pdf
type=application/postscript exts=ai,eps,ps
...
type=magnus-internal/cgi exts=cgi,exe,bat
```

Line Count: 66

LISTING 8-7   GET INFORMATION ABOUT A FILE.

TABLE 8-23. Read a fixed number of bytes from a file.

`fileobj.read(count)`	
Parameter	**Description**
count	The number of bytes to read from the file starting at the current file position.
Return Value	**Condition**
string	Returns a string containing the data read.

TABLE 8-24. Read a line of text from a file.

`fileobj.readln()`	
Return Value	**Condition**
string	Returns a string containing the line read. The string does not contain the ending newline character(s).

TABLE 8-25. Read a single byte from a file.

`fileobj.readByte()`	
Return Value	**Condition**
integer	Returns an integer value for the next byte, starting at the current file position.

In server-side JavaScript, all file I/O is buffered. If you want to be sure that the data just written have been committed to disk, you must use the `flush()` method.

tip   The write() and flush() methods of the File object are not the same as the top-level write() and flush() functions used to send data to the client browser.

Tables 8-26 through 8-29 give the syntax of the methods associated with writing to a file.

TABLE 8-26.* *Write a string to a file.

fileobj.write(*string*)	
Parameter	**Description**
string	A string corresponding to the data to be written to the file.
Return Value	**Condition**
true	Returns true if the write was successful.
false	Returns false if it was unable to write the data to the file.

TABLE 8-27.* *Write a string with a newline to a file.

fileobj.writeln(*string*)	
Parameter	**Description**
string	A string corresponding to the data to be written to the file.
Return Value	**Condition**
true	Returns true if the write was successful.
false	Returns false if it was unable to write the data to the file.

TABLE 8-28.* *Write a single byte to a file.

fileobj.writeByte(*integer*)	
Parameter	**Description**
integer	A number corresponding to the byte to be written to the file, i.e., 65 would write A'.
Return Value	**Condition**
true	Returns true if the write was successful.
false	Returns false if it was unable to write the data to the file.

TABLE 8-29. Force the buffered data from a write operation to be sent to a file.

fileobj.flush()	
Return Value	**Condition**
true	Returns true if the flush was successful.
false	Returns false otherwise.

Byte/String Data Conversion

The readByte() and writeByte() functions both use integer values to represent a single byte quantity. The File object-type has two methods: byteToString(*integer*) and stringToByte(*string*). These methods can be used to convert an integer byte value to its string equivalent, and vice versa.

All of the other methods of the File object-type are accessed by declaring a new object and using that name to access the methods, i.e., *fileobj.methodname()*. However, with these two methods you access them directly using the "File." prefix. Tables 8-30 and 8-31 show the syntax of these two methods.

TABLE 8-30. Convert the numeric value of a byte to a single character string.

File.byteToString(*integer*)	
Parameter	**Description**
integer	A number corresponding to the ASCII code value for a character.
Return Value	**Condition**
string	Returns a single character string corresponding to the byte code value, i.e., 65 would return "A". If the *integer* is not a valid number, it returns a blank string.

TABLE 8-31. Convert a single character string to its equivalent numeric value.

File.stringtoByte(*string*)	
Parameter	**Description**

TABLE 8-31. (Continued) Convert a single character string to its equivalent numeric value.

string	A single character string.
Return Value	**Condition**
integer	Upon success, it returns a numeric value corresponding to the ASCII code for the character; otherwise, it returns 0.

Listing 8-8 is an example of a file copy routine in server-side JavaScript that makes use of `readByte()`, `byteToString()`, and `writeByte()` methods.

Detecting Errors

The following functions give more details about file I/O failures. For example, if an `open("r")` fails, it may be because the file doesn't exist, you don't have permission to access it, or a number of other things. The `error()` function allows you to determine the operating system error returned by a file.

- *fileobj*.`error()` returns an integer corresponding to an operating system error status for the file.
- *fileobj*.`clearError()` clears the operating system error status.

Keep in mind that the error number returned is operating system-specific. Refer to your operating system documentation for details (For UNIX, look at the `fopen()` man page).

Summary

This chapter has focused on the nuts and bolts of server-side JavaScript functions, objects, and object-types. The server-side JavaScript object framework provides a powerful mechanism for collaboration between different users and different applications using the `project` and `server` objects. The `client` object is also an important component of maintaining information about each individual client.

Perhaps the most significant components for developing real applications is the database access and server-side file I/O support. These services are accomplished through the `database` object and `File` object-type respectively.

This chapter is intended to be a reference on server-side JavaScript components. We have given many examples, but have not addressed how the components interact with each other. In Chapter 9, we will show how the components mentioned can be used with each other to develop a real application.

```
<SERVER>
// Displays source in browser window and copy source to
destination
// Returns true on success, otherwise false
function display_and_copy_file(source, destination)
{
    var src = new File(source);
    var dst = new File(destination);
    var mybyte = 0;
    var rc = true;

    if (!src.exists())
    {
      write("<B>Error:</B> Source file does not exist!<P>");
       rc = false;
    }
    else
    {
       if (dst.exists())
          write("<B>Notice:</B> Destination file already
exists and will be overwritten!<P>");

       if (src.open("rb") && dst.open("wb"))
       {
         write("Copying server file <TT>" + source + "</TT>
to ");
         write("the destination <TT>" + destination + "</TT>
in ");
          write("addition to your browser window:<P>");
          write("<HR><PRE>");
          while (!src.eof())
          {
              mybyte = src.readByte();
              if (mybyte != -1)
              {
                 write(File.byteToString(mybyte));
                 dst.writeByte(mybyte);
              }
          }
          write("</PRE><HR>");
       }
```

LISTING 8-8   A FILE COPY ROUTINE USING THE BYTE ROUTINES OF THE FILE OBJECT.

```
    else
    {
        write("<B>Error:</B> Unable to open files!<P>");
        rc = false;
    }
    src.close();
    dst.close();
  }
  return(rc);
}

display_and_copy_file("mime.types", "mime.types.orig");
</SERVER>
```

Notice: Destination file already exists and will be
overwritten!

Copying server file mime.types to the destination
mime.types.orig in addition to your browser
window:

```
#--Netscape Communications Corporation MIME Information
# Do not delete the above line. It is used to identify the
file type.

type=application/octet-stream   exts=bin,exe
type=application/oda            exts=oda
type=application/pdf            exts=pdf
type=application/postscript     exts=ai,eps,ps
type=application/rtf            exts=rtf
...
```

LISTING 8-8   (CONTINUED) A FILE COPY ROUTINE USING THE BYTE ROUTINES OF THE FILE OBJECT.

Pulling
It All
Together

- Specify, Design, and Implement a Full-blown JavaScript application.
- Learn some unique tricks for verifying and storing form data.
- Learn how to access server-side files and SQL databases.

Overview

Up to this point, we have mostly talked about client-side and server-side JavaScript separately. However, their real strength is in being used together. By using them together, application development is much less complicated than an approach using the Common Gateway Interface (CGI). This is because you are using the same consistent language on both the client and the server. You don't have to artificially separate the code for the client and the server because they are embedded in the same page. If you were to use CGI in place of server-side JavaScript, you would have to create a special data handler script on the server separate from the HTML document.

The best way to show how client-side and server-side JavaScript work together is to create a non-trivial application that incorporates both and exploits some of their most significant features. We will do this by specifying, designing, and implementing a message board application.

Message Board Application Requirements

We would like to create our message board application so that it supports these requirements:

REQUIREMENT #1: Each message should consist of a handle for the person submitting the message and the actual message content. This information should be entered in an HTML form.

REQUIREMENT #2: The user should have the ability to clear the contents of the HTML form or to recall information entered in the previous submission.

REQUIREMENT #3: When the submit option is selected, the user should have the option to go ahead and send the message or to cancel it.

REQUIREMENT #4: The user should not be allowed to submit a form with blank fields or with characters that would compromise the integrity of our data.

REQUIREMENT #5: When the form is actually submitted, a unique message ID number and a time-stamp should be assigned.

REQUIREMENT #6: Once the message is sent, an HTML table containing all of the messages posted up to this point should be updated. This table should always be displayed below the data entry form. Each row should contain a message number, the handle of the person that posted the message, the content of the message, and the time the message was posted.

REQUIREMENT #7: Multiple client browsers should be allowed to post messages at the same time, so the user will need to have the ability to refresh the HTML table to contain the most current list of messages posted.

REQUIREMENT #8: The user should be able to select online help or information about the application.

Message Board Design Constraints

In addition to the application requirements, we need to make some design decisions about our message board application. These decisions will affect the ease of use, accessibility, and speed of the application.

CONSTRAINT #1: The message board application will only support Netscape Navigator 2.x or higher. This is because we want to use client-side JavaScript to verify form data, confirm submission of those data, and extract previously entered information stored in the browser's cookie file.

In this situation, we value ease of use over universal accessibility to the application. Data verification could be moved to the server, but it would put more load on the server and would not be as elegant.

If an invalid browser connects to the application, we will not attempt to run the application, but will display a page explaining the need for Netscape Navigator 2.x or higher. In this application, we have made some assumptions about things that must be performed on the client, so if client-side JavaScript is not supported, our application is crippled and will not meet all of its requirements.

CONSTRAINT #2: We will implement the storage of messages in two different ways—one will use a server-side file to store the messages and the other will use an SQL database. They will be implemented as a group of functions in two separate `.js` files. Depending on which approach you want to use, you will compile the desired `.js` file with the rest of the application files.

We will implement the database routines using the non-locking approach. However, we must always use locking with server-side files to ensure their integrity. So, in theory at least, the database version of our storage routines should allow for more parallelism, i.e., one client won't have to wait for another client to perform an operation.

CONSTRAINT #3: The application will be configured to use the `client-cookie` client object maintenance technique, otherwise we will not be able to recall the last message posted from a particular browser without a page reload.

Message Board Design

Program Logic

The flowchart in Figure 9-1 illustrates the overall logic of the message board application. After certain required operations are performed, the application goes into a state where it waits for form events to occur (mainly buttons being pressed). On the flowchart, the transition to this state is represented by dashed lines.

In general, the detailed steps in the flowchart could be summarized as follows:

1. Verify user environment.

2. Perform data initialization, if necessary.

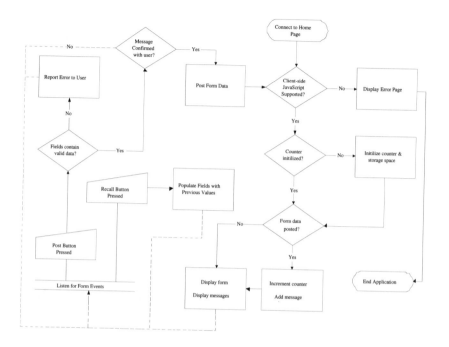

FIGURE 9-1   Logic of the Message Board application.

3. Add currently posted message, if any.

4. Setup user interface, including data entry form and message table.

5. Wait for form events.

6. Process form events when they occur.

User Interface

We would like the data entry form and message table to be on the same HTML page. The form should contain text boxes for the user's handle and message. It should also post messages, recall a previous message, clear the form, display program and help information, and refresh the message table. These operations may be performed using the following form buttons:

- **Post** - Submits the contents of your message to the server if the data meet the validation criteria.

- **Clear** - Clears the data fields that don't have a default value.
- **Refresh** - Refreshes the page to show you any new messages posted to the message table since it was last displayed.
- **Recall** - Recalls the last message entered by the current client browser.
- **Help** - Displays application help information in a separate window.
- **About** - Displays information about the program and its author in a separate window.

The message table should contain the message number, user, message content, and time-stamp for each message posted. Figure 9-2 gives a preliminary design of the user interface for the message board application, which includes the data entry form and message table.

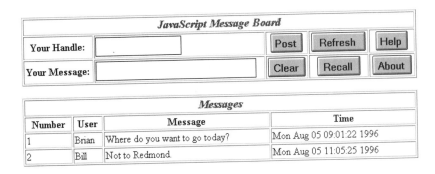

Number	User	Message	Time
1	Brian	Where do you want to go today?	Mon Aug 05 09:01:22 1996
2	Bill	Not to Redmond.	Mon Aug 05 11:05:25 1996

FIGURE 9-2   Preliminary design of the user interface.

Functional Organization of Message Board Application

Based on the program logic and user interface design, we can now identify the basic structure of the source files:

- `home.htm` - This will be the main page for the message board application. It will contain standard HTML for the data entry form. It will include client-side JavaScript functions for data verification, form interaction, and confirmation of message submission. It will also call external server-side JavaScript functions to perform message storage and retrieval.
- `invalid.htm` - This page will display when an invalid browser tries to connect to the application. It should state what version of browser is supported and allow the user to download a supported version. Of course, it should contain no JavaScript whatsoever.
- `help.htm` - This page should contain online help for the message board application.

- `about.htm` - This page should contain information about the application, version number, and programmer.
- `common.js` - This file should contain those server-side JavaScript functions that could potentially be called by multiple files in the application.
- `storage.js` - This file should contain all of the server-side functions used for the storage and retrieval of messages. We will be implementing this group of functions using two different approaches. The actual name of the file will be `iofunc.js` for server-side file storage and `dbfunc.js` for SQL database storage.

Figure 9-3 shows the functions that will be included in each application source file. A "**CS:**" before a function definition means that the function is to be executed in client-side JavaScript, and an "**SS:**" means that the function is to be executed in server-side JavaScript. When a function is subordinate to another function in the hierarchy of Figure 9-3, it means that the parent function needs the subordinate function to complete its operation.

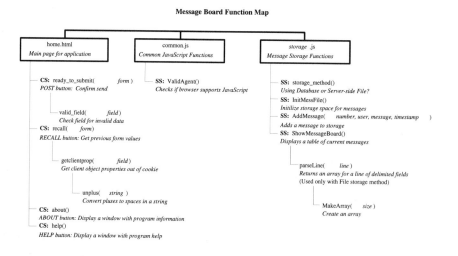

FIGURE 9-3 Message Board function map.

Partitioning the Application between the Client and the Server

Deciding whether a function gets executed in client-side JavaScript or server-side JavaScript is not arbitrary. Those functions that need to interact with the client browser are implemented in client-side JavaScript by necessity, and those functions that need to access server files and data use server-side JavaScript by necessity. In this application, we will use client cookies to pass data between the two.

Functions that make use of only the common components of the language could be included in either client-side or server-side code. For example, the `MakeArray()` function referred to in Figure 9-3 is needed in the server-side function `parseLine()`. However, this same function could be used to make an array in client-side JavaScript because it doesn't make use of any server-specific language components.

Implementing the Message Board Application

Based on the specifications and design, we can now begin implementing our message board application. The full source for the message board application, without any clarifying discussion, is included on the CD-ROM as explained in the Preface. However, in this section we will have a detailed step-by-step discussion of the implementation.

Creating the Main Application Page

We will start with the creation of the `home.htm` file. This will be the main page for the application and will be coded according to the application requirements previously mentioned. We will begin this file as we would a normal HTML file with an appropriate <HEAD> section:

```
<HTML>
<HEAD>
<TITLE>JavaScript Message Board</TITLE>
</HEAD>
```

Now, let's check to see if the current browser supports client-side JavaScript. We'll do this by calling the `ValidAgent()` function that we created in Chapter 8 in the section entitled "Using the `request.agent` Property to Verify a Browser".

We will not include the source for the `ValidAgent()` function in `home.htm`, but we will include it in `common.js` instead. This way, we will not have to duplicate the function for each page that needs client-side JavaScript support. Instead, we will include this code:

```
<BODY>
<SERVER>
// Verify that the browser supports client-side
JavaScript
if (!ValidAgent()) redirect("invalid.htm");
```

If execution continues, we know that we don't have a crippled browser and we can proceed with the meat of the application.

We will use a user-defined `counter` property of the server-side `project` object to generate a unique message ID for each message submitted. As we learned in the variable initialization discussion in Chapter 3, if a value has not yet been initialized, it has a value of `null`. Whenever a program is restarted in the LiveWire Application Manager, all user-defined properties of server-side objects set previously no longer exist. We can check if a value is `null` to determine if we need to initialize the `counter` variable and message storage file. These operations will be performed when the application is started for the first time and every time it is restarted.

The `InitMessFile()` function initializes the storage space used to store all of the messages. The source for the `InitMessFile()` function will be contained in our storage routines `.js` file.

```
// If the message counter hasn't been initialized
// then both the message file and the counter need
// to be initialized
if (project.counter == null)
{
    project.lock();
    project.counter = 0;
    project.unlock();
    result = InitMessFile();
    if (!result)
    {
        write("<BLINK>Error!  Unable to initialize Message
File.</BLINK><P>");
    }
}
```

Since the same `home.htm` will both accept form input and process its submission, we need to check each time the page is loaded to see if form data have been posted to it. This should be the first thing done after initialization to insure that the message table displayed on the page is up-to-date. If data are being posted, we need to increment the message counter and add the message.

In addition, before the message is added, a copy of the user and message are saved in the browser's cookie file using the server-side `client` object with the `client-cookie` maintenance technique. We will retrieve this information later from the browser's cookie file when using the `Recall` feature.

```
// If data is being posted from a form submission,
// then add the message
```

```
if (request.method == "POST")
{
    // Increment the message number
    project.lock();
    project.counter = 1 + parseInt(project.counter, 10);
    request.counter = project.counter;
    project.unlock();

    // Store the user and message in the client object so
it can
    // be recalled on the browser
    client.user = request.user;
    client.message = request.message;

    result =
AddMessage(request.counter,request.user,request.message,
request.timestamp);
    if (!result)
    {
        write("<BLINK>Error!  Unable to Add
Message.</BLINK><P>");
    }
}
</SERVER>
```

In client-side JavaScript, we need to create the OnClick event handler functions for the Post button. For the Post button, the function called when the button is selected is ready_to_submit(form) as shown in Figure 9-3. This function calls valid_field(field) to determine if each field contains valid data. At that point, the ready_to_submit function prompts the user for confirmation on sending the message. After confirmation, a time-stamp is generated by assigning a new Date() to a hidden form field (form.timestamp) and the data are actually submitted.

```
<SCRIPT>
// Checks text fields to ensure they aren't blank and
don't contain the
// "|" character
function valid_field(field)
{
    success = true;
    if (field.value.length > 0)
    {
        if (field.value.indexOf("|") != -1)
        {
```

```
            alert("You can't have a vertical bar character
in your input!");
            success = false;
        }
    }
    else
    {
        alert("You can't have a blank field!");
        success = false;
    }
    return success;
}


// Function executed before submission to verify input and
confirm sending
function ready_to_submit(form)
{
    if (valid_field(form.user) &&
valid_field(form.message))
    {
        if (confirm("Are you sure you want to post this
message?"))
        {
            // Sets the hidden timestamp field with the time
of submission (on the client)
            form.timestamp.value=new Date();
            form.submit();
        }
    }
}
```

We also need to create the OnClick event handler functions for the Recall button. For the Recall button, the function called when the button is selected is recall(form). This function calls getclientprop(field) to retrieve the last values for user and message from the cookie file. Properties are stored in the cookie file with pluses in place of spaces. We will use the unplus(old_str) function to convert the pluses back to spaces. For a more detailed discussion of getclientprop() and unplus(), see the section in Chapter 8 entitled "Using the client-cookie Technique to Communicate between Client-side and Server-side JavaScript".

Once the values are retrieved from the cookie file, recall() actually updates the form text boxes to contain those values.

```
// Replaces the plus (+) encoding with a space and returns
// the new string
```

```
function unplus(old_str)
{
    new_str = "";
    for (index = 0; index < old_str.length; index++)
    {
        if (old_str.charAt(index) == "+")
            new_str+=" ";
        else
            new_str+= old_str.charAt(index);
    }
    return new_str;
}

// Retrieves server-side JavaScript client object
// properties from cookie
function getclientprop(field)
{
    if (document.cookie.length > 0)
    {
        var search_in = document.cookie;
       var search_for = "NETSCAPE_LIVEWIRE." + field + "=";

        start = search_in.indexOf(search_for);
        if (start != -1)
        {
            start+=search_for.length;
            end = search_in.indexOf(";", start);
            if (end == -1) end = search_in.length;
            value =
unescape(unplus(search_in.substring(start, end)));
        }
        else
            value = null;
    }
    else
        value = null;

    return value;
}

// Used by the recall button to get the values from the
// previous posting
function recall(form)
{
    user = getclientprop("user");
    message = getclientprop("message");
```

```
      if (user != null && message != null)
      {
         form.user.value = user;
         form.message.value = message;
      }
   }
```

Now we need to create `OnClick` event handler functions for the `About` and `Help` buttons. These are very simple functions that use the `window.open()` client-side JavaScript function to pop up a new Navigator window and display the appropriate HTML page.

```
// Pop up about window
function about()
{
   aboutWin = window.open("about.htm", "about",
      "toolbar=no,location=no,directories=no,status=no,
      menubar=no,scrollbars=no,resizable=no,width=400,
      height=250");
}

// Pop up help window
function help()
{
   helpWin = window.open("help.htm", "help",
      "toolbar=no,location=no,directories=no,status=no,
      menubar=no,scrollbars=yes,resizable=yes,
      width=600,height=500");
}
</SCRIPT>
```

Next we need to create the HTML form for message submission. This form will include text boxes for the user handle and message, as well as buttons for all of the features mentioned in the user interface design section of this chapter and in Figure 9-2.

If a value for the user handle was entered in a previous posting to this page, it will become the default value for the user handle text box. This will be done using server-side JavaScript backquotes within the <INPUT> tag to supply a dynamic VALUE parameter.

We will also refer to the `OnClick` functions created previously for the `Post` and `Recall` buttons in the `OnClick` parameter of their respective <INPUT> tags. To implement the `Refresh` button, we will simply force a page reload by setting the client-side `window.location` property to `'home.htm'`.

```
<FORM METHOD="POST" ACTION="home.htm">
<TABLE BORDER WIDTH=100%>
<TR>
<TD ALIGN="center" COLSPAN="5"><FONT SIZE=+1
COLOR="red"><B><I>JavaScript Message Board using
<SERVER>storage_method();</SERVER></I></B></FONT></TD>
</TR>
<TR>
<TD ALIGN="center"><B>Your Handle:</B></TD>
<TD><INPUT TYPE="TEXT" NAME="user" SIZE="15"
MAXLENGTH="30" `(client.user != null) ? "VALUE='" +
client.user +"'" : " "`></TD>
<TD ALIGN="center"><INPUT TYPE="BUTTON" VALUE="Post"
onClick="ready_to_submit(this.form)"></TD>
<TD ALIGN="center"><INPUT TYPE="BUTTON" VALUE="Refresh"
onClick="window.location='home.htm'"></TD>
<TD ALIGN="center"><INPUT TYPE="BUTTON" VALUE="Help"
onClick="help()"></TD>
</TR>
<TR>
<TD ALIGN="center"><B>Your Message:</B></TD>
<TD><INPUT TYPE="TEXT" NAME="message" SIZE="50"
MAXLENGTH="80"></TD>
<TD ALIGN="center"><INPUT TYPE="RESET"
VALUE="Clear"></TD>
<TD ALIGN="center"><INPUT TYPE="BUTTON" VALUE="Recall"
onClick="recall(this.form)"></TD>
<TD ALIGN="center"><INPUT TYPE="BUTTON" VALUE="About"
onClick="about()"></TD>
</TR>
</TABLE>
<INPUT TYPE="HIDDEN" NAME="timestamp" VALUE="None">
</FORM>
```

Now we need to display an HTML table of the current messages posted to the message board. We will call the ShowMessageBoard() function contained in the message storage .js file to accomplish this.

```
<SERVER>
// Dumps a table of the current messages
ShowMessageBoard();
</SERVER>
</BODY>
</HTML>
```

We are done with the creation of `home.htm`. At this point, the page is completely displayed and is waiting to process form events. In the code for this page, we referred to some server-side JavaScript functions that we have not yet coded: `ValidAgent()`, `InitMessFile()`, `AddMessage()`, and `ShowMessageBoard()`. You will need to create the `common.js` file and include the `ValidAgent()` function in it as implemented in Chapter 8.

Implementing Message Storage Using a Server-side File

We are now ready to begin implementing the message storage functions `InitMessFile()`, `AddMessage()`, and `ShowMessageBoard()` using the server-side `File()` object-type. We will store these functions along with any supporting functions in `iofunc.js`.

To determine which message storage technique we are using, we will create a `storage_method()` function that reports the current method. We will display this message as part of the header to our HTML form in `home.htm`.

```
// Reports which set of storage routines are being used
function storage_method()
{
    write("Server-Side File I/O");
}
```

Now we need to create the `InitMessFile()` function. We will store the messages in the file `messages.txt` in the server's `config` subdirectory. If the file already exists, we need to discard the previous contents; if it doesn't exist, we should create it.

```
// Initializes the message file
function InitMessFile()
{
    // Create an empty message file
    project.lock();
    messfile = new File("messages.txt");
    success = messfile.open("w");
    messfile.close();
    project.unlock();
    return success;
}
```

Now we need to come up with a convention for storing messages in the text file:

- We will store one message per line of the text file, with the new-line character terminating a line.
- We will separate fields on the line by using the vertical bar character, "|". It is for this reason that we do not allow a form field to contain the vertical bar character.

```
// Appends a message to the end of the message file
function AddMessage(number, user, message, timestamp)
{
    project.lock();
    messfile = new File("messages.txt");
    success = messfile.open("a");
    if (success)
    {
        success =
messfile.writeln("|"+number+"|"+user+"|"+message+"|"+tim
estamp+"|");
    }
    messfile.close();
    project.unlock();
    return success;
}
```

The message file will look similar to Figure 9-4.

```
|1|Larry|Hello.|Mon Jun 03 09:01:22  1996|
|2|Moe|Goodbye.|Mon Jun 03 09:10:52  1996|
|3|Curly|Huh?|Mon Jun 03 09:11:41  1996|
```

FIGURE 9-4   Sample content of `messages.txt` server-side file.

Now that we have determined the form the messages will be stored in, we can create the routines to retrieve that information. The `parseLine()` function will take a line from the file and separate the individual fields into an array. This function makes use of the `MakeArray()` function to accomplish this.

```
// Creates an empty array
function MakeArray(size)
{
    this.length = size;
    for (var index = 1; index <= size; index++)
    {
        this[index] = 0;
```

```
        }
        return this;
}

// parses a line of "|" separated fields into an array
function parseLine(line)
{
    previous = 0;
    counter = 0;
    element = new MakeArray(4);
    for (index = 1; index < line.length; index++)
    {
        if (line.charAt(index) == "|")
        {
            end = index;
            element[counter++] =
                line.substring(previous+1,end);
            previous = end;
        }
    }
    return element;
}
```

The ShowMessageBoard() function reads each line of the file, calls parseLine() to return each line in an array, and displays the individual elements in an HTML table.

```
// Reads the entire message file, parses each line into
// fields, and dumps to a table
function ShowMessageBoard()
{
    project.lock();
    messfile = new File("messages.txt");
    success = messfile.open("r");
    if (success)
    {
        write ("<TABLE BORDER WIDTH=100%>");
        write ("<TR><TD ALIGN=center COLSPAN=4>"+
            "<FONT SIZE=+1 COLOR=red><B><I>Messages</I>"+
            "</B></FONT></TD></TR>");
        write ("<TR><TH>Number</TH><TH>User</TH><TH>"+
            "Message</TH><TH>Time</TH></TD>");
        while (!messfile.eof())
        {
            line = messfile.readln();
            if (!messfile.eof())
```

```
        {
            write("<TR>");
            element = parseLine(line);
            for (i=0; i < 4; i++)
            {
                write("<TD>" + element[i] + "</TD>");
            }
            write("</TR>");
        }
    }
    write ("</TABLE>");
    }
    messfile.close();
    project.unlock();
}
```

Implementing Message Storage Using an SQL Database

Now we will implement these very same message storage functions using the server-side `database` object and `database.cursor` object-type. We will store these functions in `dbfunc.js`.

As before, we will create a `storage_method()` function to report which storage routines we are using (either file or database).

```
function storage_method()
{
    write("Server-Side Database Support");
}
```

Next we need to create the `InitMessFile()` function. When implemented using the database routines, `InitMessFile()` performs these operations:

- Connect to the database.
- Drop the existing `Messages` table, if any.
- Create a new `Messages` table.

```
// Opens the Database then Drops and Recreates the
// Messages Table
function InitMessFile()
{
    if(!database.connected())
    {
        database.connect("INFORMIX", "dbhost", "livewire",
            "livewire", "livewire");
```

```
   }

   if (!database.connected())
   {
      write("Error: Unable to connect to database.");
      success = false;
   }
   else
   {
      // Create an empty messages table
      database.execute("DROP TABLE Messages");
      success = !database.execute("CREATE TABLE
         Messages (Number INTEGER NOT NULL, User
         VARCHAR(30,0) NOT NULL, Message VARCHAR(80,0)
         NOT NULL, Time DATETIME YEAR TO FRACTION(3)
         NOT NULL)");
   }
   return success;
}
```

Keep in mind that the data-types in the CREATE TABLE command may vary slightly depending on which DBMS you are using. This example uses Informix.

We will implement the database version of the AddMessage() function using an updateable cursor. This way, we will not introduce any database vendor-specific SQL statements. This code should work with any of the databases supported by LiveWire.

```
// Inserts the Message into the Messages Table
function AddMessage(number, user, message, timestamp)
{
   cursor = database.cursor("SELECT * FROM Messages",
            true);
   cursor.next();
   time = new Date(timestamp);
   cursor.Number = number;
   cursor.User = user;
   cursor.Message = message;
   cursor.Time = time;
   // insertRow returns 0 if OK
   error = cursor.insertRow("Messages");
   cursor.close();
   if (error == 0)
      return true;
   else
```

```
   {
      debug("Database Error #" + error);
      return false;
   }
}
```

Now we will implement the database version of the ShowMessage-Board() function. It will be very similar to the prettyresults() function created in the section entitled "Retrieving the Results of the Query associated with a Cursor" in Chapter 8.

```
// Dump Message Table using Cursors
function ShowMessageBoard()
{
   cursor = database.cursor("SELECT * FROM Messages
            ORDER BY Number", false);
   write ("<TABLE BORDER WIDTH=100%>");
   write ("<TR><TD ALIGN=center COLSPAN=4>"+
          "<FONT SIZE=+1 COLOR=red><B><I>Messages</I>"+
          "</B></FONT></TD></TR>");
   write ("<TR><TH>Number</TH><TH>User</TH>"+
          "<TH>Message</TH><TH>Time</TH></TD>");
   while (cursor.next())
   {
      write("<TR>");
      write("<TD>" + cursor.Number + "</TD>");
      write("<TD>" + cursor.User + "</TD>");
      write("<TD>" + cursor.Message + "</TD>");
      write("<TD>" + cursor.Time + "</TD>");
      write("</TR>");
   }
   write ("</TABLE>");
   cursor.close();
}
```

Compiling and Installing the Message Board Application

We have completed all of the code for the message board application. We are now ready to compile and install the application on the Web server using LiveWire. We will actually install two different versions of the application:

- messfile - This will be the version of the message board application that uses a server-side file to store the messages.
- messdb - This will be the version of the message board application that uses an SQL database to store the messages.

To compile each version, we will enter the following commands at the operating system prompt:

- **lwcomp -v -o** messfile.web home.htm invalid.htm about.htm help.htm *iofunc.js* common.js
- **lwcomp -v -o** messdb.web home.htm invalid.htm about.htm help.htm *dbfunc.js* common.js

Refer to the CD-ROM for sample content of the `invalid.htm`, `about.htm`, and `help.htm` files. Make sure these files exist before actually trying to compile the projects.

Once you have successfully compiled the two projects into `.web` files, you are ready to go to the LiveWire Application Manager and install them. Tables 9-1 and 9-2 show the parameters that must be entered into the Add Application form for each of the two versions of the message board application. Refer to Chapter 7 for more details on using the LiveWire Application Manager to install applications.

TABLE 9-1. *Application Manager parameters to install the file I/O version of the message board application.*

Name	messfile
Object File Path	C:/.../develop/messages/messfile.web
Default URL	home.htm
Initial URL	home.htm
External Libraries	None
Maximum Database Connections	None
Client Mode	client-cookie

TABLE 9-2. *Application Manager parameters to install the database version of the message board application.*

Name	messdb
Object File Path	C:/.../develop/messages/messdb.web

TABLE 9-2. (Continued) Application Manager parameters to install the database version of the message board application.

Default URL	home.htm
Initial URL	home.htm
External Libraries	None
Maximum Database Connections	10
Client Mode	client-cookie

The maximum database connections in Table 9-2 will depend on your application needs and database licensing. Of course, the object file paths in Tables 9-1 and 9-2 will vary depending on where you actually compiled the .web files.

Testing and Verifying the Message Board Application

We are now ready to begin testing the message board application to see if it meets the requirements specified earlier in this chapter. To connect to the message board, we can choose the desired URL of either http://*hostname*/messfile/ or http://*hostname*/messdb/, where *hostname* is the actual name of the Web server running LiveWire.

The first time anyone connects to the application we should see something similar to that of Figure 9-5 where the message board has no messages on it.

JavaScript Message Board using Server-Side File I/O				
Your Handle:		Post	Refresh	Help
Your Message:		Clear	Recall	About

Messages			
Number	User	Message	Time

FIGURE 9-5   A view of the initial connection to the message board.

Now, let's see how well we did at meeting the application requirements:

Requirement #1. Each message should consist of a handle for the person submitting the message and the actual message content that will be entered in an HTML form. As shown in Figure 9-5, this requirement has been met.

Requirement #3. This states that when the submit option is selected, the user should have the option to go ahead and send the message or to cancel it. Let's enter a message and confirm submission. Figure 9-6 shows the confirmation window and Figure 9-7 shows the resulting page after confirmation. Notice in Figure 9-7 that the value entered for the user in Figure 9-6 is retained as the new default value for that field.

FIGURE 9-6   Confirm sending a message to the message board.

Requirement #5. When the form is actually submitted, a unique message ID number and time-stamp should be assigned. Figure 9-7 shows that this was actually done for our first message.

Requirement #6. An HTML table of messages will always be displayed below the data entry form. Each row will contain a message number, the handle of the person who posted the message, the content of the message, and the time the message was posted. Again, Figure 9-7 verifies this.

Requirement #2. The user will have the ability to clear the contents of the HTML form or recall information entered in the previous submission. If

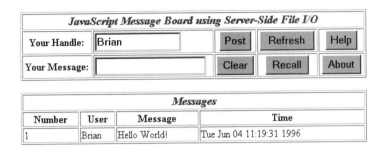

FIGURE 9-7   A view of the message board after the first message is posted.

we click the Recall button, the previously posted message from this client will appear in the message text box as shown in Figure 9-8.

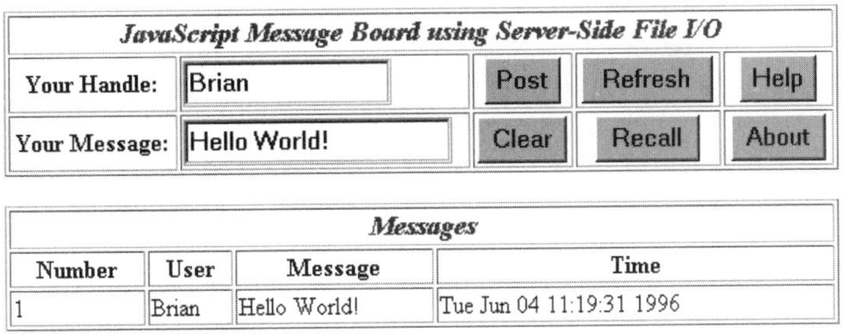

FIGURE 9-8   The result of recalling the previously posted message.

Requirement #4. The user should not be allowed to submit a form with blank fields or with characters that would compromise the integrity of our data. Let's try to submit a form with a blank message. Figure 9-9 shows the alert that results. A similar message will appear if a field contains the vertical bar character.

This completes our verification of the most significant requirements of the message board application. We did the verification for the `messfile` version but you should have the exact same results for the `messdb` version.

Summary

In this chapter we have created a non-trivial message board application that made use of many significant aspects of JavaScript. You learned how to

FIGURE 9-9 The message board application alerts the user to input errors.

use client-side JavaScript to verify and confirm form data. You also used it to extract properties stored in cookies. You learned how to use server-side Java-Script to create and access server files. You also learned how to use it to access and modify databases. These are some of the most useful features of client-side and server-side JavaScript.

After completing this program and the other examples in the book, you should feel confident in using JavaScript to develop real-world Web-based applications. Happy scripting!

C H A P T E R   1 0

Active Pages
with
JavaScript

- **Create Java Applets that can be accessed from JavaScript.**
- **Access the Java API from JavaScript.**
- **Update Images in an HTML page on the fly.**
- **Update elements of an HTML form pop-up or list box.**

Introduction

Up to this point in the book, we have learned how to have active pages using the following approaches:

- Updating the contents of form text boxes using JavaScript.
- Using JavaScript to cause an entirely new page to display in a frame.
- Using JavaScript to force a page reload. This causes the browser to get the most current data from the server for the creation of the page.

With the introduction of Netscape Navigator 3.0, there are some new JavaScript extensions that allow for even more flexibility in displaying dynamic content:

- Java/JavaScript communications.
- Updateable images.
- Updateable form select options

These new extensions to JavaScript go a long way in making an HTML page seem much more like a traditional GUI application in Microsoft Windows, the MacOS, or X Windows.

367

Java/JavaScript Communications

We will only discuss Java in so far as it relates to JavaScript. For a more in-depth discussion of Java, you should refer to one of the Java titles in this same series published by Prentice-Hall.

As mentioned in the Preface, Java is a full-featured object-oriented programming language that creates separate applets (mini-applications) that don't interrelate with HTML like JavaScript does. These applets display in a portion of the HTML page similar to the way an embedded image does.

The source for these applets must be compiled into platform-independent machine code before it can be used by the browser. In an HTML document, the Java applet is referenced using the `<APPLET>` tag. Unlike JavaScript's use of the `<SCRIPT>` tag, Java code is not embedded within the `<APPLET>` tag. The `<APPLET>` tag only gives a reference to the compiled file. Consider the following HTML code for including a Java applet as part of an HTML document:

```
<APPLET NAME="mygraph" CODE="mygraph.class" WIDTH=300
    HEIGHT=300 MAYSCRIPT>
<PARAM NAME=myvalues VALUE="12,24,19,72,18,97">
</APPLET>
```

This HTML will load the `mygraph.class` applet into a 300x300 pixel area on the page. The applet will be passed an initial value of `"12,24,19,72,18,97"` for `myvalues` parameter. The `MAYSCRIPT` specified in the `<APPLET>` tag allows the applet to be accessed by JavaScript.

Until Netscape Navigator 3.0, there has been no way for JavaScript and Java to communicate. Previously, about the only thing you could do was have JavaScript generate the `<APPLET>` tag with dynamic values for the initial `<PARAM>` values. But once the page was displayed, those parameters could not be changed again without a page reload. However, now with the Netscape LiveConnect technology, Java applets and client-side JavaScript can now communicate with each other.

Java is a very powerful general purpose language that can solve problems which simply can't be solved using HTML and JavaScript. However, until now there was no way for a Java applet to determine things like the title of the page it is in, the value of an HTML form element in that page, and so forth. With LiveConnect, you can think of JavaScript as the communications link between an HTML page and a Java applet.

For example, you could have a user enter values into an HTML form. Based on those values, you could have JavaScript send the form data to a Java graphing applet. This applet could produce a new graph based on the entered data. There is no way within HTML or JavaScript to have a graph that is updated dynamically in this way.

Using the combination of JavaScript and Java, developers can now do things on the Web that were just not possible before. Having the ability to display Java applets in a browser was a major step forward for Web developers. Now that Java applets can communicate and interact with other elements of the page, it is even more useful.

Creating Applets that are JavaScript Friendly

Most existing Java applets up to this point were not created to be "JavaScript Friendly". In order for an applet to be "JavaScript Friendly", it must support the following guidelines:

- Import the `netscape.javascript.*` package. This package is included in the `moz3_0.zip` file that comes with Navigator 3.0. You should make sure that `moz3_0.zip` is included in your Java `CLASSPATH` when compiling "JavaScript Friendly" applets.
- Implement the applet as a `Runnable` class. Many applets perform their necessary operations and terminate. We want to be able to change the applet on the fly and we need it to still be running to do this.

Accessing a Java Applet from JavaScript

For JavaScript to be able to communicate with a Java applet, we must create methods of that applet to be called from JavaScript. These methods are used to update the current state of the applet. For example, you could create an `updategraph` public method of the `mygraph` applet:

```
public void updategraph(String newmyvalues)
{
...
}
```

To call the above method from JavaScript you would execute this statement:

```
document.mygraph.updategraph("18,14,21,45,83,7")
```

In general, you can refer to an applet in JavaScript in any of the following ways:

- `document.appletname`
- `document.applets["appletname"]`

- `document.applets[i]`, with `i` being a number between 0 and `document.applets.length-1`;
`document.applets.length` refers to the number of applets on a page.

All public variables and methods available in an applet are accessible in JavaScript as methods and properties of the applet object referred to above. For example, you could call a public method of an applet using the syntax document.*appletname.methodname(param_1, ..., param_n)* or you could access a public property of an applet using the syntax document.*appletname.propertyname.*

Accessing JavaScript from a Java Applet

In order to access any JavaScript components from a Java applet, you must get a handle for the JavaScript window using the `getWindow()` method of `JSObject`. Table 10-1 gives the syntax for the `getWindow()` method. The following is an example of its use:

JSObject mywin = **JSObject.getWindow(this)**;

TABLE 10-1. Get a handle for the JavaScript window that the applet is embedded in.

handle = JSObject.getWindow(applet_reference)	
Parameter	**Description**
applet_reference	A `java.applet.Applet` object. Usually the value will be `this`, meaning the current applet.
Return Value	**Condition**
handler	A `netscape.javascript.JSObject` object that corresponds to the JavaScript window handle returned.

Once a window handle is created, you can use the `getMember()` method of the `JSObject` type to access JavaScript objects at the current level in the object hierarchy. Table 10-2 explains the syntax of the `getMember()` method. The following Java code extracts the `document.cookie` JavaScript property and displays it on the Java console using `getMember()`:

```
JSObject win = JSObject.getWindow(this);
JSObject doc = (JSObject)
    win.getMember("document");
```

```
String cookieval = (String)
        doc.getMember("cookie").toString();
System.err.println(cookieval);
```

TABLE 10-2. *Create a new sub-object for a property of the current JavaScript object.*

mysubObject = myJSObject.getMember(member_name)	
Parameter	**Description**
myJSObject	The name of the current JavaScript object of the type JSObject for which you want to retrieve a sub-object.
member_name	A String object that refers to the name of the JavaScript sub-object that you would like to retrieve from *myJSObject*. For example, this could be "hostname" if *myJSObject* contained the "location" JavaScript object.
Return Value	**Condition**
mysubObject	Returns a Java object corresponding to the *member_name* JavaScript object.

Notice that in the final call to getMember(), we use the toString() method to convert the JSObject to a string. See Table 10-3 for the syntax of toString().

TABLE 10-3. *Return a* String *corresponding to a* JSObject*.*

myJSObjectStr = myJSObject.toString();	
Parameter	**Description**
myJSObject	The name of the JavaScript object of the type JSObject that you would like to convert to a string.
Return Value	**Condition**
myJSObjectStr	Returns a String object corresponding to the value of *myJSObject*.

In addition to being able to get the value of a JSObject property using getMember(), you can also set a value of a JSObject using the setMember() method. The syntax of the setMember() method is shown in Table 10-4.

TABLE 10-4. *Set the value of a property of the current JavaScript object.*

myJSObject.setMember(member_name, member_value)	
Parameter	**Description**
myJSObject	The name of a JavaScript object of the JSObject type for which you would like to set a property.
member_name	A String object that refers to the name of the property of *myJSObject* that you would like set.
member_value	A standard Java Object or one of its children (i.e. String) that corresponds to the value you would like to set for *member_name*.

Another way to extract the value of *document.cookie* in Java is to use the *eval()* method of the *JSObject* type. Table 10-5 shows the syntax of *eval()*. The *eval()* method takes any valid JavaScript statement and returns its value. The following code uses the *eval()* method to display the contents of *document.cookie* on the Java console like in the previous example:

```
JSObject win = JSObject.getWindow(this);
String cookieval = (String)
      win.eval("document.cookie");
System.err.println(cookieval);
```

TABLE 10-5. *Evaluate a JavaScript expression.*

myObject = myJSObject.eval(javascript_expression);	
Parameter	**Description**
myJSObject	The name of a JavaScript object of the type JSObject. Generally, this is just the object returned from the getWindow() method.
javascript_expression	This is a String corresponding to any valid JavaScript expression within the context of *myJSObject*.
Return Value	**Condition**
myObject	Returns a standard Object corresponding to the value returned from *javascript_expression*.

If you would like to call a JavaScript function or method in Java, you will need to use the call() method of the JSObject type. Table 10-6 explains the syntax of the call() method. The following example illustrates a Java method used to call the JavaScript prompt() function.

```java
// Call JavaScript prompt function
private String JSPrompt(String mess, String defvalue)
{
    JSObject win = JSObject.getWindow(this);
    Object jsargs[] = new Object[2];
    jsargs[0] = mess;
    jsargs[1] = defvalue;
    Object result = win.call("prompt", jsargs);
    if (result != null)
        return result.toString();
    else
        return null;
}
```

TABLE 10-6. Call a JavaScript function from Java.

myObject = myJSObject.call(javascript_function, param_array);	
Parameter	**Description**
myJSObject	The name of a JavaScript object of the type JSObject.
javascript_function	This is a String corresponding to a JavaScript function or method within the context of *myJSObject*.
param_array	This is an array of standard Object types that contain the parameters for the actual JavaScript function. One parameter should be stored per array element.
Return Value	**Condition**
myObject	Returns a standard Object corresponding to the value returned from *javascript_function*.

An Example of Java/JavaScript Communication

We are going to create a `rainbow` Java applet and an associated HTML file that demonstrate how to communicate between JavaScript and Java using the techniques we have learned so far. This applet will accept a text string and display each character of the string in a different color created at random. By default, each character displayed will also change color in real-time on the HTML page. The user will be allowed to change the message text or to toggle the real-time color rotation.

Listing 10-1 contains the HTML document that references the `rainbow` applet. Notice that there are no text boxes to prompt for the new message. There are two buttons—one to change the message and another to toggle the color update. On a click, both of these buttons call an associated public method of the `rainbow` class which actually makes the change.

```
<HTML>
<HEAD>
<TITLE>JavaScript Example 10-1 (Java/JavaScript
Communications)</TITLE>
</HEAD>
<BODY BACKGROUND="white">
<H2><SCRIPT LANGUAGE="JavaScript">document.write(
document.title)</SCRIPT></H2>
<HR>
<APPLET NAME="rainbow" CODE="rainbow.class" WIDTH=600
HEIGHT=50 MAYSCRIPT>
<PARAM NAME=message VALUE="Rainbow Connection!">
</APPLET>
<BR>
<FORM NAME="changeapp">
<B>Font Size: </B>
<SELECT NAME="fontsize">
<OPTION VALUE="12">12
<OPTION VALUE="24" SELECTED>24
<OPTION VALUE="48">48
</SELECT>
<I>Only updated when message is changed.</I>
<BR>
<INPUT TYPE=button VALUE="Change Message"
ONCLICK="this.form.changeattempt.value++;document.rainbow.
changeMessage()">
```

LISTING 10-1   THE HTML PAGE FOR SCRIPTABLE RAINBOW JAVA APPLET.

```
<INPUT TYPE=button VALUE="Toggle Color Update"
ONCLICK="document.rainbow.updateColors()">
<P>
<INPUT TYPE="HIDDEN" NAME="changeattempt" VALUE="0">
</FORM>
</BODY>
</HTML>
```

LISTING 10-1   (CONTINUED) THE HTML PAGE FOR SCRIPTABLE RAINBOW JAVA APPLET.

The listing `rainbow.java` gives the Java code for the `rainbow` applet. Notice the `changeMessage()` and `updateColors()` methods called from the HTML page. These two Java methods actually make use of the JavaScript `prompt()` and `alert()` functions rather that using the much more complicated approach creating dialog boxes using Java.

```
import java.awt.Graphics;
import java.awt.Font;
import java.awt.Color;
import netscape.javascript.*;

public class rainbow extends java.applet.Applet implements
Runnable
{
    // Define private class variables
    Thread mythread = null;
    String message = null;
    char letters[];
    Color fontcolor = Color.black;
    boolean updatecolor = true;
    int index;
    int fontsize = 24;
    int position = 0;
    // This is the applet initialization method
    public void init()
    {
        // Need a fixed width font so fixed spacing between
        // characters looks normal for drawChars()
```

LISTING   RAINBOW.JAVA: THE SOURCE FOR THE SCRIPTABLE RAINBOW JAVA APPLET.

```
      setFont(new Font("Courier",Font.BOLD,fontsize));
      setBackground(Color.white);

      // Get message as a parameter, otherwise supply
      // default
      message = getParameter("message");

      // Update the letters[] array for the new message
      update_letters();
   }

   // Call this method to change to contents of the message
   public void changeMessage()
   {
      // Prompt the user for a new message
      String newmessage = JSPrompt("Enter the new message:",
                                   message);
      if (newmessage != null)
      {
      // Get the current font size from the HTML form select
      // and change the font size to reflect its current
      // value
      JSObject win = JSObject.getWindow(this);
      String fontszstr =
        (String) win.eval(
        "document.changeapp.fontsize.options[
        document.changeapp.fontsize.selectedIndex].value");
      fontsize = Integer.parseInt(fontszstr);
      setFont(new Font("Courier",Font.BOLD,fontsize));

      // Display the number of change attempts on the console
      JSObject doc = (JSObject) win.getMember("document");
      JSObject form = (JSObject) doc.getMember("changeapp");
      JSObject ct =
          (JSObject) form.getMember("changeattempt");
      String ctval =
          (String) ct.getMember("value").toString();
      System.err.println("# of change attempts: " + ctval);

      // Actually Change the Message
      stop();
      message = newmessage;
```

```
      update_letters();
      start();
      repaint();
        }
  }

  // Call JavaScript alert function
  private void JSAlert(String mess)
  {
      JSObject win = JSObject.getWindow(this);
      Object jsargs[] = new Object[1];
      jsargs[0] = mess;
      win.call("alert", jsargs);
  }

  // Call JavaScript prompt function
  private String JSPrompt(String mess, String defvalue)
  {
      JSObject win = JSObject.getWindow(this);
      Object jsargs[] = new Object[2];
      jsargs[0] = mess;
      jsargs[1] = defvalue;
      Object result = win.call("prompt", jsargs);
      if (result != null)
    return result.toString();
      else
    return null;
  }

  // Call this method to toggle the continuous update of
  // colors
  public void updateColors()
  {
      stop();
      updatecolor = !updatecolor;
      start();
      JSAlert("The color update has been turned " +
              (updatecolor ? "on." : "off."));
  }

  // This method is called when the applet is started
  public void start()
  {
```

LISTING   (CONTINUED) RAINBOW.JAVA: THE SOURCE FOR THE SCRIPTABLE RAINBOW JAVA APPLET.

```java
   if (mythread == null)
   {
 mythread = new Thread(this);
 mythread.start();
   }
}

// This method is called when the applet is stopped
public void stop()
{
   mythread.stop();
   mythread = null;
}

// This is the main method for a "Runnable" class
public void run()
{
   while (mythread != null)
   {
 try {Thread.sleep(200);}
   catch (InterruptedException e){}
 if (updatecolor) repaint();
   }
   mythread = null;
}

// Draws the rainbow letters
public void paint(Graphics g)
{
   for (index=0; index < message.length(); index++)
   {
 position = 5+fontsize*index;
 fontcolor = new Color((int)(Math.random()*255),
               (int)(Math.random()*255),
               (int)(Math.random()*255));
 g.setColor(fontcolor);
 g.drawChars(letters,index,1,position,fontsize);
   }
}
// Updates the letters array with the contents of the
// message string
private void update_letters()
{
```

LISTING   (CONTINUED) RAINBOW.JAVA: THE SOURCE FOR THE SCRIPTABLE RAINBOW JAVA APPLET.

```
      if (message == null) message = "Rainbow Text!";
      letters =  new char [message.length()];
      message.getChars(0,message.length(),letters,0);
   }
}
```

Remember that `rainbow.java` must be compiled into a `.class` file using the Java compiler. The `moz3_0.zip` file must be included in `javac`'s `CLASSPATH` in order for it to find the `netscape.*` packages. Now let's view the `rainbow` applet in action and specifically point out some of the points where Java and JavaScript are interacting. Figure 10-1 shows the HTML page with the embedded `rainbow` applet.

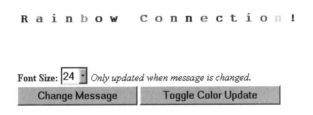

FIGURE 10-1   The rainbow applet in action.

When the *change message* button is selected, the code for its JavaScript `ONCLICK` event handler is executed. First, the `changeattempt` variable is incremented by executing `this.form.changeattempt.value++`. This variable keeps track of the number of times the *change message* button is pressed. After incrementing `changeattempt`, the `changeMessage()` method of the rainbow applet is called from JavaScript by executing `document.rainbow.changeMessage()`. Figure 10-2 shows the prompt that pops up when the *change message* button is pressed.

No where in the HTML page of Listing 10-1 is there any JavaScript code for the `prompt()` function. This JavaScript built-in function is called from the `rainbow` applet using the `call()` method of the Java `JSObject`.

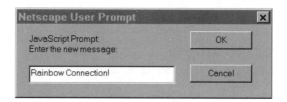

FIGURE 10-2 Changing the content of the rainbow message.

When a new message is selected, the font size of the message is updated as well. The font size is stored in a SELECT box in the HTML form. However, this value is never passed to the Java applet. The `rainbow` applet actually used the `eval()` method of the `JSObject` to retrieve the value from the form by executing `eval("document.changeapp.fontsize.options[docu-ment.changeapp.fontsize.selectedIndex].value")`.

As we can see from this example, Java and JavaScript are both made more powerful by the ability to interact with each other. JavaScript is the real key to integrating Java applets with an HTML page rather than having them be an entirely separate entity just taking up real-estate on the same page.

Accessing the Standard Java Packages from JavaScript

In addition to being able to communicate back and forth between JavaScript and a Java applet in an HTML page, JavaScript can also make use of the standard Java packages such as `java.*`, `sun.*`, and `netscape.*`. For example, Java has a `Stack` class that could be very useful in some JavaScript applications. The following code illustrates how to use Java's `Stack` class in JavaScript:

```
var mystack = new java.util.Stack();
mystack.push("25");
mystack.push("15");
mystack.push("21");
mystack.push("19");

while(!mystack.empty())
{
        document.writeln(mystack.pop());
}
```

This opens up JavaScript to the wealth of powerful Java objects available as part of the standard Java API. You can use Java's `Float` data-type rather than relying on JavaScript's basic numeric type. The following example creates a new `Float` variable and displays it both as a floating point number and an integer:

```
var myfloat = new java.lang.Float(123.451);
document.writeln(myfloat);
document.writeln(myfloat.intValue());
```

In general, to create Java objects in JavaScript use the syntax of Table 10-7. You should access the properties and methods of these Java objects using the same syntax that would be used in Java

TABLE 10-7. Create a JavaScript variable of a Java object-type.

`var varname = new packageName.class_constructor(parameters);`	
Parameter	**Description**
packageName	The name of the desired Java package such as `java.lang`, `sun.tools`, or `netscape.net`.
class_constructor	The name of the Java constructor for the desired class. For example, this could be `Float()` if the *packageName* was `java.lang`.
parameters	This could be any optional or required parameters for the specified constructor.
Return Value	**Condition**
varname	Returns a new object of the specified type.

Updateable Images

Almost all HTML writers should be familiar with the `<IMG>` tag used to imbed an image within an HTML document. Until Navigator 3.0, it was impossible to change the content of an image once the document had been loaded. Now, within JavaScript, there is a facility to create and update images within an HTML document without reloading the entire page. Updating images is done through the `document.images[]` array as explained in Table 10-8.

TABLE 10-8. Updating an Image in an HTML document.

document.images[i].src = *imageURL*;	
Parameter	**Description**
i	document.images[] is an array containing all of the images in the HTML document. The index *i* is any value between 0 and *n-1* where *n* is the number of images on a particular page.
imageURL	A string containing the URL for the new image.

It is important to note that the size of the updated image will be the same as the original image. For example, image A is a 100x200 pixel image included in an HTML page with those same dimensions in the <IMG> tag. You decided you want to change this image to image B. Image B is a 400x400 pixel image. Image B will be resized to 100x200 before it is displayed on the page.

Now let's create a simple HTML page that allows users to choose the kind of marble they want for the bathrooms in their house. When they select a certain color of marble the page will automatically show them the new color.

Figure 10-3 shows how Listing 10-2 first appears in the browser. When any of the other colors are chosen from the select box, the associated image is automatically updated as well. Figure 10-4 shows the results of selecting the color white.

As demonstrated with the previous example, having the ability to change an image on the page as a result of interaction with the user can be very useful when trying to display dynamic content.

Updateable Form Select Options

In addition to being able to update images on the fly with Navigator 3.0, you can also update the contents of pop-up menus and list boxes created using the HTML <SELECT> tag. To change the content of the text of a particular SELECT element in JavaScript, you would refer to it using the syntax of Table 10-9.

Listing 10-3 gives an example of using this technique to change the order of the elements in a list box from ascending to descending order.

Figure 10-5 shows how Listing 10-3 first appears in the browser. When descending order is chosen from the *order* select box, the list in the *nameselect* select box is updated to reflect the change as illustrated in Figure 10-6.

```
<HTML>
<HEAD>
<TITLE>JavaScript Example 10-2 (Updating an Image)</TITLE>
</HEAD>
<BODY>
<H2><SCRIPT LANGUAGE="JavaScript">
document.write(document.title)</SCRIPT></H2>
<HR>

<SCRIPT>
function changemarb(form)
{
    bg = form.marble.selectedIndex + 1;
    document.images[0].src="marble"+bg+".gif";
}

</SCRIPT>

<TABLE
BORDER=5><TD><CENTER><B><I>Marble</I></B></CENTER><IMG
HEIGHT=60 WIDTH=120 SRC="marble1.gif"></TD>
<TD>
<FORM NAME="choose">
<CENTER><B><I>Color</I></B></CENTER>
<SELECT NAME="marble" ONCHANGE="changemarb(this.form)"
SIZE=3>
        <OPTION SELECTED>Brown
        <OPTION>White
        <OPTION>Green
</SELECT>

</FORM>
</TD>
</TABLE>
</BODY>
</HTML>
```

LISTING 10-2   UPDATING AN IMAGE IN AN HTML PAGE ON THE FLY.

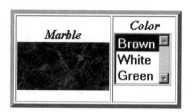

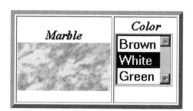

FIGURE 10-3   The initial appearance of the updateable image page.

FIGURE 10-4   The appearance of the updateable image page after white is selected.

TABLE 10-9. Updating an element of an HTML SELECT.

`formName.selectName.options[i].text = newValue;`	
Parameter	**Description**
i	`options[]` is an array containing all of the elements of the SELECT. The index *i* is any value between 0 and *n-1* where *n* is the number of elements in particular select statement.
newValue	A string containing the new text for the ith element of the select.

Summary

As previously mentioned, JavaScript is a work in progress and there will probably be incremental improvements in each new release of Netscape Navigator. However, the introduction of Java/JavaScript communication and having the ability to update images and selects within an HTML page goes along way in making JavaScript the tool of choice for developing full-featured interactive Web applications.

```
<HTML>
<HEAD>
<TITLE>JavaScript Example 10-3 (Change Elements of a
Select)</TITLE>
</HEAD>

<BODY>
<H2><SCRIPT LANGUAGE="JavaScript">
document.write(document.title)</SCRIPT></H2>
<HR>

<SCRIPT>
function changeorder(form)
{
    if (form.order.selectedIndex == 0)
    {
       for (i = 0; i < document.nameform.nameselect.length;
i ++)
       {
       document.nameform.nameselect.options[i].text =
namearray[i];
       }
    }
    else
    {
       for (i = 0; i < document.nameform.nameselect.length;
i ++)
       {
       document.nameform.nameselect.options[i].text =
namearray[namearray.length-1-i];
       }
    }
}
</SCRIPT>

<FORM NAME="nameform">

<B>List Order:</B><BR>
<SELECT NAME="order" ONCHANGE="changeorder(this.form)">
<OPTION SELECTED>Ascending
<OPTION>Descending
</SELECT>
```

LISTING 10-3   UPDATING THE CONTENT OF HTML SELECT OPTIONS.

```
<P>

<B>List Content:</B><BR>
<SELECT NAME="nameselect" SIZE=7>
    <OPTION>Aaron
    <OPTION>Brian
    <OPTION>Carl
    <OPTION>Dan
    <OPTION>Eric
    <OPTION>Fred
    <OPTION>Gordon
</SELECT>
</FORM>

<SCRIPT>
// Puts the Names into an Array
namearray = new
Array(document.nameform.nameselect.length);
for (i = 0; i < document.nameform.nameselect.length; i ++)

{
    namearray[i] =
document.nameform.nameselect.options[i].text;
}
</SCRIPT>
</BODY>
</HTML>
```

LISTING 10-3 (CONTINUED) UPDATING THE CONTENT OF HTML SELECT OPTIONS.

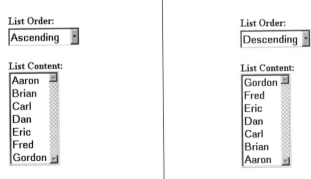

FIGURE 10-5   The original state of the updateable SELECT example.

FIGURE 10-6   The result of selecting descending order in the updateable SELECT example

Index

Symbols

!, Boolean NOT operator 94
!=, not equal to comparison operator 91
"this" Statement 269
&&, Boolean AND operator 94
&, Bitwise AND Operator 88, 90
*, multiplication operator 84
++, increment operator 85
+, Addition Operator 84
+, String concatenation operator 95
--, decrement operator 85
-, negation operator 85
-, subtraction operator 84
/, division operator 84
<, less than operator 92
<=, less than or equal to operator 92
<<, Bitwise Left Shift Operator> 91
=, assignment operator 84
==, equal to comparison operator 91
>, greater than comparison operator 91
>=, greater than or equal to comparison operator 92
>>, Bitwise Sign-propagating Right Shift 91
>>>, Bitwise Zero-fill Right Shift 91
^, Bitwise Exclusive OR Operator 91
|, Bitwise OR Operator 90
||, Boolean OR operator 94

A

abs() Method 240
acos() Method 240
action Property 193
Adding an Application 277
Addition Operator, (+) 84
alert() Method 138, 145, 152
alinkColor Property 170, 175
anchor() Method 245
anchors Array 173, 182
    length Property 173
appCodeName Property 141
APPLET Tag 368
    MAYSCRIPT parameter 368
Appliation Manager
    Modifying an Application 277
Application Manager 277
    Adding an Application 277
    Debugging an Application 280
    Deleting an Application 278
appName Property 134, 141
appVersion Property 141
Array Operator 81
    extending the size of an array 83
    length property 83
asin() Method 240
assignment operator (=) 84
atan() Method 240

B

back() Method 186
Backquote (`) Character 273
bgColor Property 171, 176
big() Method 245
Bitwise AND Operator, (&) 88
Bitwise Left Shift Operator, (<<) 91
Bitwise Operators 86
   AND, (&) 88, 90
   conversion of strings to numbers 86
   Exclusive OR, (^) 91
   left shift 91
   OR, (|) 90
   Sign-propagating Right Shift, (>>) 91
   Zero-fill Right Shift, (>>>) 91
Bitwise Sign-propagating Right Shift, (>>)
   91
Bitwise Zero-fill Right Shift, (>>>) 91
blink() Method 245
blur() Method 208, 218, 225, 230
bold() Method 245
Boolean Data Type 77
   !, NOT operator 94
   !=, not equal to comparison operator
     91
   &&, AND operator 94
   <, less than operator 92
   <=, less than or equal to operator 92
   ==, equal to comparison operator 91
     confusion with assignment opera-
       tor (=) 92
   >, greater than comparison operator
     91
   >=, greater than or equal to compari-
     son operator 92
   ||, OR operator 94
   FALSE, zero evaluates to 94
   logical evaluation of String data types
     94
   TRUE, non-zero evaluates to 94
break Statement 117

Built-in Methods 256
Built-in Objects 232
button Object 196, 198
   click() Method 199
   name Property 198
   onClick Event 199
   value Property 198

C

C/C++ 14, 71
   comparison of arrays 82
   comparison of String data type 77
   conditional expression 95
   Similarities to 1, 133
CD-ROM
   Code Examples xvii, xix
   Installing Netscape Navigator xviii
ceil() Method 240
charAt 245
charAt() Method 245
checkbox Object 196, 200
   checked Property 202
   click() Method 203
   defaultChecked Property 202
   name Property 203
   onClick Event 203
   value Property 203
checked Property
   of checkbox Object 202
   of radio Object 210
clear() Method 172, 180
clearTimeout() Method 145, 157, 167
click() Method 223
   of button Object 199
   of checkbox Object 203
   of radio Object 211
   of reset Object 213
client Object 296
   destroy method 296
   expiration method 296
   Maintenance Techniques 297

client-cookie 298
client-url 303
server-cookie 305
server-ip 304
server-url 305
Client-side JavaScript
Relationship to server-side JavaScript 4
close() Method
of document Object 172, 180
of window Object 145
of window object 156
Comments 10, 126, 127
Hiding JavaScript from non-JavaScript browsers 128
Common Components of JavaScript 286
Common Gateway Interface (CGI) 25, 70
Communicate between Client-side and Server-side JavaScript 298
Compiler, LiveWire 275
Conditional Expressions 95, 110
else Statement 110
for Statement 110, 112
for (variable in object) Statement 113
if Statement 110
while Statement 110, 111
confirm() Method 145, 152
continue Statement 116
cookie Property 171, 176
cos() Method 240

D

Data Types 76
Boolean 77
See also Boolean Data Type
Date 250
Math 76
See also Math Data Type
Special Values
null 81
<undefined> 81

String 77
See also String Data Type
database Object 308
beginTransaction method 314
commitTransaction method 314
connect method 310
connected method 310
disconnect method 310
execute method 313
Locking Connection 311
majorErrorCode method 316
majorErrorMessage method 316
minorErrorCode method 316
minorErrorMessage method 316
Non-locking Connection 309
rollbackTransaction method 314
SQLTable method 313
database.cursor Object-type 317
blobImage method 321
blobLink method 321
close method 319
columnName method 319
columns method 319
deleteRow method 328
insertRow method 328
next method 319
updateRow method 328
Data-typing 3
Date Object 250
Methods 251
debug Function 287
Debugging an Application 280
decrement operator, (--) 85
defaultChecked Property
of checkbox Object 202
of radio object 210
defaultSelected Property 218
defaultStatus Property
of window Object 145, 150
defaultValue Property
of password Object 207
of text Object 225

of textarea Object 229
Deleting an Application 278
division operator, (/) 84
do, while Statement missing from JavaScript 111
document Object 15, 136, 169
    alinkColor Property 170, 175
    anchors Array 173, 182
        length Property 173
    bgColor Property 171, 176
    clear() Method 172, 180
    close() Method 172, 180
    cookie Property 171, 176
    defined using BODY and HEAD tags 170
    fgColor Property 171, 177
    forms Array 173, 184
    forms Property
        length Property 173
    history Object 173, 186
        See history Object
    lastModified Property 171, 177
    linkColor Property 171, 177
    links Array 173, 187
        length Property 173
    location Property 173, 190
    Methods 179
    open() Method 172, 180
    Properties 175
    referrer Property 177
        referrer 171
    title Property 171, 178
    vlinkColor Property 171, 179
    write Function 14, 23
    write() Method 172, 181
    writeln() Method 172, 181

E

E Property 233
elements Array 193, 196
encoding Property 193

Error Messages
    JavaScript alert() method of the window Object 138
    JavaScript error message 139
    Object has no properties 135
escape Function 289
escape() Method 245, 256
eval() Method 114, 116, 256
    JavaScript Evaluation 259
    Numeric Evaluation 259
Events 139
    See also MouseOver
    See also onBlur
    See also onClick
    See also onFocus
    See also onSelect
    See also onSubmit
    executing multiple JavaScript statements 157
MouseOver Event 190
exp() Method 240

F

fgColor Property 171, 177
File Object-type 329
    byteToString method 338
    close method 332
    eof method 331
    exists method 331
    flush method 338
    getLength method 331
    getPosition method 333
    open method 332
    read method 336
    readByte method 336
    readln method 336
    setPosition method 333
    stringtoByte method 338
    write method 337
    writeByte method 337
    writeln method 337

fixed() Method 245
floor() Method 240
flush Function 288
focus() Method 208, 218, 225, 230
fontcolor() Method 245
fontsize() Method 245
for (variable in object) Statement 113
for Statement 110, 112
form Object 136, 192
    action Property 193
    button Object 196
    checkbox Object 196
    element Array 196
    elements Array 193
    encoding Property 193
    hidden Object 196, 204
    method Property 193
    onSubmit Event 195
    password Object 196, 206
    radio Object 196
    reset Object 196
    select Object 196
    submit Object 196
    submit() Method 195
    target Property 193
    text Object 196
    textarea Object 196
Forms 24, 136
forms Object 184
    button Object 198
    forms Array 173
    length Property 173
FORTRAN 102
forward() Method 187
frame Object 136, 161
    clearTimeout() Method 167
    frames Array 165, 168
    length Property 166
    name Property 166
    setTimeout() Method 167
Frames 25, 63, 136, 159
    BODY HTML Tag 67

Function Files 273
function Statement 118
    Passing Parameters 123
    placing in HEAD section 120
Functions 62

G

getDate() Method 251
getDay() Method 251
getHours() Method 251
getMinutes() Method 251
getMonth() Method 251
getSeconds() Method 251
getTime() Method 251
getTimeZoneoffset() Method 251
getYear() Method 251, 256
go() Method 187
GOTO statement missing from JavaScript
    102

H

hash Property 191
hidden Object 196, 204
    name Property 205
    value Property 205
history Object 62, 173, 186
    back() Method 186
    forward() Method 187
    go() Method 187
host Property 191
hostname Property 191
href Property 191
HTML Tags
    A 182, 188
    APPLET 368
    BODY 67, 170
        See onLoad Event and window Object
        See onUnload Event and window Object

CHECKBOX 202
Comments 127
Comments as Meta-commands 10
FORM 26, 184, 192
   INPUT
      BUTTON 198
      CHECKBOX 202
      HIDDEN 205
      PASSWORD 206
      RADIO 209
      RADO 42
      RESET 212
      SUBMIT 222
      TEXT 225
   SELECT 27, 140, 216
      OPTION 216
   TEXTAREA 228
FRAME 40, 161
   BODY 67
   COLS 162
   FRAMESET 31, 67, 161
   NAME 165
   ROWS 162
   SRC 162
   TITLE 65
HEAD 10, 161, 170
HTML 9
HTML Comments 10
OPTION 216
PASSWORD 206
PRE 17, 78
RADIO 42
SCRIPT 13, 23, 72
   LANGUAGE 13
SELECT 216
SUBMIT 222
TEXT 225
TEXTAREA 228
TITLE 12, 65
HyperTalk 14, 78, 133, 139

I

if Statement 28, 43, 110, 118
   else Statement 110
   partial evaluation of 72, 102
Images, Updateable 381
increment operator, (++) 85
index Property 218
indexOf() Method 143, 245
Internet
   History of, xiv
isNaN() Method 261
ISO Latin Character Set 29, 100
italics() Method 245

J

Java 14
   Relationship with JavaScript xv, 133
Java API, Accessing from JavaScript 380
Java Applet
   Accessing from JavaScript 369
   Netscape API
      call 373
      eval 372
      getMember 371
      getWindow 370
      setMember 372
      toString() 371
JavaScript
   legal locations in a document 73
   Printing 69
   Timing of Execution 74
JavaScript Properties
   read-only 137

L

lastIndexOf() Method 245
lastModified Property 171, 177
length Property 217

of anchors Array of document Object 173

of elements Array 196

of forms Object of document Object 173

of frame Object 166

of links array of document Object 173

of options Object 218

of radio Object 210

of select Object 217

of String Object 244

Less Than Operator, (<) 92

Less Than or Equal To Operator, (<=) 92

link() Method 245

linkColor Property 171, 177

links Array 173, 187

   length Property 173

   MouseOver Event 190

   onClick Event 190

LiveConnect 368

LN10 Property 237

LN2 Property 237

location Object 190, 191

   hash Property 191

   host Property 191

   href Property 191

   pathname Property 191

   port Property 191

   protocol Property 191

   search Property 191

   See document Object, location property

location Property 173

log() Method 240

LOG10E Property 237

LOG2E Property 237

M

Math Data Type 76

   +, addition operator

      compared to String concatenation (+) operator 96

+, String concatentation operator used with Math Data Types 99

decimal representations 76

floating point representation with exponent 76

hexadecimal representation 76

octal representation 76

Math Object 233

   E Property 233

   LN10 Property 237

   LN2 Property 237

   LOG10E Property 237

   LOG2E Property 237

   Methods 240

   PI Property 237

   SQRT1_2 Property 239

   SQRT2 Property 239

max() Method 240

method Property 193

Methods 138

Microsoft Windows 57

min() Method 240

Modifying an Application 277

multiplication operator, (*) 84

N

name Property

   of button Object 198

   of checkbox Object 203

   of frame Object 166

   of hidden Object 205

   of password Object 207

   of radio Object 210

   of reset Object 213

   of select Object 217

   of submit Object 223

   of text Object 225

   of textarea Object 229

   of window Object 145

navigator Object 136, 141

   appCodeName Property 141

appName Property 134, 141
appVersion Property 141
userAgent Property 141
negation operator, (-) 85
Netscape Communications
    Frames 63
    Home Page 7
    Navigator, version 2.0 7, 81
    Navigator, version 3.0 81
Netscape Navigator, Installing xviii
new Operator 81
null, special data value 81

O

Object-oriented Languages 2, 14, 133
    C++ 14
    HyperTalk 14
    Java 14
    SmallTalk 14
onBlur 139, 218, 227, 230, 231
onChange 140, 218, 227, 230, 231
onClick 42, 139, 190, 199, 200, 203, 212,
    213, 223
onFocus 139, 218, 227, 230, 231
onLoad 147, 158, 173
onSelect 139, 227, 230, 231
onSubmit 195
onUnload 147, 158, 173
open() Method
    of document Object 172, 180
    of window Object 145, 154
Operator Precedence 100
options Object 196, 217
    blur() Method 218
    defaultSelected Property 218
    focus() Method 218
    index Property 218
    length Property 218
    onBlur Event 218
    onChange Event 218
    onFocus Event 218

See select Object
selected Property 218
selectedIndex Property 218
text Property 218
value Property 218

P

parent 42, 66, 67, 134, 168
    synonym for window or frame Objects.
        See window and frame Ob-
        jects.
parse() Method 251
parsefloat() Method 240, 256
parseint() Method 240, 256
Partitioning Applications 4, 348
Pascal 15, 78
Passing Parameters 123
password Object 196, 206
    blur() Method 208
    defaultValue Property 207
    focus() Method 208
    name Property 207
    select() Method 208
    value Property 207
pathname Property 191
Perl 70
PI Property 237
port Property 191
pow() Method 240
Printing JavaScript 69
project Object 306
    Locking 307
prompt() Method 145, 153
protocol Property 191

R

radio Object 196, 208
    checked Property 210
    click() Method 211

defaultChecked Property 210
length Property 210
name Property 210
onClick Event 212
value Property 210
random() Method 240
redirect Function 288
referrer Property 177
request Object 292
    agent property 293
    ip property 293
    method property 293
    protocol property 293
reset Object 196, 212
    click() Method 213
    name Property 213
    onClick Event 213
    value Property 213
return Statement 121
round() Method 240

S

Scope of Statements 268
search Property 191
select Object 196, 214, 217
    name Property 217
    options Property 217
    selectedIndex Property 28, 217
Select Options, Updateable 382
select() Method 225, 230
    of password Object 208
selected Property 218
selectedIndex Property 217, 218
self 144, 149
    Synonym for a window or frame Object
SERVER Tag 272
Server Application Program Interface 70
server Object 307
    host property 308
    hostname property 308
    port property 308

protocol property 308
Server-side JavaScript
    Relationship to client-side JavaScript 4
    Using to redirect non-JavaScript-capable browsers 131
setDate() Method 251
setHours() Method 251
setMinutes() Method 251
setMonth() Method 251
setSeconds() Method 251
setTime() Method 251
setTimeout() Method 145, 156, 167
setYear() Method 251
sin() Method 240
small() Method 245
SmallTalk 14
Software Required xvii
sqrt() Method 240
SQRT1_2 Property 239
SQRT2 239
SQRT2 Property 239
status Property
    of window Object 145, 151
Storage of Server-side Objects 54
strike() Method 245
String Data Type 77
    +, concatenation operator 95
        compared to addition (+) operator 96
        used with Math data types 99
    maximum string literal length 77
    non-printing characters 77
String Methods
    indexOf() Method 143
String Object
    length Property 244
    Methods 245
string Object 244
sub() Method 245
submit Object 196, 221
    click() Method 223

name Property 223
onClick Event 223
value Property 223
submit() Method 195
substring() Method 245
subtraction operator, (-) 84
sup 245
sup() Method 245

T

tan() Method 240
target Property 193
text Object 196, 224
blur() Method 225
defaultValue Property 225
focus() Method 225
name Property 225
onBlur Event 227
onChange Event 227
onFocus Event 227
onSelect Event 227
select() Method 225
value Property 225
text Property 218
textArea Object
no formatting within the object 229
textarea Object 196, 227
blur() Method 230
defaultValue Property 229
focus() Method 230
name Property 229
onBlur Event 230
onChange Event 230
onFocus Event 230
onSelect Event 230
select() Method 230
value Property 229
"this" Statement 27
title Property 171, 178
toGMTString() Method 251
toLocaleString() Method 251

toLowerCase() Method 245
top 144, 149
Synonym for a window or frame Object
Top-level Functions, Server-side JavaS-
cript 286
toUpperCase() Method 245

U

<undefined>, special data value 81
unescape Function 289
unescape() Method 29, 245, 256
UNIX 57
userAgent Property 141
UTC() Method 251

V

value Property
of button Object 198
of checkbox Object 203
of hidden Object 205
of options Object 218
of password Object 207
of radio Object 210
of reset Object 213
of submit Object 223
of text Object 225
of textarea Object 229
var Statement 75
Variable Declaration 75
on-the-fly creation of variables 135
See also, var Statement
Variable Initialization 54
Variables 62
global 122
local 122
scope of 122
weak data typing 78
Verify Form Data 351
vlinkColor Property 171, 179

W

while Statement 110, 111
window Object 57, 63, 144
    See also Frames and <FRAME> tag
    accessing from JavaScript 144
    alert() Method 138, 145, 152
    clearTimeout() Method 145, 157
    close() Method 145, 156
    confirm() Method 145, 152
    defaultStatus Property 145, 150
    Events 157
    name Property 145
    onLoad Event 147, 158
    onUnload Event 147, 158
    open Method 154
    open() Method 145
    prompt() Method 145, 153
    setTimeout() Method 145, 156
    status Property 145, 151
    Synonyms
        self 144, 149
        top 144, 149
        window 144, 149
with Statement 243, 268
World Wide Web
    History of, xiv
write Function 14, 288
write() Method
    of document Object 172, 181
writeln() Method
    of document Object 172, 181